Triangle design pattern and related antipatterns

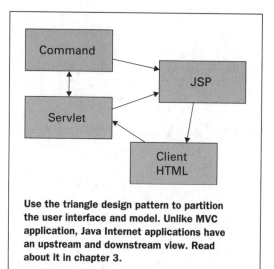

Use the triangle design pattern to partition the user interface and model. Unlike MVC application, Java Internet applications have an upstream and downstream view. Read about it in chapter 3.

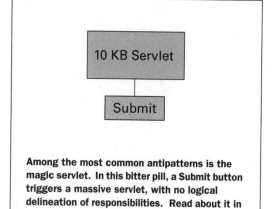

Among the most common antipatterns is the magic servlet. In this bitter pill, a Submit button triggers a massive servlet, with no logical delineation of responsibilities. Read about it in section 3.2, page 59.

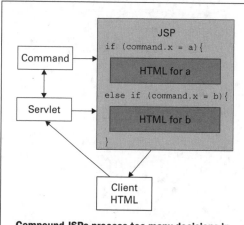

Compound JSPs process too many decisions in the JSP. Decision logic should be pushed into the controller. Read about them in section 4.3, page 88.

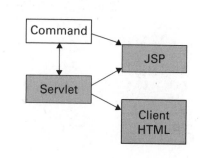

Sometimes, utilities, model logic, or view logic can creep into Fat commands. In this antipattern, performance and maintenance costs suffer. Read about them in section 4.5, page 102.

Bitter Java

BRUCE TATE

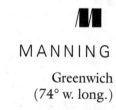

MANNING

Greenwich
(74° w. long.)

For Maggie

For electronic information and ordering of this and other Manning books,
go to www.manning.com. The publisher offers discounts on this book
when ordered in quantity. For more information, please contact:

Special Sales Department
Manning Publications Co.
209 Bruce Park Avenue   Fax: (203) 661-9018
Greenwich, CT 06830   email: orders@manning.com

Manning Publications Co.   Copyeditor: Liz Welch
209 Bruce Park Avenue   Typesetter: Tony Roberts
Greenwich, CT 06830   Cover designer: Leslie Haimes

ISBN 1-930110-43-X

Printed in the United States of America

1 2 3 4 5 6 7 8 9 10 – VHG – 05 04 03 02

contents

2 *The bitter landscape* 23

PART 2 SERVER-SIDE JAVA ANTIPATTERNS 51

10   *Bitter scalability*   283

foreword

It is the rare computer-science book that truly captivates me. Sometimes, it's the raw power of the writer's deep intellect and mastery, as with Guy Steele's *Common LISP: The Language*, which I remember reading straight through while lying on a sunny Hawaiian beach. Some would certainly chuckle at such "geekiness"— and maybe they are right to do so—but for me, each of Steele's successive chapters awoke a hunger to understand more and more. I couldn't put it down.

Then there's the seeming fairy tale packed with amazing revelation after revelation. A book that simultaneously forces you to suspend reality, yet hammers you in the cerebellum with the deep-but-fleeting truths you've been desperately seeking, truths you know you should have already recognized but have somehow missed. Tom DeMarco's *The Deadline: A Novel About Project Management* was such a book. I couldn't put it down.

Bruce Tate has, with *Bitter Java*, created another of these rare, captivating works. As with DeMarco's Morovian kidnapping, Bruce's personal "extreme sports" kayaking, mountain biking, and hot-air ballooning adventures carried me from "hydraulic" point to point, paddling as fast as I could to get to the next pattern or point. As with Steele, I couldn't wait for the next successive insight— and as with DeMarco, I just couldn't put *Bitter Java* down.

My advice? Don't start reading this book unless you can drop everything else on your schedule for the rest of the day. If it's late in the day, I feel for you, because you're going to be very tired tomorrow. If you're on a sunny Hawaiian beach, you'd better use SPF 99. There's no escaping it.

Bitter Java was a thrill for me, and I fully expect it will be for you too. If you develop software or work with those who do, you'll relate to chapter after chapter. I fully expect to be quoting Bruce in my next design review. *Bitter Java* is simply loaded with the wisdom and experience any good software engineer seeks. I found chapter 9's Java coding standards worthy of being its own publication—one that I sincerely wish all Java programmers would read and heed.

As Bruce's analogies clearly express, software engineering is very much like running dangerous rivers, and even though it's not necessarily as life-threatening as your standard class IV+ hydraulic, failure can be just as catastrophic to your livelihood and that of those you lead. So I recommend that you study this excellent guidebook very carefully. Bruce has packed it solid with the clearly written, fun-to-read, hard-earned wisdom of a true *white-water* master.

Prepare yourself well so you can maximize the thrill of the ride *and* live to do it again—and don't drop your paddle unless you've got your "hands Eskimo roll" down pat!

Have fun!

Hays W. "Skip" McCormick III
Coauthor of *AntiPatterns: Refactoring Software,
Architectures, and Projects in Crisis*

preface

In the summer, Texas rivers are dry. To find white water, kayakers have to follow the storms. One summer day in 1996, a partner and I left Austin at 8 P.M. to drive into the teeth of a huge thunderstorm and to follow it to the Cossatot River in Arkansas. When we arrived, the bad weather had played a cruel joke, swinging right around the river. Exhausted and disappointed, we pitched our tent on the bank of the river. We heard no raindrops that night.

In the morning, groggy and still disappointed, I stepped out of the tent and almost tripped … right into the river. The Cossatot, notorious for rapid flooding, had gotten 6 inches of rain in 2 hours a scant 10 miles upstream. Now we were facing the prospect of running a river that was too *high*. We decided to save the difficult white water for the following morning and run the easier sections upstream. The meandering, beginner-level Class I creek had become a Class III cauldron of turbulence. It took us just 20 minutes to complete what the guide-books called a "4-hour run." The "intermediate" section downstream was even worse: a Class IV flume of exploding violence. After extensive scouting, we took turns standing on the bank with a safety rope while the other worked the section. We then parked our kayaks at the tents and hiked down to check out the advanced section. To our surprise, dozens of locals on lounge chairs relaxed on the banks. They faced what is normally a series of Class IV waterfalls now completely hidden beneath a maelstrom of mayhem. We had never seen more than a handful of spectators before. They were there to see the local hotdogs crash and burn. Surprised by the scene, my buddy and I each sat on a boulder to watch the action ourselves.

Fast-forward to 2000. I leave a comfortable and successful career at IBM to join a startup called allmystuff, Inc. The economy is beginning to falter, but the company has just received funding while other Austin startups are biting the dust. This startup's business model does not depend on now dwindling advertising revenues, and the talent on allmystuff's team is amazing. When I join the company, it has $10 million in the bank and customers and technology that indicate a likelihood of success. I have seen many of my friends leave IBM for less money and security, but plenty of adventure. I reason that I can always go back in a pinch. In the approaching darkness, I head out into the storm.

As the Austin reporters gleefully chronicle the demise of the once high-flying Austin startups one by one, allmystuff too begins to struggle. We work insane hours to deploy solutions for our few customers. In spite of our strong record for quality, the waning economy eventually catches up to us too. The venture capitalists opt to close down and restart with a new concept better suited to a receding economy. Despite the harshness of the events, I learned more during that time than any other in my career.

Like the locals on the bank of the Cossatot, most of us cannot resist a story when it involves real excitement and adventure, and even danger. Whether we are viewing a well-honed Greek tragedy or the latest pop-culture offering like the *Survivor* television series, we cannot get enough. Programmers are no different. We love what we call *merc talk*, mercenaries chatting about the latest battle's adventures, for many of the same reasons. Some of my most vivid memories of work are from around the ping-pong table at allmystuff. We talked about what prompted the brutal hours we were working. We talked about management philosophy, whether the code base was getting out of control, and whether XML with specialized viewers would give us a simpler solution than our increasingly complex JSP model. We talked about whether our graphic designer could handle the mapping of her user interfaces onto increasingly complex Java commands, in light of our increasingly delayed schedules. The enthusiasm generated by these conversations is what had prompted me to leave a safe career for a pay cut, insecurity, and a whisper of a hope at millions. And these experiences make me more valuable as a programmer, as a manager, and as an architect.

In a context I no longer remember, previous IBM Chairman John Akers once said that there were too many people "hanging around the water cooler." I remember that we were outraged. He didn't get it. Around a water cooler, or bar, or ping-pong table is where you will hear the stuff that makes or breaks a project—or a company. This, the programmer's mythology, must be nurtured and fed, for it is the stuff of life. I attempt to capture some of it in *Bitter Java*.

Turning time back again to before allmystuff, I am speaking at a conference. The title of my presentation is "Bitter Java." During the conference I meet a well-respected Java programmer who is one of the inventors of JSP. He tells me he's been in Pamplona and has run with the bulls. He was even gored. He proceeds to explain his bull-running strategy. My mind resists. Of all the people in Pamplona that day, he should be the last to tell me about how to avoid getting gored. I might as well consult O. J. Simpson about marital relations. Tens of thousands of crazed, adrenaline junkies run every year, and only a handful ever gets gored. But gradually my mind focuses: if I were to run, he might well be just the person I'd want to talk to. I would want to know how he planned his run, how he executed that plan, and what went wrong. That's information I could use. As it turns out, the gored programmer is the vice president of engineering at allmystuff, and he recruits me to help start his services organization. Back to my presentation, although it might put the allmystuff job at risk, I decide to use the Pamplona story to start my talk. It captures the fundamental concepts of *Bitter Java* perfectly. If it helps avoid a subtle trap or process pitfall, a story about failure can be worth 10 stories about success. The story catches the audience's attention, and ... I get the job anyway.

Like many programmers, I love extreme sports. We boaters are drawn to tragedy and sometimes play dangerous games. A well-known cautionary kayaking rule by author William Neely is that the time spent staring at a nasty hydraulic is directly proportional to the amount of time you'll spend getting trashed in it. Said another way, if that hole looks nasty enough to eat you, it probably will. Kayakers have a good strategy for describing a run down a river. The guidebooks will point out a route *and the dangerous spots outside and along the route.* A guidebook might say, "Next, you will see a boulder in midcurrent. Go left. Should you blunder to the right, the *Terminator* hydraulic will certainly show you the error of your ways." I learned long ago that even if you don't know a river intimately, you will want to know its trouble spots. I want to know if a rock is undercut, and if that undercut is likely to trap me. I want to know where to punch that riverwide hydraulic, or how to miss the rocks on the bottom of the waterfall. I want to know if anyone has ever died on the river and how it happened. With enough information, I can usually avoid the hazards with skill or even by walking around them on the bank with my boat firmly on my shoulder.

The programmer in me wants to do the same. I need to understand where applications and projects fail. I need to know if I am making too many communications over that interface, and the techniques that can steer me through that turbulent spot. I need to understand where a technology is likely to break and if it is likely to scale.

It is my conviction that in order to be successful, our software development culture must embrace failure and learn from it. I have yet to see an example of an organization that systematically learns from its mistakes and is diligent at capturing the reasons behind the modification of a flawed design pattern or process in a regular, systematic way. I have seen a lot of code and not all of it was sweet. I have learned to love bitter Java. I hope you will too.

acknowledgments

Bitter Java as a concept began three years ago, as a one-hour presentation. Braden Flowers helped shape the early message, and I am immensely grateful to him for that. The Bitter Java website followed two years later. Though the ideas have percolated (ahem) for some time, the Manning staff, many reviewers, some friends, other authors, and I formed a cohesive virtual team, spanning three continents, that was able to produce this book on a tighter timeframe and with better quality than I ever thought possible. Though I must try to mention all of you individually by name, the many contributions and insights that I have received make doing so impossible.

Having written two other technical books, I was shocked and delighted by the world-class support Manning provided. I thank Marjan Bace twice: first for your patient guidance and insistence on excellence at every step in the process, and second for your gentle hand in guiding my style and shaping my craft. Your skill with the written word inspires the artist in me, and your understanding of people—your customers, your competitors, and your authors—impresses me beyond words.

Special thanks go to Ted Kennedy, who provided outstanding, professional reviews that challenged me, but who also supported me when I needed it the most. Thanks to all of those who spent countless hours reviewing the book: Jon Eaves, John Crabtree, John Mitchell, Steve Clafin, Sean Koontz, Max Loukianov, Greg Wadley, Tim Sawyer, Braden Flowers, Ted Neward, Eric Baker, Jon Skeet, and especially Juan Jimenez, who would make a fine editor. Your compliments were of incalculable worth, and your criticisms, both harsh and kind, helped me to shape a better book. I want each of you to know that though I did not incorporate all comments, I carefully considered each one individually, and there were thousands. I hope that I will be able to do the same for each of you someday.

My thanks also go to the production team: Liz Welch for your kindness, efficiency, and superb editing skill (especially your insistence on clarity and consistency); Susan Capparelle, Helen Trimes, and Mary Piergies for your competent and timely skill in managing and promoting this project; Dan Barthel for supporting the project and "discovering" Braden and me; Leslie Haimes for a beautiful cover; Bruce Murray and Chris Hillman for outstanding technical support; Lee Fitzpatrick for signing the checks as the team kept shifting; and Tony Roberts for your craftsmanship in shaping the look of the book.

Thanks to all who contributed ideas and content to this book: Brian Dainton and the team at Contextual for contributing your style guide; Tony Leung for the sample code from *Plugging Memory Leaks*; Amandeep Singh for the read/write lock code; and Mike Conner for use of the diagrams in *Scaling Up E-business Applications with Caching*. Thanks also to Mike Conner for shaping the team that sharpened "the Triangle"—the core design pattern in *Bitter Java*. Thanks to Mark Wells for pointing me toward the read/write lock idea. Special thanks go to Skip McCormick III, both for starting the antipatterns ball rolling and for writing a foreword that captures my imagination and the spirit of the book. And once again, thank you, Braden Flowers, for contributing the EJB examples.

2001 was a difficult year for the nation, the high-tech industry, and my family. Through it all, Maggie, you were by my side, supporting, inspiring, and encouraging me. You were editor, gopher, scheduler, encourager, and especially friend. I thank you, and my love for you grows always.

about this book

The study and application of antipatterns is one of the next frontiers of programming. In *Bitter Java* we explore the topic with personal narrative and specific examples. There is a lot of code, and I refactor a common example many times to improve the performance and readability until the final examples are decidedly sweeter.

How the book is organized

This book contains 11 chapters, 3 sections, and an appendix. Additional details about the book's organization and structure can be found in chapter 1, section 1.5. Here is an overview.

Part 1 covers the foundations of design patterns, antipatterns and standards supporting Internet server-side development.

- Chapter 1 compares antipatterns to other industries that use similar concepts. For example, the medical industry uses preventative care (design patterns) and cures (fixes), but the best doctors diagnose the root causes like weight or stress (antipatterns). I also explain in more depth the organization of this book.

- Chapter 2 covers the base Internet standards, plus Java, plus a little process: all of the things that you'll need for server-side Java. It's not a comprehensive tutorial, but it might let you know where you need more study.

Part 2 covers server-side antipatterns in detail. In it, I start with a poor bulletin board application, and refactor it to solve individual antipatterns.

- Chapter 3 introduces the basic server-side antipatterns, and defines the Triangle design pattern common at allmystuff (now Contextual) and IBM. The core antipattern is the Magic Servlet: a servlet that tries to do all of the work.

- Chapter 4 covers the antipatterns from Java Server Pages. Since JSP has a tag language, this chapter has a decidedly different feel.

- Chapter 5 makes a case for caching by showing that caching at multiple levels of an enterprise can improve performance by an order of magnitude.

- Chapter 6 identifies the Java problems that lead to memory leaks, and discusses troubleshooting techniques.

- Chapter 7 deals with antipatterns related to connecting two systems. Connection thrashing anchors the discussion of tightly coupled systems, and XML with Web Services form the foundation for loosely coupled systems.

- Chapter 8 introduces EJBs. I lay out the fundamentals, and draw a bitter design that breaks out the model component of the bulletin board application as EJB entity beans.

Part 3 covers the higher level details outside of the context of the bulletin board example.

- Chapter 9 addresses programming hygiene. It includes a real coding standards guideline from Contextual, and has many suggestions to make code more readable and understandable.

- Chapter 10 lays out performance antipatterns, from implementation to process to tuning. I also discuss deployment architectures for scalability.

- Chapter 11 sums it all up, and shows how you can apply antipatterns to your project, your career, and your enterprise.

The three tables in the appendix cross-reference antipatterns by name, scale, and symptom.

How to use the book

I suggest initially reading or skimming the chapters sequentially to get an overall feel for antipatterns, then returning to specific chapters and examples for reference material.

If you still need help or have questions for the authors, please read about the unique online resources described below.

Who should read this book?

Bitter Java is for the intermediate server-side Java programmer or architect, but others will benefit as well. Beginning programmers will appreciate the clear, understandable language, and the philosophy of striving to understand antipatterns. Advanced programmers will find some new antipatterns for XML, and will also benefit from a new angle of pattern study.

Your quest for Bitter Java need not end when you've read this book from cover to cover. No book stands alone, and you should make good use of the many online resources and books listed in chapter 1, as well as the online resources at http://www.manning.com and http://www.bitterjava.com. There also is a bibliography at the end of the book with sources listed by subject.

While the Java is bitter, I hope that we have helped to make your reading experience smooth and sweet.

Source code

The book contains extensive source code examples, most of which are server-side examples based on servlets. The book also contains EJB programming examples by Braden Flowers.

Source code examples are available online at http://www.bitterjava.com or from the publisher's website http://www.manning.com/tate.

Typographical conventions

Italic typeface is used to introduce new terms and to define personal narratives. These extreme sports stories have a brief opening at the beginning of a chapter, and a moral within the body of the chapter that illustrates a key antipattern concept.

Courier typeface is used to denote code samples, as well as elements and attributes, method names, classes, interfaces, and other identifiers. Bold face

`Courier` identifies important sections of code that are discussed within the chapter text.

Code annotations accompany many segments of code. Certain annotations are marked with chronologically ordered bullets such as ❶. These annotations have further explanations that follow the code.

Code line continuations are indented.

Online resources

Two outstanding Internet resources are at your fingertips:

- Manning's Author Online provides private forums for all book owners. You can reach Manning's *Bitter Java* forum by pointing your browser to http://www.manning.com/tate. Follow the directions to subscribe and access the forum.

- The *Bitter Java* website at http://www.bitterjava.com provides open forums for Java antipatterns and sample programs. Through these forums you can take part in general antipatterns discussions and even analyze specific topics from the book. Shortly after *Bitter Java* is released, you'll be able to download the programming examples. And don't forget to register for the *Bitter Java* email newsletter, which is published every other month, or whenever I have enough interesting information for one. Back issues are also available.

Feel free to use either resource to ask questions, make comments about *Bitter Java*, and receive help from other readers and authors. We have formed the infrastructure for an online community. The rest is up to you.

about the cover illustration

The figure on the cover of *Bitter Java* is an Azanaghi man, whose people lived for centuries in the northernmost sections of present-day Mauritania. The details of his life and position are for us lost in historical fog, and the artist has further added to the mystery of the man by not showing us his face. The illustration is taken from a Spanish compendium of regional dress customs first published in Madrid in 1799. The book's title page states:

> *Coleccion general de los Trages que usan actualmente todas las Nacionas del Mundo desubierto, dibujados y grabados con la mayor exactitud por R.M.V.A.R. Obra muy util y en special para los que tienen la del viajero universal*

Which we translate, as literally as possible, thus:

> *General collection of costumes currently used in the nations of the known world, designed and printed with great exactitude by R.M.V.A.R. This work is very useful especially for those who hold themselves to be universal travelers*

Although nothing is known of the designers, engravers, and workers who colored this illustration by hand, the "exactitude" of their execution is evident in this drawing. The mysterious Azanaghi man is just one of many figures in this colorful collection. Their diversity speaks vividly of the uniqueness and individuality of the world's cultures and regions just 200 years ago. This was a time when the dress codes of two regions separated by a few dozen miles identified people uniquely as belonging to one or the other. The collection brings to life the sense of isolation and distance of that period—and of every other historic period except our own hyperkinetic present.

Dress codes have changed since then, and the diversity by region, so rich at the time, has faded away. It is now often hard to tell the inhabitant of one continent from another. Perhaps, trying to view it optimistically, we have traded a cultural and visual diversity for a more varied personal life. Or a more varied and interesting intellectual and technical life.

We at Manning celebrate the inventiveness, the initiative, and the fun of the computer business with book covers based on the rich diversity of regional life of two centuries ago, brought back to life by the pictures from this collection.

Part 1

The basics

In 1993, I made my first descent down a Class IV river: the Cossatot River in Arkansas. To prepare, I first spent many hours on easier Class II rivers in Texas with experienced paddlers. I was learning the common vocabulary and the repetitive motions that I would need to survive in a new kayaking community. Though the rivers were easy, those enjoyable hours prepared me for the challenges to come.

Chapters 1 and 2 lay the foundation for patterns, antipatterns, and server-side Java programming. In chapter 1, we discuss the impact that design patterns have had on modern programming, and we make the argument that antipatterns are a necessary and complementary topic of study. We provide some tips for detective work, exploring ways to establish patterns of repeated Java problems. In chapter 2, we discuss the current landscape of server-side Java programming, from the basic Internet standards and languages to the improvements in methodology, with a twist. Along the way, we will look for the nooks and crannies that are likely hiding places for antipatterns and the process improvements that help us combat them.

Bitter tales

1

This chapter covers

- A programming horror story
- Techniques for finding and fixing antipatterns
- Examples of antipatterns in other industries

On a cold day in Eastern Tennessee, my kayak is perched precariously atop a waterfall known as State Line Falls. The fall has a nasty reputation among kayakers. One of our team is walking this one. He was injured and shaken up last year at the same spot. This time around he wants no part of it.

From the top, there is no clue of the danger that lurks around the bend, but we know. We have been thinking ahead to this rapid for several days. We have read about what I cannot yet see. Five truck-sized boulders guard four slots. The water rushes through the slots and plunges to the bottom of the fall. I will see the entire waterfall only seconds before I go over it. Most of the water lands on boulders barely covered by two feet of water. Three of the four slots are reputed to be too violent and dangerous for your mother-in-law. Through the fourth, the river rips into the narrows and picks up speed. It drops sharply over the lip and crashes onto the jagged rocks 16 feet below. I am a programmer by trade, a father of two, and a kayaker of intermediate skill. I have no business going over a Class V waterfall described in guidebooks as "marginal." But here I am, looking for the landmarks. I pick my slot, sweep left, and brace for the soft landing—or the crash. I am in free fall.

1.1   A Java development free fall

The sales team was strong. They got all the right sponsors, lined them up, and marched them into the executive's office. They all said the same thing. The development cycle times were outrageous. Each project was longer than the last, and the *best* project overshot deadlines by 85 percent. It did not take the CIO long to add up the numbers. The cost overruns ran well into seven figures.

The answer was Java. The lead rep presented a fat notebook showing references from everywhere: the press, the news, and three major competitors. The proposed tools won awards and added to the outrageous productivity claims promised by even the most conservative vendors. They never cited the downside or training requirements. In early 1996, hardly anyone did. The sales team brought in the big gun: a proof-of-concept team that quickly hammered out an amazingly robust prototype in a short time. The lead rep had practiced the close many times, but in this case, the deal was already sealed. She was able to get even more of the budget than she expected. After all, a product and language this easy and this similar to C++ should not require much training, so she got most of that allocated budget too.

But a year and a half later, the lead programmer was sitting behind a desk in the middle of the night while the sales rep celebrated her third National Circle sales award in Hawaii. In truth, the programmer seemed genuinely happy to be there. He knew that he was in over his head, and he needed help badly. He could see that clearly now. When the project started, the programming team had just enough time to learn the syntax of the new language. They had been using an object-oriented language for four years without ever producing an object-oriented design. Their methodology called for one large development cycle, which provided very little time to find all of the mistakes—and even less time to recover. The insane argument at the time was that there was no time for more than one iteration.

As a member of the audit team dispatched to help the customer pick up the pieces, I was there to interview the programmer. My team had composed a checklist of likely culprits: poor performance, obscure designs, and process problems. We had written the same report many times, saving our customers hundreds of thousands of dollars, but the interviews always provided additional weight and credibility to back up our assertions.

"Is your user interface pure HTML, then?" I asked.

"Yeah," the programmer replied. "We tried applets, but that train crashed and burned. We couldn't deal with the multiple firewalls, and our IT department didn't think they would be able to keep up with the different browser and JVM configurations."

"So, where is the code that prints the returning HTML?"

He winced and said, "Do you really want to go near that thing?" In truth, I didn't want any part of it. I had done this long enough to know that this baby would be too ugly for a mother to love, but this painful process would yield one of the keys to the kingdom. As we reviewed the code, we confirmed that this was an instance of what I now call the Magic Servlet antipattern, featured in chapter 3. The printout consisted of 30 pages of code, and 26 were all in a single service method. The problem wasn't so much a bad design as a lack of any design at all. We took a few notes and read a few more pages. While my partner searched for the code fragment that processed the return trip, I looked for the database code. After all, I had written a database performance book, and many of the semiretired database problems were surfacing anew in Java code.

"Is this the only place that you connect to the database?" I asked.

"No," he answered. "We actually connect six different times: to validate the form, to get the claim, to get the customer, to handle error recovery, to submit the claim, and to submit the customer." I suppressed a triumphant smile and again reviewed the code. Connection pooling is often neglected but incredibly powerful. In chapter 7, the Connection Thrashing antipattern shows how a method can spend up to half of its time managing connections, repeating work that can usually be done once.

I also jotted down a note that the units of work should be managed in the database and not the application. I noticed that the database code was sprinkled throughout, making it difficult to change this beast without the impact rippling throughout the system. I was starting to understand the depth of the problem. Even though most of these audits were the same, at some point they all hit me in the face like a cold glass of water.

Over the next four hours, we read code and drew diagrams. We found that the same policy would be fetched from 4 to 11 times, depending on the usage scenario. (The caching antipatterns at this customer and others prompted discussions in chapter 5, where you'll learn about the caching and serialization techniques that can make a huge difference.) We drew interaction diagrams of the sticky stuff and identified major interfaces. We then used these diagrams to find iteration over major interface boundaries and to identify general chatty communications that could be simplified or shifted.

We left the customer a detailed report and provided services to rework the problem areas. We supplied a list of courses for the programmers and suggested getting a consulting mentor to solidify the development process. When all was said and done, the application was completed *ahead* of the revised schedule and the performance improved *tenfold*. This story actually combines three different customer engagements, each uglier than this one. I changed some details to protect the names of the guilty, but the basic scenario has been repeated many times over the course of my career. I find problems and provide templates for the solutions. While most of my peers have focused on design patterns, I find myself engaged with *antipatterns*.

1.1.1 Antipatterns in life

On the Watauga River, with all of the expectations and buildup, the run through State Line is ultimately anticlimactic. I land with a soft "poof" well right of the major turbulence. The entire run takes less than 20 seconds. Even so, I recognize this moment as a major accomplishment.

How could a journeyman kayaker successfully navigate such a dangerous rapid? How could I convince myself that I would succeed in light of so many other failures? I'd learned from the success and failure of those who went before me. The real extremists were those that hit rock after rock, breaking limbs and equipment, while learning the safest route through the rapid. I see a striking similarity between navigating rivers and writing code. To make it through State Line Falls, I simply did three things:

- *I learned to use the tools and techniques of the experts.* As a programmer, I attend many conferences to learn about best practices, and to find the new frameworks and tools that are likely to make a difference on my projects.
- *I did what the experts did.* I learned the easiest line and practiced it in my mind. We can do the same thing as programmers, by using design patterns detailing successful blueprints to difficult architectural problems.
- *I learned from the mistakes before me.* The first time down a rapid, it's usually not enough to take a good plan and plunge on through, torpedoes be damned. Good plans can go bad, and it's important to know how to react when they do. As a programmer, I do the same thing. I am a huge fan of "merc talk," or the stories told around the table in the cafeteria about the latest beast of a program. This is the realm of the antipattern.

When I was told how to run State Line Falls, I asked what-if questions. What should my precise angle be? How can I recover if I drift off that angle? How far left is too far? What's likely to happen if I miss my line and flip? I got answers from locals who had watched hundreds of people go down this rapid with varying degrees of success. The answers to these questions gave me a mental picture of what usually happened, what could go wrong, and what places or behaviors to avoid at all cost. With this knowledge, I got the confidence that it took to run the rapid. I was using design patterns and antipatterns.

1.2   Using design patterns accentuates the positive

Design patterns are solutions to recurring problems in a given context. A good example is the Model-View-Controller design pattern introduced in chapter 3. It presents a generic solution to the separation of the user interface from the business logic in an application. A good design pattern should represent a solution that has been successfully deployed several times. At State Line Falls, when I read about the successful line in guidebooks and watched experienced kayakers run the rapid, I was essentially using design patterns. As a programmer, I use them for many reasons:

- *Proven design patterns mitigate risk.* By using a proven blueprint to a solution, I increase my own odds of success.
- *Design patterns save time and energy.* I can effectively use the time and effort of others to solve difficult problems.

- *Design patterns improve my skill and understanding*. Through the use of design patterns, I can improve my knowledge about a domain and find new ways to represent complex models.

Embracing design patterns means changing the way we code. It means joining communities where design patterns are shared. It means doing research instead of plowing blindly into a solution. Many good sources are available.

Books

This is a sampling of books from the Java design pattern community and the definitive source for design patterns (*Design Patterns: Elements of Reusable Object-Oriented Software*). As of this writing, five or more are under development, so this list will doubtlessly be incomplete. Amazon (http://www.amazon.com) is a good source for finding what's out there.

- *Design Patterns: Elements of Reusable Object-Oriented Software*, by Erich Gamma, Richard Helm, Ralph Johnson, and John Vlissides (The Gang of Four)
- *Refactoring: Improving the Design of Existing Code*, by Martin Fowler, Kent Beck (contributor), John Brant (contributor), William Opdyke, and Don Roberts
- *Core J2EE Patterns*, by John Crupi, Dan Malks, and Deepak Alur
- *Concurrent Programming in Java: Design Principles and Patterns*, by Doug Lea
- *Patterns in Java, Volume 3: A Catalog of Enterprise Design Patterns Illustrated with* UML, by Mark Grand
- *Data Structures and Algorithms with Object-Oriented Design Patterns in Java*, by Bruno R. Preiss
- *Java Design Patterns: A Tutorial*, by James William Cooper

1.2.1   Design patterns online

Manning Publications has a series of author forums for discussion. These authors discuss server-side architectures, Java programming techniques, Java Server Pages (JSPs), Extensible Markup Language (XML), and servlets. The author of this book also has an online community to discuss Java antipatterns.

Manning authors

- Manning author forums: http://www.manning.com/authoronline.html
- Java antipatterns: http://www.bitterjava.com

Java vendors

- IBM: http://www-106.ibm.com/developerworks/patterns/
- Sun: http://java.sun.com/j2ee/blueprints/

1.2.2 UML provides a language for patterns

The design pattern community has exploded in recent years partially because there is now a near universal language that can be used to express patterns. Unified Modeling Language (UML) brings together under one umbrella several of the tools supporting object-oriented development. Concepts such as scenarios (use cases), class interactions (class diagrams), object interface interaction (sequence diagrams), and object state (state diagrams) can all be captured in UML. Though this subject is beyond the scope of this book, there are many good UML books, tools, and resources as well.

Books

- *UML Distilled: A Brief Guide to the Standard Object Modeling Language*, by Martin Fowler and Kendall Scott
- *Enterprise Java with UML*, by C. T. Arrington
- *The Unified Modeling Language User Guide*, by Grady Booch, et al.

Tools

- Rational: http://www.rational.com
- Resource center at Rational: http://www.rational.com/uml/index.jsp
- TogetherJ from Together Software: http://www.togethersoft.com

1.3 Antipatterns teach from the negative

AntiPatterns: Refactoring Software, Architectures, and Projects in Crisis by William J. Brown, et al., is an outstanding book dedicated to the study of antipatterns. The antipattern templates that follow each chapter in this book come from Brown's text. In it, the authors describe an antipattern as "a literary form that describes a commonly occurring solution to a problem that generates decidedly negative consequences." The words that caught my attention are *commonly occurring solution* and *decidedly negative consequences*. Many others have presented some of the negative examples in this book as the right way to do things. Some, like the Magic Servlet, are forms of programs published in tutorials, created by wizards, or captured in frameworks. As for negative consequences, anyone who has followed software engineering closely knows that a high percentage of software projects fail. The *AntiPatterns* text cites that five of six software projects are considered unsuccessful. Java projects are not immune. Earlier this weekend, I heard about a canceled Java project using servlets and JSPs at a Fortune 100 company that will be replaced with a new project using CICS and C++!

Some of the madness in our industry is caused by outright malice. Some vendors sell software that they know isn't ready or doesn't work. Some managers resist change and sabotage projects. Some coworkers take shortcuts that they know they will not have to repair. Most of the time, though, it is simple ignorance, apathy, or laziness that gets in the way. We simply do not take the time to learn about common antipatterns. Ignorant of software engineering history or the exponentially increasing cost of fixing a bug as the development cycle progresses, we might kid ourselves into thinking we'll take a shortcut now and fix it later.

1.3.1   *Some well-known antipatterns*

As programmers, we will run across many antipatterns completely unrelated to Java. For the most part, we will not go into too many of them, but here are a few examples to whet your appetite:

- *Cute shortcuts*. We've all seen code that optimizes white space. Some programmers think that the winner is the one who can fit the most on a line. My question is, "Who is the loser?"

- *Optimization at the expense of readability*. This one is for the crack programmers who want you to know it. In most cases, readability in general is far more important than optimization. For the other cases, aggressive comments keep things clear.

- *Cut-and-paste programming*. This practice is probably responsible for spreading more bugs than any other. While it is easy to move working code with cut and paste, it is difficult to copy the entire context. In addition, copies of code are rarely tested as strenuously as the originals. In practice, cut-and-paste programs must be tested *more strenuously* than the originals.

- *Using the wrong algorithm for the job*. Just about every programmer has written a bubble sort and even applied it inappropriately. We can all find a shell sort if pressed, and if we understand algorithm analysis theory, we know that a bubble sort is processed in $O(n^2)$ time, and a simple shell sort is processed in $O(n\log(n))$ time, which is much shorter for longer lists.

- *Using the wrong class for the job.* In object-oriented languages, we've got to choose between classes like tables and arrays that have similar function but different characteristics. If our algorithm calls for random access of a collection, using a b-tree or hash table will be much faster than an array. If we're going to frequently index or enumerate the collection, an array is faster.

1.3.2 Antipatterns in practice

The study and application of antipatterns is one of the next frontiers of programming. Antipatterns attempt to determine what mistakes are frequently made, why they are made, and what fixes to the process can prevent them. The practice is straightforward, if tedious. The benefits are tremendous. The trick to the study of antipatterns is to:

1 *Find a problem.* This might be a bug, a poor-performing algorithm, or unreadable method.

2 *Establish a pattern of failure.* Quality control is a highly specialized and valued profession in manufacturing circles. A good quality engineer can take a process and find systemic failures that can cost millions. Software process can create systemic failure, too. The Y2K bug was a systemic failure of a very simple bug that was created and copied across enterprises hundreds of millions of times. Sometimes, the pattern will be related to a technology. Most often, process problems involve people, including communications and personalities.

3 *Refactor the errant code.* We must of course refactor the code that is broken. Where possible, we should use established design patterns.

4 *Publish the solution.* The refactoring step is obvious but should be taken a bit further than most are willing to go. We should also teach others how to recognize and refactor the antipattern. *Publishing the antipattern is as important as publishing the related solution.* Together, they form a refactoring guide that identifies the problem and solves it.

5 *Identify process weaknesses.* Sometimes, frameworks or tools encourage misuse. Other times, external pressures such as deadlines may encourage shortcuts. We must remember that a process must ultimately be workable by imperfect humans. In many cases, education may be the solution.

6 *Fix the process.* This is the most difficult, and most rewarding, step. We effectively build a barrier between our healthy enterprise and the

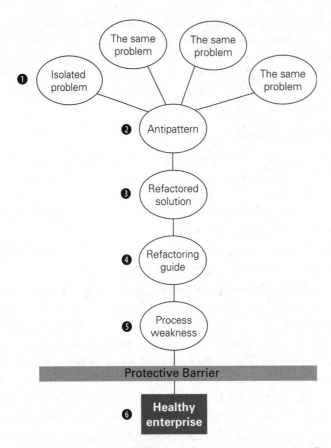

Figure 1.1 The antipattern process involves finding a problem ❶, establishing a pattern and publishing an antipattern ❷, refactoring the solution ❸, building a guide so that the problem can be resolved and fixed en masse ❹, identifying process weaknesses ❺, and building a barrier between the healthy enterprise and the antipattern ❻.

disease. Here, we take a hard look at what's broken. In simple cases, we fix the problem. In more extreme cases, we might need to establish a risk/reward analysis and win sponsorship to fix the problem.

Figure 1.1 illustrates the antipattern process.

1.3.3   *Antipattern resources*

The antipattern community is gathering momentum, looking for things that break in a methodical way and capturing those experiences. Some engines use pattern recognition to find bugs from software *source code*. Many programmers are starting to publish *bug patterns* for common programming mistakes. The http://www.bitterjava.com site has some links to Eric Allen's series "Bug Patterns."

The design pattern community also has a counterpart: the *antipattern* community. This group is interested in learning from common experience and capturing that knowledge in a uniform, methodical way.

AntiPatterns: Refactoring Software, Architectures, and Projects in Crisis brings these concepts together better than any other source I have seen. With Brady Flowers, who contributed the Enterprise JavaBeans (EJB) examples for this book, I had started to do bitter Java sessions at conferences before we found *AntiPatterns*. When we found it, we immediately fell in love with the ideas expressed in this book. Most of the book's antipatterns went beyond theory and explained the cultural conditions prompting a problem. The book is extraordinarily useful to programmers who strive for excellence. We hope to take these concepts into the Java community to continue the momentum that *AntiPatterns* has created. We will go beyond generic antipatterns and dive into those that are most prevalent to the Java community. These are some online resources for antipatterns:

- The authors have an online source for Java antipatterns. You can find it at http://www.bitterjava.com. On the site, we will attempt to provide you with articles, discussion boards, and useful links.
- The http://www.antipatterns.com site has articles, events, and message boards.

1.4   *Antipattern ideas are not new*

Should developers spend more time on the study of antipatterns or design patterns? I will answer this with another true adventure story. Throughout the better part of this past century, mountain climbers across the world had an ultimate goal: to scale Mt. Everest, the highest summit in the world. Over time, mountaineers tried many different approaches that would allow political passage to the mountain, solid expedition logistics, and the best chances for success. Two routes go through Tibet. George Mallory was an early British mountain climber, famous for saying he climbed Everest "Because it is there." He made his attempts on the north face, over terrain called the North Col. The other northern route was considered much too dangerous for early mountaineers. Edmund Hillary, who became the first to climb Everest, eventually succeeded on the southern face, through Nepal. That route is called the South Col route. After the first ascent, expeditions climbed this dangerous mountain with greater regularity and greater margins of safety. They began to unlock the secrets of operating at high altitude and to find where the inevitable danger spots were likely to be. They began to understand when the summer monsoons directed the jet stream away from Everest to provide a window of acceptable weather. They learned to leave their tents at midnight so that they would not be trapped on the summit in the afternoon, when the weather frequently deteriorated. They were using design patterns.

Inevitably, people started to guide trips up the mountain with increasing success. Many debated that some of the paid clients did not have the appropriate skills to be on the mountain and would not be able to handle themselves in the event of an emergency. These criticisms turned out to be prophetic. Two expeditions led by the strongest guides in the world got trapped at the top of Everest through a series of poor decisions and bad luck. An afternoon storm killed many of them, including three of the six guides and several of the clients. Jon Krakauer made this incident famous in the book *Into Thin Air*. The design patterns were able to get them to the top but were unable to get them safely back down. Good application of climbing antipatterns, like avoiding the top of the mountain at dangerous times and holding fast to a prescribed turn-around time, could have made the difference.

1.4.1 Learning from the industry

In many real-world situations, the principles of design patterns and antipatterns are combined. In heath care, aggressive preventive care (design patterns) is combined with systematic diagnostics of health-related issues (antipatterns). In manufacturing, quality certification programs like ISO 9000 (design patterns) are combined with aggressive process analysis, problem identification, and continuous improvement (antipatterns). Road signs are combined to point out good driving behaviors like "Pass on left" and hazards like "Watch for falling rock." In many other fields, the two practices go hand in hand. Software engineers should try to combine these two approaches.

A powerful movement in the quality industry, from the late '70s through the '80s, sought to involve front-line assembly workers in the quality process. These teams were tightly integrated with quality professionals. The teams, sometimes with light-handed management direction, would identify problems and contribute a block of time weekly toward solutions to those problems. My father, Robert G. Tate, Jr., became so attached to this process that he left a high-level position at Dover Elevators to pursue a consulting career installing "quality circles" around the world. He found that something magical happened with the involvement of the actual blue-collar plant floor. The relationships changed. Management, quality control, and the product builders began to work together. The process was remarkably simple:

- Quality circles would form for the purpose of solving quality problems.
- Participants would become involved in the identification and solution of quality problems.
- Management would empower them to deal with quality problems directly.
- Participants were educated to perform these tasks.

Many of the quality groups showed staggering returns. Other programs, such as Zero Defects, also thrived. Awards and accreditations, like Malcolm Baldrige and ISO 9000, gathered steam. The United States again discovered the value of quality.

In a very real sense, this book represents the same ideas that we see in other areas and places them in the context of Java application development. We are taking responsibility for bringing quality code to the desk of the common programmer. We want to identify places where our assembly line is broken. We want to spot holes in process and procedure that can cripple our customers or even ourselves down the road. We want to *know* when major systematic problems, like the routinely late turnaround times on Everest, occur. We then want to systematically solve them and save others from repeating our mistakes. Most of this book deals with antipatterns that are already well entrenched in Java programs, processes, and programmers. We should now talk briefly about the discovery process.

1.4.2 Detective work

Experienced, conscientious programmers find most antipatterns. While teaching the instincts of a detective may be difficult, I can provide some rules of thumb from my consulting experience. These tips represent the places and methods that I use to find antipatterns hiding in a customer's process, or my own.

Bug databases contain a bounty of wealth

Most organizations already track quality metrics in the form of bug databases. We can look to establish patterns based on keyword searches and spot checks. Are we seeing a pattern of memory leaks? If so, misconceptions or frameworks could be a source of bad behavior. Are the change lists for view-related maintenance particularly long? If so, this could point to tight coupling. Are certain objects or methods particularly vulnerable to bugs? If so, they might be refactoring targets.

Early performance checks can point out design flaws

Sanity checks for performance early in a process can point to design flaws. Some of these might be isolated incidents. Some, even at an early stage, are likely to be common enough to warrant special attention. Internet applications are particularly vulnerable to communication overhead. Several of the antipatterns in this book deal with round-tripping, or making many communications do a relatively isolated task. Sloppy programming, including many of the issues in chapter 9, can also cause performance problems, especially in tight loops.

Frequent code inspections and mentors help

Beginners and early intermediates can be a common source of antipatterns. Pairing them with more experienced programmers and architects for code reviews and mentoring can head off many bad practices before they start. At allmystuff, the engineering department did a nice job of mentoring the solutions development staff, which typically consisted of weaker developers with better customer skills. Even a five-minute code inspection can reveal a surprising amount of information. Are the methods too long? Is the style readable and coherent? Are the variable names appropriately used? Does the programmer value her intelligence above readability?

End users are unusually perceptive

Later in my career, I began to appreciate the impact of end-user involvement at all stages of development. I found that end users can be brutally honest, when we allow them to be. When I began to truly listen to feedback, I could tell very early if my team would need to bear down or change direction. Too often, we ask for the questions and listen only if we hear what we want or expect.

Outsiders can use interviews

The most powerful tool for someone outside a development organization is the interview. People are put off when we try to propose answers without asking questions. Getting them to open up in an interview is usually not difficult but may occasionally be troublesome. When we are digging for trouble, people are much more perceptive if they perceive that we are helping to solve problems and not looking for someone to blame. Interviews are most useful if we can script at least a set of high-level questions, as well as anticipate some low-level questions.

Establishing a pattern

By itself, a problem is only a bug. We should already have processes and procedures for identifying and fixing bugs. Indeed, many of my father's customers had adequate measures for detecting and removing bad products from the line. The problems with these reactive approaches are twofold. First, we will never find all of the bugs. Second, if we do not fix the machinery or the process, we will create more bugs! After we have established a pattern, we need to elevate it from bug to antipattern.

1.4.3 Refactoring antipatterns

After we find a problem and establish a pattern, our strategy calls for refactoring it to form a better solution and process. Here, we are overlapping the realms of design patterns and antipattern. My intuition is that this combination is part of what is missing in the software quality industry. The combination of design patterns and antipatterns is practical and powerful. Poor solutions can be identified through antipatterns and redesigned into more proven and practical alternatives using design patterns. The process of continually improving code through restructuring for clarity or flexibility and the elimination of redundant or unused code is called *refactoring*.

Many experts advocate the rule "If it isn't broke, don't fix it." In the realm of software development, following this rule can be very expensive, especially at the beginning of a program's life cycle. The average line of code will be changed, modified, converted, and read many times over its lifetime. It is folly to view a refactoring exercise as time wasted without considering the tremendous savings over time. Instead, refactoring should be viewed as an investment that will pay whenever code is maintained, converted, read, enhanced, or otherwise modified. Therefore, refactoring is a cornerstone of this book.

1.5 Why Bitter Java?

In the Java community, the study and promotion of design patterns, or blueprints for proven solutions, has become well established and robust. The same is not true of the antipattern. As an architect and consultant, I have seen an amazing sameness to the mistakes that our customers tend to make. While the problem of the month may change slightly in a different domain or setting, the patterns of poor design, culture, and even technology stay remarkably consistent from one engagement to the next. I strongly believe that the study of antipatterns inherently changes the way we look at the software process. It keeps us observant. It makes us communicate. It helps us to step beyond our daily grind to make the fundamental process changes that are required to be successful.

Most of the antipatterns in *Bitter Java* have a relatively limited focus compared to the more general antipatterns in the *AntiPatterns* text. Each is applied to the server-side programming domain, which is popular right now and young enough to have a whole new set of common mistakes. Our hope is that this book will continue the evolution of the study of antipatterns and bring it into the Java community.

1.5.1   *The Bitter Java approach*

Bitter Java will take a set of examples, all related to a simple Internet message board, and redesign them over many chapters. Each iteration will point out a common antipattern and present a refactored, or redesigned, solution that solves the problem. In many cases, there may still be problems in the refactored solution. In most cases, these problems are addressed in later chapters. The others are left as an exercise for the reader. Regardless, the focus of the antipattern is to refactor a single problematic element.

The focus of *Bitter Java* is on server-side programming. The base architecture uses common server-side standards of servlets, JSPs, Java connectors, and EJBs. Where possible, the solutions are not limited to any vendor, though EJB implementations are currently platform specific.

1.5.2   **Bitter Java *tools***

Based on my experience, I have chosen VisualAge for Java, WebSphere, and DB2 because the software and support are readily available to the authors. All of the implementations stress open Java designs and software architectures. Free, open alternatives to our software include:

- The home page for Java, with pages for base toolkits and specifications for J2EE extensions, can all be found at http://java.sun.com.
- A free servlet container, for the execution of servlets and JSPs either in a stand-alone mode or with a web server, can be found at http://jakarta.apache.org/tomcat/.
- A free web server can be found at http://apache.org.

BEA Systems' WebLogic also supports all of the classes and constructs used in this book, though they have been tested only on the original toolset. We do use the IBM database drivers (and I feel that the native database driver is almost always the best option), but we do not use the IBM-specific framework for databeans or servlet extensions, opting for the open counterparts instead.

1.5.3 *The* Bitter Java *organization*

Bitter Java presents some background information in chapters 1 and 2, and subsequent chapters present a series of antipatterns. The patterns are collected into themes. Chapters 3 and 4 focus on a design pattern called Model-View-Controller, and an associated Java design pattern called the Triangle. Chapters 5 and 6 concentrate on optimizing memory and caching. Chapters 7 and 8 concentrate on EJBs and connections. Chapters 9 and 10 address programming hygiene and good performance through scalability. The chapters are organized in the following manner:

- Background material for the chapter.
- A basic description of the antipattern, including some of the root causes and problems.
- Sample code illustrating the use of an antipattern.
- One or more refactored solutions.
- Sample code illustrating the refactored solution.
- A summary containing the highlights of the chapter.
- A list of all antipatterns covered in the chapter.

Antipatterns and templates

Each antipattern is presented twice: once in the main text, and once in template form at the end of each chapter. The templates that we have chosen, both within the chapters and at the end of most chapters, are based on the templates suggested in the *AntiPatterns* book. Those in the chapter text choose a minimalist organization with the keyword *antipattern* followed by its name in a heading, followed by some background material. Finally, we present a refactored solution following the *solution* keyword. At the end of each chapter is a more formal template, following the conventions in *AntiPatterns*. In this way, we make this initial contribution to the initial collection of Java antipatterns.

If you are looking for particular technologies or techniques, this is where to find them:

Table 1.1 The technologies and techniques in *Bitter Java* are presented in an order that suits the ongoing refactoring of a set of examples. This table can help you navigate to particular concepts that might interest you.

Technologies	Chapter
JSP design and composition	3, 4
Servlet design and composition	3, 4
JDBC, database programming	3, 4, 5, 6, 7
Connections framework	7
XML antipatterns	7
Web services	7
EJBs	8
Caching	5
Model-view-controller	3, 4
Performance antipatterns, tuning, and analysis	10
Antipatterns and the development process	1, 2, 11
Connection pooling	6
Coding standards and programming hygiene	9

For the programming examples, http://www.manning.com/tate/ has the complete code for all of the examples, as well as forums for discussing the topics of the book. The code in the book will be in the Courier style:

```
code = new Style("courier");
```

Where possible, long programs will have embedded text to describe the code. In other places, there may be in-line code that looks like this. Most of the programming samples are based on VisualAge for Java, version 4, and WebSphere Studio version 4. Most Java examples are based on JSP 1.1 and on Java 1.2. We'll tell you if the version is different. Some of the code examples for the antipatterns are for instructional purposes only and are not running programs. We have compiled and tried all of the good programming examples. They work.

1.5.4 *The* **Bitter Java** *audience*

Bitter Java is not written like a traditional technical manual or textbook. To keep things lively, we will mix in real-life adventure stories at the beginning of each chapter, with a programming moral later in the chapter. We hope that the style will engage many, and it might put off a few. If you are a reader who likes to cut to the chase, you will probably want to skip to chapter 3, and you may even want to skip the story at the front of each chapter. If you are looking for a dry reference with little extraneous content, this book is probably not for you.

The skill level for bitter Java is intermediate. If you have all of the latest Java design pattern books and have bookmarks for all of the key design pattern communities, this book is probably not for you. If you do not yet know Java, then you will want to try some introductory books and then come back to this one. If, like most Java programmers, you are an intermediate who could use some advice about some common Java pitfalls, then this book *is* for you. Those who have converted to Java from a simpler language, a scripting language, or a procedural language like C may find this book especially compelling.

Finally, *Bitter Java* is intended to be at a slightly lower level of abstraction than project management books, or the first *AntiPatterns* text. We intend to introduce code and designs that do not work and to refactor them. From these, we will show the low-level impact of process flaws, a failure to educate, and shortcuts. From this standpoint, architects and programmers will find appropriate messages, but they may find following the examples challenging. Project managers may also find some compelling thoughts, though the programming content may be slightly advanced. For both of these communities, antipattern summaries are listed at the end of each chapter in a concise template based on those in the original *AntiPatterns* text.

1.6 *Looking ahead*

Bitter Java is about programming war stories. Books like *The Mythical Man Month,* by Fredrick P. Brooks, have left an indelible impression in the minds of a whole generation of programmers. We aim to do for Java programmers what Brooks did for project managers. *Bitter Java* is about the quest for *imperfection.* We are not looking for isolated examples. We are looking for problems in process and culture, demonstrated by technically flawed designs. We are setting out to find the repeated mistakes that have bite. We are recording some of the useful mythology of the Java programmer.

In the next chapter, we will focus on the current landscape of the industry and why it is so ripe for antipatterns. Next, we will look at basic server-side designs and some antipatterns that plague them. Then, we will focus on common problems with resources and communication. Finally, we will look at advanced antipatterns related to enterprise Java deployments. So, settle down with this cup of bitter Java. We hope that when you're done, your next cup will be a smoother, more satisfying brew.

The bitter landscape

2

This chapter covers
- Standards supporting server-side programming
- Early antipatterns plaguing Java programmers
- The emergence of extreme programming practices

With four kayaks on top of the jeep, two local guides, a close friend, and I are driving up the Piedra River in Colorado. The river is pristine and intensely beautiful. Its steep gradient and the huge water volume remind us of the formidable reputation it has among kayakers, but I feel confident. We have asked our guides to take us to the easy section. We drop off our car and put in.

I follow our local guide closely. The plan is to blow through the first few less technical rapids without scouting and then head downstream. I paddle around a river bend and, as I take in the sight and sound, my stomach tightens. The river explodes around me. I am not moving nearly fast enough—and I haven't scouted. As I plunge over the waterfall, I realize I have no chance. I flip quickly, miss my roll, and I am now struggling to pull out of my kayak in the middle of a Class IV+ rapid.

2.1   Fertile grounds for antipatterns

Over the last decade, open Internet standards supported by components and frameworks have relieved us of the burden of writing complex communication layers. After a couple of decades of struggling with memory management and multiple inheritance in C and C++, programming environments like Java have allowed us to concentrate on the application more than the programming language. Traditional struggles with distributed communication, database programming, and inadequate object packaging are now handled by EJBs and even Common Object Request Broker Architecture (CORBA), which hides much of the complexity of these problems.

This rich and fertile soil has made it easier for us to grow increasingly sophisticated applications. But rich soil is fertile for weeds, too. With the increased power of frameworks comes the danger of increased laziness. New layers can also add complexity and heavier processing burdens.

Antipatterns love to hide, and we generally give them plenty of opportunity to do so. In this chapter, we will review the basic building blocks of server-side Java. We will explore its landscape and, along the way, expose many of the crevices that conceal antipatterns. We will also lay a common foundation so we can begin the discussion of Java antipatterns with a shared perspective and terminology.

2.1.1   The benefits of layering

Modern programming systems organize increasingly complex ideas by building increasingly complex and abstract services using layers. Early computers did not layer services at all. Programs were necessarily small because hardware systems and software organization could not support large software projects. Twenty-five years ago when we wrote our first Basic programs, they typically went through very few layers: the program, the Basic interpreter, Basic services, and thin hardware-support layers. The Basic and hardware-support layers were burned onto read-only remory (ROM). Of course, we did not get any of the benefits of a dynamic operating system, either.

Over time, operating systems and languages have increased layering, masking complexity and improving productivity. Today, a simple "Hello, World" servlet could go through many layers, networks, and computers. Figure 2.1 on the next page shows some of them, along with the supporting Internet standards. On the client, the HTML presentation layer renders the user interface. HTTP provides a standard messaging protocol that in turn is layered over standard communication and addressing protocols, such as Transmission Control Protocol (TCP) and Internet Protocol (IP). A domain name service (DNS) server provides a software layer to resolve the name to a formal IP address. The server has TCP and IP layers for communication, HTTP layers to receive a client request and process static content, a Java virtual machine (JVM) that supports the Java programming language, and a servlet container that processes the servlet. It would not be unusual for a simple Hello, World servlet, called through a proxy server or firewall, to touch hundreds of hardware and software layers.

The architect for each layer made assumptions that work in your favor. Imagine a casual Internet programmer who uses the Microsoft software development tools (Visual Basic, Access, and FrontPage) to create a simple website for his home business over a weekend or two. Consider the complexity of the possible application:

- Through HTML and extensions, he may give it a sophisticated graphical user interface (GUI). For this, he may use some complex structures such as tables, layers, prebuilt components, and even multimedia.
- The site could directly communicate with other user interfaces through links, even when the programmer knows little about the environment supporting them.
- He could link it to a database without any programming, and even link it to other applications on the desktop.

Compared to programs written just 10 years ago, this application is amazingly sophisticated thanks to the supporting layers. Microsoft architects correctly assumed that home developers are willing to trade performance for ease of

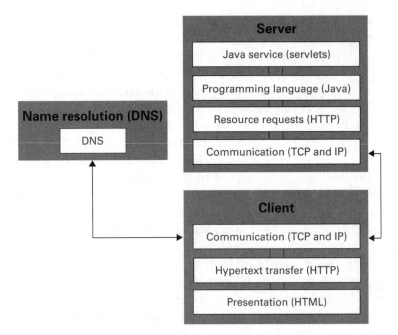

Figure 2.1   Here are some of the layers an Internet application typically uses. On the client, the browsers encapsulate layers for communication, message transfer, and presentation. Name resolution is handled through DNS, and the server contains layers for communication, messaging, and application program support.

use. Similarly, the architects of the Internet assumed that we are willing to trade some of the power of each native platform for a least common denominator that allows open interoperability.

2.1.2   *Layering can work against us*

Students of antipatterns also know that an architect's assumptions can work against them. A website you create using Access, Visual Basic, and FrontPage can be ramped up quickly, but consider the disadvantages:

- Maintenance is likely to be a challenge.
- The site will be difficult to scale and extend.
- You must deal with serious security risks.
- The site's architecture may render it slow and unstable.

- The site's lack of support for important standards, sensible within a homogeneous environment, makes it difficult to integrate with the rest of the enterprise.

The original layer architect's assumptions in this case are working against us. Many of the antipatterns in this book have their roots in this conflict between initial development simplicity and subsequent needs for scalability, extensibility, and performance. Initial assumptions can lead to shortcuts that burn you badly as your project evolves. I spent the first four years of my consulting career picking up broken glass from this type of scenario. In many instances, a customer takes a simplistic, oversold technology; builds a system in a short time without a concrete design; and pushes it broadly into production. I recall chatting on a plane with executives of an airline reservation system. Just before, one of our salespeople tried to sell a version of Basic as the best tool to build the next generation of one of the largest reservation systems in the world! These executives got a good chuckle, but many will take the bait. The lure of simplicity makes them believe outrageous sales claims: the simplistic environment is just as robust and scalable as any other environment. The trick to success is to ask relevant questions like these:

- What does each layer bring to the table? We should understand the *value* of each additional layer, and ask the vendors to provide references and prove their worth.

- What is the cost? We need to be insistent about establishing *cost*. The lure of something for nothing can often cloud the judgment of the most sensible. Java technologies are no different. EJBs have often been over-sold, and to customers who have little or no chance for success.

- Under what circumstances are those layers likely to break? What is our *risk*? In essence, we want to find the traps. This book explores some likely traps surrounding server-side Java. In this overview, as we build up the various layers of the Internet, we will also notice the types of nooks and crannies that conceal other traps.

- What can we do to protect ourselves from the trap, and how can we extricate ourselves once we've fallen in?

- Finally, we want to establish our *risk mitigation*. This is the realm of the antipattern.

2.2   *Internet technologies*

The technology that has probably shaped Java programming more than any other is the Internet. This huge, loose collection of disparate systems is connected by broadly adopted open standards. These standards form a large part of the foundation for Java servlets that are used heavily in this book. The Internet standards technologies are far from spectacular. Faster, more flexible, and more reliable communication protocols than TCP exist. The power of markup languages like Standard Generalized Markup Language (SGML) dwarfs the standard Internet markup language, HTML. HTTP is simple and unsophisticated. The Internet works because the open standards are simple, widely adopted with just enough flexibility and power to allow meaningful development.

To find out more about a standard, the ultimate source is the RFC. The standards board that has oversight responsibilities for the engineering of the Internet is the Internet Engineering Task Force (IETF). A party submits a standard on a form called a request for comments (RFC). When an RFC is adopted, it becomes the standard. The process works like this:

- The IETF forms a committee that drafts a document (the RFC).
- Interested parties review the RFC and make comments.
- If the reviews warrant change, the comments are incorporated into the RFC.
- When debate is closed, the final version of the RFC becomes the standard and no further comments or changes are permitted.
- From that point forward, changes occur through subsequent RFCs, which can enhance, clarify, or even supersede previous RFCs.

Unlike proprietary standards, RFCs for all Internet standards are at our fingertips. They can be found at the IETF website: http://ietf.org/rfc.html. Problems can be debated in a formal and open forum. If our understanding is ever muddy or unclear, we should go right to the source of the standard: the RFC.

2.2.1   *Internet topologies affect our applications*

Let's examine the composition of the Internet with an eye toward the places that antipatterns may develop. The nodes of the Internet interoperate through a defined set of standard networking protocols. Since most organizations and corporations have security concerns, attaching all computers directly to the Internet is not practical. Instead, several layers are used for protection, as shown in figure 2.2.

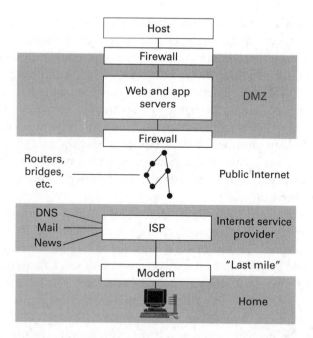

Figure 2.2 The Internet can have many layers between clients and their ultimate destination. The enterprise layers are typically broken into two zones, separated by firewalls, called the DMZ. The web server, and sometimes the web application server, resides in the DMZ.

2.2.2 *Enterprise layers add security and overhead*

Most enterprises use firewalls and proxies to shield them from basic security problems. A *firewall* is simply a machine placed between the Internet and the HTTP servers of a corporation so that hackers cannot attack directly. Most modern architectures call for two firewalls, placed on either side of the web servers, to create an area called the *DMZ* (*demilitarized zone*). The DMZ defines an area between the internal intranet and the external Internet. The Internet includes both benevolent customers and malevolent hackers. The DMZ provides a necessary compromise: access is open enough for meaningful communication and security is tight enough to protect assets. Each firewall enables different protocols, so hackers must coordinate two different types of attacks to reach the systems on the private intranet. The systems in the DMZ are more vulnerable to attack but are perfectly situated to provide access to corporate resources from the public Internet so that effective commerce can take place.

Figure 2.2 shows the communication hops that a typical customer-to-business HTML page request might take. The request goes from the browser to a modem. There, the modem connects over a phone or cable network to the Internet service provider (ISP). This area, called the *last mile*, is seen as the last major obstacle to widely available high-speed connections. The ISP provides such services as domain name lookup and mail and news servers, and it provides an entry point to the Internet. Once the request is on the Internet, it could take any number of steps before it reaches its ultimate destination. The request then must make its way through a number of hops in the intranet. In this case, we have a firewall, a combined web and application server, another firewall, and a host.

As firewalls are added for security, sprayers and caches are added for performance. *Sprayers* take a single Universal Resource Locator (URL) and map it onto many different web servers. The sprayer may allocate requests using sophisticated load balancing, or it may opt to simply serve them round-robin, allowing a distribution of work across many servers. *Caches* are boxes that store frequently accessed, static items like images, web pages, or multimedia files. Since these files are not likely to change, a hardware cache can resolve many requests before they even reach the web server, resulting in better throughput and faster response times.

While sprayers, firewalls, and caches serve inbound traffic, *proxies* are machines that protect outbound traffic. A proxy will make requests on the outside Internet on behalf of a browser. The proxy gives users inside a firewall secure access to the Internet, based on corporate policies.

These hardware layers serve us well, but they also add length to the communication path between our customers and our server-side code. The added firewalls might also conspire to foil us, if we are not careful.

Objects in the mirror appear closer than they are

The additional path length is completely transparent to us, so it is easy to assume that our users are closer to our applications than they might physically be. Many of us are accustomed to controlling the network between our clients and servers. With the Internet, that is simply not the case. Assumptions that our communications are near instantaneous can be disastrous. *We must make every communication count.* Many of our antipatterns in the book are due to making too many round-trip communications.

In late 1998, my Java proof-of-concept team designed an application that was to be deployed in a Canadian government organization and used by Canadian citizens. We treated round-trip communications like gold because the quality of the Canadian phone system is not uniformly as strong as the U.S. counterparts. In some cases, we could not even expect a 14.4 connection. Our deployment succeeded, where our competition failed, with fewer programmers, less advanced technology, and less support for the latest standards because our solution made fewer round-trip communications.

The security policy of the firewalls is out of our control

If we are building server-side code and our customer is a corporate customer, then we must deal with one or more firewalls *on each side of the communication*. In most cases, we do not fully control the security policy of the firewalls on both sides of the communication. Therefore, we must make sure that our applications use only the most basic communication protocols and standards.

In early 1996, my Java proof-of-concept team was asked to build a prototype of a Java application for a city government to show legal cases to government employees. We were told that the applications and users would all be within the same firewall. Due to complex user-interface requirements, we built a sophisticated applet with lots of bells and whistles. We connected directly to the database with Java Database Connectivity (JDBC). (After all, it was only a prototype.) Our project was a huge success.

We were later called back to the customer to fix a few bugs in our prototype. The customer had a consultant come in and deploy the prototype with very few changes. The application was so successful that many outside the city legal department wanted to see it and use it. Though we had recommended against deploying this application in its prototype state for this reason, we wound up fixing it because an executive played a round of golf with our customer. My team never again assumed that we controlled the deployment topology or security policy of a firewall. Let's explore the open standards that are fair game for our deployments.

2.2.3 Standards enable the Internet and add layers

If hardware has powered the Internet, software has united it. Though there are tens of thousands of disparate hardware platforms doing the grunt work, standards have allowed them to work together with remarkable cohesion. Post Office Protocol (POP3) and SMTP are standards for email. Emerging standards like Wireless Markup Language (WML) serve pervasive computing. Several standards are particularly important to us; for example, TCP and IP are networking protocols that are the Internet standard; HTTP is a protocol used to transfer documents; HTML is a tag language specifically used for documents; XML is an emerging markup language for giving structure and meaning to generic data. Table 2.1 lists the standards that will form the foundation for the Java server-side standards.

Table 2.1 The standards that enable the Internet. They will insulate our server-side Java applications from the details of low-level message transfer, data presentation, and parsing.

Standard	Meaning	Purpose
TCP	Transmission Control Protocol	System layer for reliable message transmission protocol.
IP	Internet Protocol	System layer for distributed addressing and routing protocol.
HTTP	Hypertext Transfer Protocol	Application layer for data transfer.
HTML	Hypertext Markup Language	Tag language used to add structure and meaning to documents for presentation. It has evolved to include increasing application content.
XML	Extensible Markup Language	Tag language used to add structure and meaning to generic data.

2.2.4 *TCP and IP provide low-level communications*

TCP/IP is a combination of two standards. TCP is used to provide message transmission. That means it provides these services:

- Data will get from the source to the destination, or an error will be reported.
- The data will reach the destination in the right order.
- The data will reach the destination without duplication.

TCP establishes a connection and disconnection protocol and a data-transfer protocol. Attached to each message is a TCP header of 20 bytes or so that contains the source address, destination address, sequence, acknowledgment number, size, and a checksum for reliability.

IP specifies a header, an address, and a routing protocol, among other things. An IP header contains source, destination, size, and reliability information.

IP addresses are like mailboxes, and they uniquely identify every logical site on the Internet. Four numbers, separated by dots, represent an IP address. If you are currently online, on most systems you can find your dotted address by typing "ping localhost" in a command window. This address is unique to your system and can be reached by any point on the Internet. Some IP addresses are static; some are issued dynamically. A DNS takes a friendly name and translates it to a valid IP address, which allows us to type (and remember) names like http://www.bitterjava.com.

IP routing is handled hop-to-hop. A node delivering an IP message does not need to know how to get to the ultimate destination. It only needs to know the address of the next hop. A message being delivered from bruce.bitterjava.com to braden.austin.oberon.com might be delivered to bitterjava.com, then oberon.com, then austin.oberon.com, and finally braden.austin.oberon.com. The IP message has a timeout built in that prevents infinite looping in the delivery process. If a message eventually times out, it is discarded and the source is notified so that the message can be retransmitted. Each node has a routing table, which contains the rules for individual message dispatch.

Given these standards, we have the primitives necessary to create distributed applications. Since we can now assume that other Internet servers also adhere to these standards, we can build additional application layers that will enable increasing levels of cooperation. Following are some application-level standards.

2.2.5 *HTTP provides application-level transport*

TCP and IP are basically at the network and transport layers. HTTP, the protocol that browsers use to transfer web pages, moves up to the application layer. It does not specify a connection, instead it uses TCP/IP for networking services.

In its simplest form, HTTP is a client/server protocol. In reality, HTTP has matured to a library-level transport given its popular use for tunneling all sorts of application-specific protocols. For example, HTTPS can be used to send secure messages. The base HTTP protocol shields the application developer from the complexities of basic client/server communication. The client specifies a resource in the form of a URL. The URL specifies the protocol, a domain name, and a path. Once the URL is specified, a TCP session is established, and the client can issue commands. The most common commands are GET and POST.

A GET request is used to request server documents. When the client issues a GET, the server then sends back a content message consisting of status, header, and data. The Multipurpose Internet Mail Extension (MIME), the type standard, determines how the browser will display the data. Common types are text/html for formatted text, text/plain for plain text, and image/

jpeg or image/gif for other images. MIME types also exist for XML, multimedia, and applications.

A POST request instructs the server to execute an application to process a block of information. A POST request can be issued within HTML to send user-specified form data to the server for processing. The server then processes the request and sends back a response, as in the GET. The traditional method for processing the request is the Common Gateway Interface (CGI) command. CGI simply starts a program on the server on behalf of the client. This architecture can result in poor performance, because each request starts a process, makes any required enterprise connections, processes the request, takes down the connection, and then kills the process—an extraordinarily cycle-expensive process. A significant advance over CGI, and the application architecture for Java that we will use in this book, is called a *servlet*. A Java servlet is a Java program that stays resident after use. Chapter 3 will begin to describe some antipatterns of servlet architectures.

2.2.6   *HTML and XML*

We have been working our way up the food chain to progressively higher level layers. HTML was originally created as a standard way to format documents for display, but it has grown to be rich enough to build basic application user interfaces. Though there are many extensions and versions, its user interfaces can be flexible, portable, scalable, and efficient. HTML consists of plain text, marked up with tags. Known as *metadata*, or data about data, these tags define how HTML documents are interpreted and rendered.

Where HTML tags attach a structure and meaning to documents, XML attaches structure and meaning to generic data. With XML, standard types can be built to do many different things. Hundreds of XML standards already exist. XML types can be used in a number of ways. XML documents can be translated with Extensible Stylesheet Language (XSL). This translation technology can generate HTML from XML for easy presentation; it can even *repurpose* data, or translate content from one XML form to another. Within an application, the Document Object Model (DOM) interface can be used to parse even the most complex XML documents. You can find additional information about XML, including the base specifications, at http://www.xml.org. Numerous other great websites and books on XML are available as well.

Internet layers solve client/server problems

Each successive Internet standard forms an increasingly abstract software layer. The combination that is the Internet has shown incredible power and promise. It solves many of the antipatterns that were introduced with client/server technology:

- Where client/server standards were proprietary, these standards are open. The increased abstraction layers make it possible for disparate systems to communicate with ease.

- The standards make it easy to deploy applications. Since the HTML user interfaces are lightweight and delivered automatically, the client-side administration burden is reduced significantly. Though visions of enterprisewide thin clients have still not materialized as expected, Internet systems still significantly reduce the pain of administration.

- The standards make it easier to develop common client user interfaces. Supporting many different client types is inherently expensive. The Internet's thin-client model can ease that burden significantly.

Few deny the impact of open Internet standards on modern application development. We need to understand that there is a cost. Our user interfaces are not going to be as sophisticated as the client/server counterparts. Distributed networks are also not going to be as fast as local networks. If we are not paying attention, the top-level abstractions can easily hide the amount of work that must be done to move data. We can easily be complacent and neglect to take into account the cost of round-trip communications.

2.2.7   *Mini-antipattern: Too Many Web Page Items*

Throughout this book, we will discuss explicit antipatterns, but also what we call "mini-antipatterns"—small but common problems. The first antipattern is an example dealing with the cost of Internet communications. Though each Internet layer is incredibly efficient, we can easily underestimate communication costs. We have already seen that the path of an Internet request can be deceptively long, including many Internet hops and layers. With the growing sophistication of the artwork and dynamic content on many pages, the number of communications can exacerbate the problem. Let's take a look at a simple page and one with more complex graphics. Page Detailer is a tool that shows the load times of all the individual HTTP items on a screen. Figure 2.3 shows a page detail of the simple introduction page for http://www.yahoo.com. The page is deceptively simple and loads extremely quickly. For this entire page, despite the dynamic nature of the content, only three graphics and five distinct items loaded. The entire site loaded in half a second.

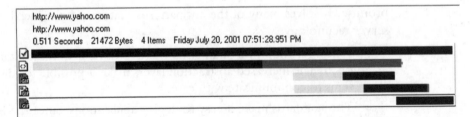

Figure 2.3 This page detail shows the power of simple page design. The bars represent the total time required to load the various objects on the Yahoo! site.

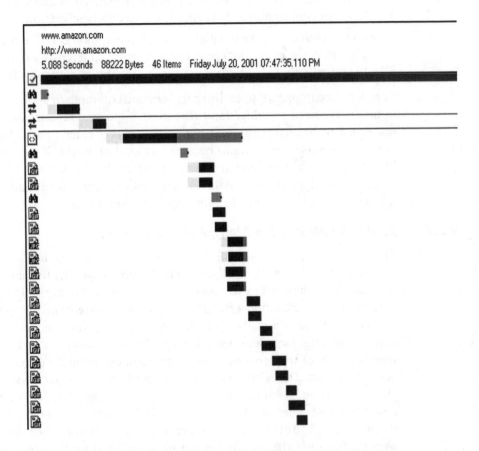

Figure 2.4 This page detail shows the cost of building a more sophisticated page. True, the Amazon site loaded in a quick 5 seconds, but on a client with a high-speed modem. Together, these sites illustrate the power of simple web pages with few objects.

By contrast, figure 2.4 shows the Page Detailer output for http://www.amazon.com. There were 10 times the number of items, and the load time was roughly 10 times as long. Though this test does not prove that the longer load times are due to the higher number of graphics, the circumstantial evidence is interesting. Since each of these objects will trigger a separate HTTP GET, there is a distinct performance penalty, and though small graphics are blocked by many browsers in groups of four and should load quickly, the effects are cumulative. For a Java programmer, the lesson is clear: a Java Internet application can be only as good as its supporting architectures and page designs. Reducing the number of web objects can reduce the load time, especially when transactions are very short or resources are constrained.

We have seen the basic building blocks that will support Java server-side programming. As we move up the food chain, we begin to discuss the applications that incorporate these layers. We will now briefly examine the organizational principles of Java through object orientation. We will consider the traditional view that the supporting layers can help us, and we will also look at some ways those layers can work against us.

2.3   *Object technologies and antipatterns*

Although object-oriented programming (OOP) requires a different methodology and thought process than its procedural predecessor, the fundamental concepts are few and simple. In structured programming, one divides data into data structures and programs into functions. If a procedure or function is too complex, it is decomposed into several simpler procedures. Complex problems are decomposed into smaller and smaller units until each is of a manageable size. Figure 2.5 shows the typical organization of a structured

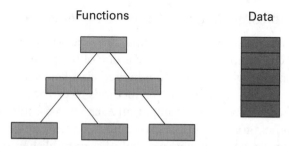

Functions   Data

Figure 2.5 Structured programming calls for the separate creation and maintenance of major data structures and programs. Taking larger procedures and decomposing them into smaller ones control complexity but can make maintenance problematic. The famous Y2K bug thrived under conditions of structured programming.

program. Procedures are in a hierarchy and data exists in data structures. In most cases, data and applications are managed by very different subsystems.

2.3.1   Encapsulation helps to isolate change

A basic idea of object technology is that things that belong together are packaged together. We encapsulate basic building blocks with both functions and variables that belong together, as in figure 2.6. The building blocks are the same, but the organization is different. In this way, we can package data together with the functions that manipulate it. This organization is much more like the way that we think, and leads to more maintainable and elegant designs.

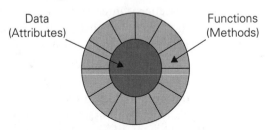

Data (Attributes)   Functions (Methods)

Figure 2.6   Encapsulation packages methods and the data structures that they use together. This packaging scheme allows implementation hiding, which in turn leads to formal interfaces that improve maintenance by containing major changes to smaller areas.

A *class* is a template where attribute types and methods are defined. It is a complex data type. In this case, the data type not only defines the data, but also the things that can be done to the data. We call the variables *attributes* and the functions *methods*. For example, a tax-form object may have data for the customer and the individual line items, and a method to calculate the form. It might also have methods to create and destroy the form and validation methods. A class is like a cookie cutter, and an object is like the cookie. To create an object, a program *instantiates* a class. For a class called Author, we might have objects for Tate and Hemingway.

2.3.2   Inheritance enables packaging of common behavior

Inheritance captures real-world relationships, allowing packaging of common behavior without cut and paste. Inheritance is one of the primary ways that we can customize frameworks for reuse. An inherited class keeps the interface and features of its parent, and can override the methods to provide new behaviors, or add new instance variables. For example, an Author class could inherit from Person. The designers for the Author class could concentrate on building in functionality related to being an author—say a list of published books. All of the functionality in Person—such as the name, birth date, address, and phone number—could be inherited. Combined with good encapsulated component design, inheritance is another tool for reuse, and also provides better reliability.

When we reuse a piece of code, we tap the developers who built it, as well as the testers, technical writers, and users who have used the original.

But inheritance is not a panacea. Deep inheritance trees are complex to read and use, and they can hide some unpredictable behaviors. Using inheritance as a shortcut can cause serious trouble. If a sales department, for example, wants special extensions of the corporate customer class, a temptation is to create a `SalesCustomer` class. If other departments follow suit, we will rapidly lose the ability to create real-world subclasses of the `Customer` class. Still, it is another tool in our bag of tricks that can elegantly capture powerful, real-world relationships.

2.3.3 *Polymorphism enables flexible reuse*

With inheritance, many different forms of an object can use the same type of interface. A real-world appliance is a good example of polymorphism. Many forms of an appliance do different things through the same interface. Every electrical appliance has the same interface with the wall—a plug. Though appliances can have dramatically different functions, the builders of a house need to install a single kind of interface—the electric outlet. Polymorphism works the same way.

A good example is the desktop document. To print it, we simply drag and drop it on a printer object. The desktop documents are like polymorphic appliances because we can have many different forms of documents with different behaviors and the same interface. The printer object is like the power outlet. Whether the object is a spreadsheet, document, or graphic, though the logic to print is different, we print it with the same gesture. The interface is the same, even though the implementation may be dramatically different. The printer object does not need to know that a document is a spreadsheet. It can simply execute a generic print method specified in a standard interface, and let the specific print method do the specialized job. In this way, application programmers are able to tap the functionality of specialized documents through a standard interface.

2.3.4 *Mini-antipatterns: Excessive Layering*

I successfully exit my boat just as my body is sucked over yet another waterfall. After a protracted swim through three rapids with drops, jagged trees, and boulders, I am lucky to escape unscathed.

The guides misunderstood our request for an easy section. Up to that day, their "advanced" section was a new, expert-level Class V run that had not yet made it into guidebooks. Though the easy section in the guidebooks had no rapids harder than intermediate Class III, their "easy" section started with a Class IV+ 8-foot twisting waterfall.

Object technology, and associated iterative methodologies, have been the most significant, and oversold, development improvements since structured programming. While many see dramatic improvement in development cycle times, others fall short of expectations. The journey into the unknown domain of objects can quickly turn for the worse. As with my trip down the Piedra River, you can suddenly find your plans working out badly. In the kayaking community, I easily qualify as conservative. I do extensive research on everything that I run. I scout anything bigger than a ripple. I set safety and carry rescue gear. On the Piedra we had not communicated clearly with our well-meaning guides. Against my better judgment, we had not scouted the river and failed to see the real danger. We did not stop to ask critical questions of the experts.

Often when we are being sold a new technology, external forces get in the way. Others promote the new run as easier than Basic, more flexible than C++, and faster than Assembler. We can get the Class V thrill with Class III risk. Our eagerness and job pressures drive us to look for shortcuts. We may not get the appropriate education or leadership, and may not even know that we are in way over our heads until we are swept over that 8-foot fall and left swirling in the river.

Object-oriented systems add layers to shield us from complexity. We have seen that necessary additional layers add value at a cost. Extraordinarily complex frameworks can be built with relatively easy reuse. Each layer has the potential to have an interface simpler than the last. If we ignore the cost of each added layer, we can get into trouble quickly. If a system design has too many layers through excessive wrapping, deep inheritance, or poor design, performance problems can grow exponentially. Code can also grow too deep to maintain. It is easy for increasing complexity to be hidden until we integrate at the end of a project, only after huge investments have already been made.

In seven years as a systems programmer at IBM and in another five years as a consultant, I saw this happen many times to experienced and talented teams. Some problems are notorious for attracting solutions that are elegant but slow. These are a few examples I participated in:

- In the early and mid-1990s, graphical frameworks were such a problem. I was a member of one of 20 or 30 teams throughout the industry that were racing to build an object-oriented user interface framework. We placed general wrappers around Windows and OS/2 graphical objects.

When we did so, we lost many of the specialized optimizations that the graphical framework designers built in, such as event filtering and repainting. The original Java architecture for user interfaces, the Abstract Window Toolkit (AWT) library, also had this problem. It was easy to produce heavily layered user interfaces. All of the inheritance layers and the generalized event management without adequate filtering made it easy for one user event to generate thousands of messages with simple gestures like resizing. The term "event storm" was coined to describe this common antipattern.

- Early versions of a fully object-oriented operating system called Taligent also suffered from the over-layered user interface antipattern. I worked alongside many of the brightest minds in the industry in a department responsible for porting Taligent to other operating systems. The fundamental premise of the operating system was that everything was an object, from semaphores to file handles. This came at a price, but it was one that we thought that we could manage. As Apple and IBM worked to merge IBM's microkernel architecture with Apple's critical user-interface technology and operating system abstractions, scope grew and fundamental assumptions also changed. We would work to integrate massively complex systems at the last hour. The debugging process was much faster than I would have thought possible, but the thing was s-l-o-w. There were simply too many layers for the operating system or supporting hardware. We had not even layered on user applications yet.

- In the mid- to late 1990s, early persistence frameworks, which allowed a network of objects to be transparently saved to a database, were also perilous. Many customers rolled their own. Very few were successful. The reasons were twofold. First, the frameworks, implemented on relational databases, could not take advantage of many of the features of the database engines for sorts, stored procedures, or complex queries. When these functions were handled at the application layer, the performance was hideous. Second, the frameworks were usually very complex, adding many layers to the most basic of object models. When complex and heavily layered object models are defined, even the most robust architectures can break down.

Not all of these projects had happy endings. Some of the time, simplification with faster hardware and better designs were able to take up the slack and save us. Occasionally, we never recovered. When you're developing complex object-oriented designs, you must build layers for simplicity and modular design. You should also control the proliferation of layers to essential well-defined abstractions for the sake of performance. Integration testing throughout the lifecycle helps you identify where the bottlenecks and excessive layering are likely to occur so that you can spot problem areas early enough to make design changes and set early expectations.

2.3.5 Setting the stage for Java

Over time, C++ established object technology in systems labs and even in traditional information technology shops across the world, and newer languages began to include object-oriented features. In early 1996, CORBA was floundering with both leading vendors, IBM and Iona, struggling to reach a critical mass for their products and Microsoft struggling with DCOM, an alternative architecture. Object technologies had established an effective beachhead, but application programmers were lashing out at C++ and Microsoft development environments and operating systems were under increasing criticism. Java and Netscape were about to take the world by storm. Hydrogen, meet oxygen.

2.4 Java technologies solve antipatterns

In early 1995, Sun built a proprietary browser with a language allowing tiny applications, called applets, to be distributed like web pages. In late 1996, with help from Sun, Netscape built the Java language and applet architecture into its popular browser. The Internet was beginning to explode and suddenly Netscape, and thus Java, were everywhere. It's not a perfect language by any stretch. Its types are an awkward blend of primitives and true classes. It is still controlled by Sun instead of an open standards board. And the Java community still bickers about where to take the language and major extensions like J2EE.

But Java *is* right for the time. The C++ syntax, though awkward at times, provides an instant community of programmers hungry for a cleaner and higher level language. The Internet foundations positioned Java early on as the premiere language for web class applications. *One of the key factors to Java's success is its resolution of problems and antipatterns common in other languages!* The C++ and Smalltalk communities both had significant challenges that Java addressed, at least partially. Here are some of the major problems that programmers of other languages encountered:

- *Pointer arithmetic in C and C++, leading to instability and inherently poor security.* C++ and C instructions could be used to write to just about any memory in the computer, including maliciously or in error. If a block copy went one byte too far, it was likely stomping on someone else's data. Java placed necessary constraints around pointer use for significant gains in security and stability.

- *Poor memory management in* C++. Java is a "garbage-collected" language, which means that the memory management is much more automatic. Where each object in C++ must be explicitly allocated and freed, Java objects can be automatically removed from memory when the last reference to them is removed. Chapter 6 will show us that we still have to pay cursory attention to Java memory management, but the issues are much less complex and absorb much less time.

- *Problematic multiple inheritance.* C++ programmers had a difficult time with *multiple inheritance*, or inheritance from more than one parent. For example, a person could be a customer and also a father. When frameworks got complicated, programmers had a difficult time determining which methods were inherited from which parent. Many a masters thesis was written on the C++ diamond inheritance problem, an artifact of C++ multiple inheritance. Java addresses this problem by allowing only single inheritance. Interfaces can still be used to implement classes with more than one characteristic.

- *Runtime type errors in Smalltalk.* Java is strongly typed, so programs have fewer instances of runtime type errors. The compiler can catch many instances of type collisions.

- *Frustration with the proliferation of compiler directives.* Includes, defines, and typedefs were convenient at times but difficult to manage. In C++, cascading include files were very difficult to maintain, understand, and debug. Java forbids include files, and it does not have compiler directives.

Though Java has its own set of problems, it did address some significant complaints of C++ and Smalltalk programmers. It is a fine example of the industry looking at the antipatterns of a technology and then solving them with an improved technology. Languages and standards layers can play a role in antipattern development. Frequently, the development process will play a larger role in the antipattern life cycle.

Java allows us to take significant steps forward from its predecessors. The capabilities of the language and libraries are improving rapidly. But a language in itself is only a tool. It cannot protect us from major antipatterns. The methodologies and procedures that we define to employ the tool have a much larger bearing on success or failure.

Figure 2.7   Jimmy Vick over the Sinks. This photograph shows a literal interpretation of major problems with a waterfall. In kayaking, cascades are tough because each dramatic drop can take a paddler further off of his line, eventually dooming the run. Programming schedules can be doomed when fixed in a sequence, slipping further with every major step in the cycle.

2.5   *Major problems with the waterfall*

Java eases many C++ complexities, such as multiple inheritance and memory management. We have a good start, but *the process that we use to build applications is as important as the basic building blocks.* In this review, we will briefly explore the impact of methodologies on antipatterns. Traditional application development, called the *waterfall development methodology,* can allow complex and large projects to be attacked but falls short as requirements get more dynamic (figure 2.7). In general, the waterfall methodology can also provide safe harbor for antipatterns:

- The process resists change in general, especially new requirements. This resistance to change leads to fertile grounds for antipatterns, because we have fewer opportunities to refactor.

- The waterfall process can delay high-risk elements (such as integration) until late in the cycle, when it may be too late to recover. Antipatterns can thrive in such an environment. Quality control is back-loaded, and antipatterns found near the end of the cycle might never get fixed because of political pressures and expense.

- The process forces complex one-time translations between major documents, with no built-in accountability. For example, it is difficult to be sure that a program matches the original requirements. It is also difficult to determine where a functional requirement maps onto an end user's requirement. This characteristic is called *traceability*. Process-related antipatterns can thrive because of the relative lack of accountability.

2.5.1   *Iterative methodologies*

Iterative methodologies improve this process by providing short cycles with increased accountability throughout each cycle. We can adapt to change and address key risk elements early. Iterative methodologies help to thwart antipatterns by doing the following:

- Iterative methodologies provide more opportunities to refactor, usually after each cycle. We then have an antidote for antipatterns that are discovered.

- Deliverables, called *artifacts*, trace end-user requirements from the beginning throughout the entire process after each iteration. This traceability improves accountability and quality. In such an environment, process antipatterns are more easily exposed and addressed.

- One of the cornerstones of a good development process is to build in increasing value as the cycle matures. With an iterative process, it is much easier to do so. Managers can define functional releases from a very early stage, with extra functionality delivered throughout the process that builds in additional use cases with each successive iteration. Reducing scheduling pressures by accurate sizing can also help code quality.

2.5.2   *Mini-antipatterns: Incomplete Process Transitions*

Many projects never see the full benefits of object-oriented technologies and related methodologies. They fail to make an effective transition from the traditional waterfall process. Here are some common mistakes:

- *Poorly defined iterations.* It is easy to look at an iterative methodology and incorrectly infer that the process is unstructured. Many project managers do not attempt to set a comfortable rhythm of release cycles.

In these cases, it is tough for a team to develop a set of repeatable practices that work for the team.

- *Poorly defined stopping points.* I visited customers in the mid-1990s that are probably still iterating on a single release. It is important to specify a set of metrics that define the completion of a project or a phase. Usually, the iteration units include a finite set of use cases, with some flexibility to remove or insert additional cases as time permits. The flexibility must be constrained by the business environment, though. Sometimes, different phases of the process are overemphasized. For example, too many iterations over the requirements and design without a clearly defined exit strategy led to the term *analysis paralysis.*

- *Overmanagement of the artifact set.* Object-oriented tools and processes can produce a staggering amount of paper if left unchecked. When working at a startup, we were trying to get our cycle time down to six weeks. As we were building the Client Services organization, two managers with mostly procedural process experience produced a process that would require a staggering 30 artifacts! Each artifact must contribute to the delivery of a quality product to the customer. Additional artifacts should be added only to the extent that they patch holes in the existing development process and lead to better efficiency or quality.

- *Poor teams or inadequate education.* Most projects that succeed do so because of good teams with strong knowledge. Investments in the quality of the team, especially when teams are new to object technologies, cannot be overemphasized. In addition, it never ceases to amaze me that many extremely strong teams have completely inadequate hiring processes. Investments in consulting to shore up the interview process or good recruiting companies usually provide outstanding returns.

Effective education and leadership can go a long way toward steering clear of many of these problems. In fact, many organizations seed small projects with high-powered consultants who serve as mentors to jump-start a project. Hands-on training under effective leadership can be an extremely strong educational method.

2.5.3 *Programming horizons: Extreme programming*

Some recent refinements to iterative development have shown promise under the label of *extreme programming.* Kent Beck introduced this methodology in a book called *eXtreme Programming eXplained.* This refined process uses a collection of simple rules and practices to form a disciplined and team-oriented approach to software development. The process is described in detail at http://www.extremeprogramming.org. Most of the rules are borrowed from other processes. My intuition is that the methodology will prove to be highly effective at combating antipatterns. Here are some of the key rules of extreme programming:

- *Choose simple solutions.* Extreme programming advocates the simplest solution that will work, because of the ease of development and maintenance. Simple solutions are much less likely to create antipatterns, or to hide the ones that already exist.

- *Ensure that the customers are on site.* Throughout the programming cycle, end users should be available to provide guidance, insight, and opinions.

- *Write user stories.* These serve the same purpose as the use case. They are a few sentences of text, written by the users.

- *Divide larger projects into measured, planned, small releases.* Smaller cycles result in user feedback, diminished risk, and adaptability to change. Small cycles also allow antipatterns to be found and refactored sooner, through more frequent code examination at every cycle.

- *Refactor early and often.* Refactoring involves redesigning solutions in order to improve readability or design and remove redundancy or unused code. Extreme programming operates under the philosophy that refactoring is a wise investment. Refactoring helps eliminate antipatterns.

- *Program in pairs.* This practice seems wasteful but has tremendous power. Pair programming improves quality and reduces tunnel vision. Antipatterns are more likely to be spotted with an extra set of eyes.

- *Code test cases before the rest of the system.* This practice helps to flesh out the requirements and ensures that new classes will meet specifications.

- *Do not use overtime.* This is probably one of the most useful—and least used—ideas in extreme programming. Overtime increases available hours and reduces clear thinking, with predictable results.

Extreme programming also introduces other practices that are not outlined here. The methodology is garnering strong momentum among developers. I used many extreme programming practices at allmystuff and endorse them heartily. Such excitement and promise from a new methodology that actually simplifies the development process is promising, and many of the practices build a culture of teamwork and merciless refactoring that can thwart antipatterns before they start.

2.6   *A quick survey of the bitter landscape*

To study Java antipatterns, we must begin with an understanding of the overall landscape: the standards TCP, IP, HTTP, HTML, and XML. The performance of communications on the Internet has improved dramatically, but complex interfaces with too many objects can hinder good performance before any application code even enters the picture.

Object technologies that form the basis for the Java programming model make it easier to design and build applications. Encapsulation allows effective packaging, inheritance allows meaningful reuse, and polymorphism allows many forms of the same thing to share the same interface. Object layering is the foundation for good design, but excessive layering will hamper performance and readability.

Programming methodology also plays a significant role in Java antipatterns. Traditional methodologies such as the waterfall process allow complex projects but do not adapt to change or late-breaking requirements. Iterative development, through multiple cycles that iterate over requirements, allows better adoption of change and vastly superior risk management, but object-oriented processes are not bulletproof. Programming processes are still improving, and extreme programming shows promise. By adopting practices that have worked under many circumstances, the process is improving the reliability and efficiency of teams today.

This summarizes chapter 2. Part 2 continues with a series of chapters that iteratively improve a poor programming example. Chapters 3 and 4 will introduce model/view/controller concepts and related antipatterns in the new context of servlet designs. Chapters 5 and 6 will demonstrate effective memory use and caching techniques. Chapters 7 and 8 will focus on EJBs and connection models. Chapters 9 and 10 will deal with the bigger picture, addressing scalability and programming hygiene.

2.7   *Antipatterns in this chapter*

These are the templates for the antipatterns that appear in this chapter. They provide an excellent summary format and form the basis of the cross-references in appendix A.

Too Many Web Page Items

RELATED ANTIPATTERNS: Round-tripping. This antipattern is one form of the Round-tripping antipattern, found in chapter 8.

DESCRIPTION: Many web designers have no concept of the costs associated with loading web page items such as graphics or animations. Since items have incremental load costs, too many objects can doom performance.

MOST FREQUENT SCALE: Enterprise. Most enterprises operate from a standard template with a common look and feel.

REFACTORED SOLUTION NAME: Eliminate Extraneous Objects.

REFACTORED SOLUTION TYPE: Software.

REFACTORED SOLUTION DESCRIPTION: Often, the number of web page objects can be reduced through careful user interface design.

TYPICAL CAUSES: This antipattern can occur when graphics are used in place of text, when image is valued over performance and performance is not a priority.

ANECDOTAL EVIDENCE: "This site looks cool, but it is dog slow." "We have burned up 8 seconds, and we have not even loaded the servlet yet."

SYMPTOMS, CONSEQUENCES: Poor performance.

ALTERNATIVE SOLUTIONS: Faster connections and better deployment hardware or architecture.

Excessive Layering

DESCRIPTION: Object-oriented systems are easy to layer with excessive complexity that is not required to adequately describe the relationships and behavior in the model. The complexity of the software can easily outpace the capabilities of the hardware platform.

MOST FREQUENT SCALE: Application.

REFACTORED SOLUTION NAME: Refactor; Integrate Early and Often.

REFACTORED SOLUTION TYPE: Software.

REFACTORED SOLUTION DESCRIPTION: Layers can be combined or eliminated based on the requirements of the system.

TYPICAL CAUSES: This antipattern can occur when inexperienced developers design solutions, or when communication between teams is inadequate, such as in geographically distributed groups.

ANECDOTAL EVIDENCE: "I sure hope that this integration works. We don't have time to recover if it doesn't." "Do you really need 18 levels of inheritance in `customer`?"

SYMPTOMS, CONSEQUENCES: Poor performance, poor readability.

Incomplete Process Transition

RELATED ANTIPATTERNS: Analysis paralysis. New teams without complete education or experienced leadership can overanalyze solutions to the point of stagnation.

DESCRIPTION: Many never enjoy the full benefits of object-oriented technologies and iterative processes because they fail to make a full transition to the new development process.

MOST FREQUENT SCALE: Application or enterprise.

REFACTORED SOLUTION NAME: Education, Leadership.

REFACTORED SOLUTION TYPE: Process.

REFACTORED SOLUTION DESCRIPTION: Obtain additional education, be certain that sufficient experience and leadership is on the staff, and make sure that each document contributes to bottom-line quality. Exercise care when managing the iterations.

TYPICAL CAUSES: A company or organization might be interested in the benefits of object technologies but unwilling to pay the price.

ANECDOTAL EVIDENCE: "We seem to be chasing our tails." "I just don't get it."

SYMPTOMS, CONSEQUENCES: Teams iterate over a problem well beyond the schedule constraints, especially in the analysis phase (called analysis paralysis). Projects run over budget as frequently as before. Neutral or negative quality results are also indicators. Maintenance times are not shortened.

Part 2

Server-side Java antipatterns

W*hen my party of three ran our first Class IV river, we found that many of the paddling methods that had worked for us in the past were no longer sufficient. When we ran a series of waterfalls called Five Falls, a few of us went over the first rapid backward. One person flipped and had to swim ashore. Another flipped and was rescued mere feet away from the start of the most dangerous rapid on the river. We quickly learned to scout, ask questions, and understand where the troublesome spots were likely to be. We needed to dive into the details.*

In Part 2, we introduce common Java-based antipatterns in detail. We demonstrate the problems through poor Java examples. Variations of our ongoing application, a bulletin board system, are used throughout the book. We will iteratively improve it in chapters 3 through 8. We will attack antipatterns related to basic model-view separation, caching, memory management, connections, and EJBs.

As we dive into the details, we will see two central themes: resource management and organization. Server-side Java programmers must come to terms with efficient management of connections, memory, files, and threads. Significant portions of whole books have been written on this subject. Noted author and Java guru John D. Mitchell warns that "the lack of clear thinking and design in dealing with resources in Java is the *crux* issue for server-side Java folks." Indeed, several of the chapters focus on a single resource or technique for resource optimization. Chapter 6 (on memory management) and chapter 7 (on connection management and coupling) are especially poignant examples. Organization is undeniably the other dominant theme. Chapters 3 and 4 deal with a model-view-controller organization that will improve maintenance and readability.

You should be aware of several assumptions I make as I build the examples in the book:

- In many cases, examples are bitter *by design*. Our approach is to refactor the same base program in order to resolve one problem at a time. Many known problems are not solved until late in the text. Obviously, code in this book should not unthinkingly be pasted into production environments.

- Most of the programming examples are complete rather than discussed through code fragments. Because they place at your fingertips all of the details that you need to follow the conversation, I hope that understanding the argument in this part will be easier.

- The exception management in the examples is intentionally sparse. This keeps them brief and helps us maintain our focus on the bitter lessons being taught.

- You can download the code from this part at your convenience from http://www.bitterjava.com.

Chapters 3 and 4 will discuss a modern version of the Model-View-Controller design pattern; chapter 5 will improve the performance of that design through caching; chapter 6 will address Java memory management; chapter 7 will deal with connections and coupling; and chapter 8 will deal with EJBs. In truth, I could have organized the book differently. I settled on this structure because it provided a logical refactoring of a single application through successive steps that flowed freely and smoothly. The initial examples build a bulletin board system. A cache improves the performance, and memory-management techniques help manage the cache. Connection pooling provides a cache of sorts for database connections. We finally look at how this project might be done with a bitter EJB implementation. While this organization provides a free-flowing book, it may be admittedly more awkward as a reference text. Such are the day-to-day compromises of a starving author.

And now, let's roll up our sleeves and attack the bitter business at hand.

Bitter servlets 3

This chapter covers

- The common Magic Servlet antipattern
- A step-by-step refactoring guide for Magic Servlets
- A core design pattern called the Triangle for server-side programming

It is springtime, and the hills are uncharacteristically green. I am mountain biking near my home in Austin. I take a fairly remote trail winding through the rocky Bear Creek pass. It traverses the steep slopes beautifully, alternately sliding on and off the ridges to provide many technical climbs and screaming descents. I am winded as I arrive at a particularly technical climb on the Outback trail. I have not ridden for a long while. Most Outback climbs are not risky because it is hard to gather dangerous speed. Hills with very steep ledges are usually too difficult to climb, but this one has teeth. It has enough rocks and ledges to make abruptly stepping off the bike on this steep terrain an adventure, as my shins remind me.

There are few good and many bad places to dismount, with cracks that can snap ankles or knees. Mentally rehearsing my dismount at a demanding ledge around a blind switchback that I seldom conquer, my mind wanders off the trail. As I begin to round the tight bend at the bottom to start the climb, my body slips backward, my front wheel lifts off the ground, my weight abruptly shifts forward, and my back wheel spins out. I have lost momentum and am still depressingly close to the bottom. I step off my bike and start to walk it toward the top.

At the top of the hill, barely visible between the cracks, on a large, flat rock is a huge rattlesnake. It is not in a defensive posture, so there is no rattle and no other hint to its presence. The snake occupies the very flat rock that I would have landed on had things gone as in my rehearsed dismount. It seems that my poor conditioning and technique today conspired to save me. I shudder, and continue to climb.

3.1   Getting off on the wrong foot

The basic gateway into most standards-compliant server-side Java applications is the *servlet*: a simple wrapper around a service, implemented in Java and reached through HTTP. This chapter lays out the most basic antipattern involving the first layer of server-side Java: the Magic Servlet. Projects bungling this first basic step have little hope for success. After examining the roots of this antipattern, we will lay out the design, the symptoms, and the problems of the Magic Servlet antipattern. Then, through a series of refactoring steps, we will transform this antipattern to the Triangle, a design pattern based on Model-View-Controller.

3.1.1   An early antipattern: The Magic Pushbutton

First, we should discuss an early version of an old antipattern. I encountered the Magic Pushbutton in many of my early consulting engagements. (Stewart Nickolas, a well-respected software architect, coined the phrase.) After I started searching for the antipattern, I found what looked like the same wretched application at many different places and different circumstances. It didn't matter what industry. It didn't matter what language was used for the implementation, though Visual Basic was the most common. The problem was more common to inexperienced programmers, but hard-core programmers were not immune. It was the simplest of antipatterns: an unstructured application consisting of a single, monolithic procedure fired by a user interface event. In a nutshell, this problem is a lack of decomposition. A simple example is an 11 KB application with 10 KB hanging off a pushbutton, as in figure 3.1. Many readers recognize this antipattern even before further description. This pushbutton is "magic" because it does most of the work for the application within a single function. These applications make me think of a fat plumber in tight Spandex. The proportions are comical and the results can be disastrous. The applications are obviously ugly and difficult to maintain, but the root cause or the refactored solution is not always obvious.

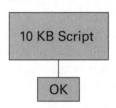

Figure 3.1
The Magic Pushbutton consists of a block of code hanging off a pushbutton and represents event-driven programming at its worst. It was most prevalent in the mid-1990s when Visual Basic, PowerBuilder, and similar languages were at their strongest.

The Magic Pushbutton can actually be traced to the graphical tools that broke onto the programming scene in the early 1990s. The tools ushered in drag-and-drop programming. Like the ancient trading clipper ships that carried rats with new diseases hidden among the treasures they bore, these tools brought a new kind of antipattern. If you bring up an old copy of Visual Basic, it's easy to see why. The program, and many others like it, first presents a screen that allows the development of the user interface. The programmer can rapidly prototype the user interface and then attach the necessary logic. The subliminal message is clear: "Go ahead and start. You're building a program, not a house. You don't need a foundation. With this new tool, you will have plenty of time to design what you need down the road." For some applications, this approach works because the back end is already defined. The back end might take the form of components built by someone else, stored procedures, or existing transactions. For these applications, the view and model are cleanly separated.

If the back-end logic is not well defined, then the application can easily adopt the user interface as the design. The programming scripts, in the form of basic functions, are attached to user interface events at key places. The biggest event, like a Submit or OK pushbutton, usually attracts the most code, much like the jam side of a piece of toast attracts the floor. The Submit function becomes the focal point of the application and, without the appropriate organization, grows like an unmanageable blob.

3.1.2 *Building with Model-View-Controller*

Of course, the right way to design this type of application is by using one of the most famous and earliest design patterns: Model-View-Controller. This common design pattern has become a staple of modern programming. It is mentioned in the introductory chapters describing the utility of design patterns in the design pattern bible, *Design Patterns*, by the Gang of Four. It has been refined and updated in such places as *Core J2EE Patterns*, by Deepak Alur, et al., and the Jakarta Struts framework. It has served as the foundation for frameworks in Java, C, C++, Smalltalk, LISP, and many others. In this chapter, we will introduce a variation called the *Triangle pattern*. With this pattern, the model is the business logic that drives the application. The user interfaces, called *views*, then present various aspects of the model. The interaction of the user and other input/output streams are managed with the controller. This design pattern is shown in figure 3.2.

3.1.3 *Failing to separate model and view*

Listing 3.1 is a program, written by a novice, that fails to use Model-View-Controller. This baby is admittedly too ugly for even a mother to love, but Java like this is more common than any of us would like to admit, especially in

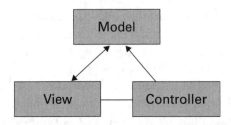

Figure 3.2 Model-View-Controller is a design pattern that advocates clear separation of the user interface, or *view*, and the business logic, or *model*. The controller helps to manage input and output. The advantages are widely recognized as easier maintenance, improved flexibility, and more readable code.

script-driven visual development environments. Listing 3.1 is an attempt at a bank account program.

Listing 3.1   A bank account without Model-View-Controller

```java
import java.util.*;
import java.text.*;

public class BitterAccount {

  public String balance;
  public String fieldValue;                        ● View logic
  public int radioButtons;
  public float balanceNumber;                      ● Model logic

public BitterAccount() {
    balance="0";
  }

public String buttonPressed() {
    radioButtons = userInterface.getRadioState();      ● View logic
    if (radioButtons == 1) {
      fieldValue = userInterface.getEntryField();
      balanceNumber = balanceNumber +                  ● Model logic
        Float.valueOf(fieldValue.trim()).floatValue(); ● View and
                                                           model logic

      balance = Float.toString(balanceNumber);         ● Model logic
      return balance;
    }  else if (radioButtons == 2) {                   ● View logic
      fieldValue = userInterface.getEntryField();
      balanceNumber = balanceNumber -                  ● Model logic
        Float.valueOf(fieldValue.trim()).floatValue(); ● View and
                                                           model logic

      balance = Float.toString(balanceNumber);         ● Model logic
      return balance;
    } else if (radioButtons == 3) {                    ● View logic
      return balance;                                  ● Model logic
    }
  }

}
```

This application is the logic for a simple ATM program. It takes the amount in an entry field and debits or credits the account appropriately, based on the state of a radio button. Notice that no attempt has been made to break out the business logic (the account) and the user interface. In fact, the model and view are so tightly intertwined that, in many places, both the model and view are serviced with a single line of code. It is ugly now, and enhancements—such as checking for an overdrawn state, adding a customer name and number, and attaching this program to a database or transaction—will keep the snowball rolling. Adding on the functionality of the account number verification will just exacerbate the problem.

3.1.4 Breaking out the model

Now, consider the first refactoring step in listing 3.2, the alternative:

> **Listing 3.2 The Model-View-Controller design pattern**

This bank account program is the model portion for the same application as listing 3.1, refactored to the Model-View-Controller design pattern.

```
public class Account {                              ● Model logic

 private float balance;

 public Account(float openingBalance) {
    setBalance(openingBalance);
 }

 public void setBalance(float amount) {
   this.balance=amount;
 }

 public float(get.balance) {
   return this.balance
 }

 public float debit(float amount) {
   setBalance(this.balance-amount);
   return (this.balance);
 }

 public float credit(float amount) {
   setBalance(this.balance+amount);
   return (this.balance);
 }

}
```

The revised program is much simpler. It is the model for the application. The name of the class is a real business object. The methods represent real business actions. We can do things that we would expect to do to an account, like debit and credit and check the balance. The logic that handles events for the user interface and marshals the data to the user interface does not belong with the model. We would add a controller object to handle these functions.

Notice the clarity of the model. It is infinitely more readable. As we have come to expect, we can answer questions about extending the model much more easily in the second example. Where could we add an overdrawn condition to the first example? What about the second? How would we credit interest in the first example? What about the second? With our first antipattern, we will review the same problem with a similar solution.

3.2 *Antipattern: The Magic Servlet*

Now we come to the most common server-side Java antipattern. The root of this antipattern is a poor understanding and application of the principles of Model-View-Controller. With this design pattern, our fundamental goal is to establish a firm separation between the data model and the view, called *model-view separation*. Both the model and the view must be implemented without assuming anything about implementation details of the other. The controller helps establish the connection between the two so that neither the view nor the model must know about the internal details of the other.

We have seen the model-view-controller architecture applied many times with client/server architectures. When we split architecture between client and server, a common assumption that is usually not far from the truth is that the model-view separation follows without much additional effort. On the client side, we have view logic. On the server side, we have the model. The controller is usually split between the two, with most of the implementation on the server and in supporting software. Most client-server user interfaces are highly interactive, so the model and view interface is not dramatically different from a localized implementation. In fact, it is easy to become lazy and assume that model-view separation will naturally fall along the client-server boundary.

We can get into serious trouble when we apply the same loose understanding to servlet programming. Let's think back to my ride up the trail in the Texas hill country. We have an easily visible danger and a hidden one. Because we are using servlets, the lines between the client and server are clearly articulated, are they not? The client, which represents the view, is simply the HTML user interface. The servlet represents the model, and the software layers of our chosen architecture will handle the tasks usually managed by the controller. As we bike up this trail, our eyes are clearly on the rocks of the trail: the separation between the HTML view and the servlet.

We are about to be bitten by the hidden rattler. Unlike many interactive client-server user interfaces, HTML has more of a batch-oriented architecture. From the HTML code on the client, we will send an *upstream* HTTP POST to submit a request, and wait for the response. When that request is complete, the server will send back a different *downstream* user interface. *We must also apply sound model-view separation to this downstream interface!* Unfortunately, many programmers usually focus on the cleanly separated upstream HTML view, missing the generated downstream interface. The servlet becomes a tangled mass of model and downstream view. This is where the rattlesnake is hiding.

3.2.1   Can we use servlets as the model?

We now have a clear evolution from the Magic Pushbutton antipattern to present implementations. Instead of hanging an interactive 10 KB script off a pushbutton, we hang a 10 KB servlet off a Submit button, with all of the code in a single service method, as in figure 3.3. To review, a servlet is a server-side, long-running Java program that conforms to an open application programming interface (API). Servlets provide a server-side interface to a service. When we click a Submit button on an HTML page, if the back end is written in Java, we are likely calling some form of a servlet first. Servlets take advantage of the HTTP GET and POST interfaces. The user invokes the servlet through one of these commands.

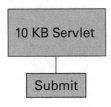

Figure 3.3
The Magic Servlet is perhaps the most common server-side Java antipattern. Programmers assume that the separation between HTML and Java servlet code represents a clean separation between user interface and business logic. For many reasons, such is not the case.

The typical servlet runs and prints some HTML that is returned to the client when the request is complete. The heart of the antipattern is here, with the downstream user interface. Figure 3.4 shows the architecture for a servlet and a request for a servlet on most commercial web application server architectures.

Listing 3.3 is an example of a servlet that prints "Hello, World" to the user.

Listing 3.3   "Hello, World," the traditional first Java server-side program

```
import javax.servlet.*;
import javax.servlet.http.*;
import java.io.*;

public class HelloWorld extends HttpServlet
{
  public void doGet(HttpServletRequest req,
```

❶ `helloWorld` **class**

❷ **HTTP** GET **interface**

```
                    HttpServletResponse res)
                    throws ServletException, IOException
  {
    res.setContentType("text/html");
    PrintWriter out=res.getWriter();
    out.println("Hello World");
    out.close();
  }

}
```

❸ Print writer prints HTML responses
❹ Printing response for the end user

❶ This servlet inherits from HTTPServlet, which is the standard communication between the client and server for this class of application.

❷ This program is triggered by an HTTP GET request. The other common HTTP command is POST. Many times, both GETs and POSTs are sent to a common method. These examples consolidate them in a method called performTask.

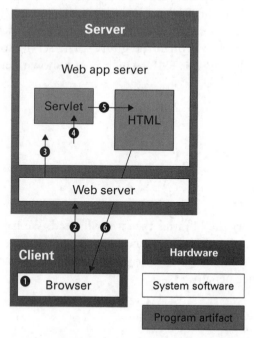

Figure 3.4 ❶ The user makes a request for a servlet. ❷ The browser does an HTTP POST. ❸ The web server passes the request through to the application server, possibly installed as a web server plug-in. ❹ The application server invokes the servlet. ❺ The servlet executes and prints out an HTML page that ❻ is returned to the user.

❸ The servlet gets a writer, which prints output that will be returned to the user.

❹ The writer is used to print HTML text that is returned to the user.

3.2.2 *Stumbling into the Magic Servlet trap*

In better designs, the servlet is only an interface point between the server-side logic and the user interface. Unfortunately, the monolithic, do-everything server script is still the design of choice for a surprising number of Internet sites. It's not always a servlet. This antipattern can take the form of a CGI script, or an Oracle PL/SQL stored procedure, or an ActiveX request. In its worst, and arguably most frequent, form, this servlet may handle the parsing of the arguments, the back-end database connections, and the printing of the resulting HTML page. The similarities to the Magic Pushbutton antipattern that I started presenting to clients in 1990 are striking.

The program which follows is an example of a do-everything Java program taken from a real-world consulting engagement. It is based on an administrative program used to print all of the pages in a bulletin board. This example is actually much cleaner than the Perl program that it replaced. It has been stripped down to the basics for clarity, and the recognizable features have been changed for readability (and to protect the guilty). The servlet logic is completely separated from the input HTML (which is not shown here), but the silent viper is hiding within.

```
package bbs;

// Imports

import COM.ibm.db2.*;
import java.sql.*;
import java.io.*;
import javax.servlet.*;
import javax.servlet.http.*;
```

These lines simply import the libraries that we will need. We have imported the libraries for JDBC, Java utilities, Java servlets, and our database driver. This sample uses DB2 drivers. Generic JDBC drivers are available as well, but may have a slight performance penalty.

```
public class PostList
    extends javax.servlet.http.HttpServlet
    implements Serializable {

    /************************************************************
     * Process incoming requests for information
     *
     * @param request encapsulates the request to the servlet
```

```
* @param response encapsulates the response from the servlet
*/
```

This is the class definition. We have elected to inherit from the most common servlet type, or HTTPServlet. We get a request object and a response object. These represent the initial request and the page that we will send back as a response.

```
public void performTask(
  HttpServletRequest request,
  HttpServletResponse response) {
```

Listing 3.4 shows the meat of the workhorse method. This is the proverbial 10 KB script. The performTask method consolidates all of the different paths into the servlet to process the request. These may take the form of HTTP GETs or POSTs. In this method, we can begin to see where we start to break down architecturally. We are printing the HTML response page directly from this method. These print statements are sprinkled throughout the method, along with database requests and a little error processing.

Listing 3.4   We hopelessly tangle the model and return-trip view

```
try {
  response.setContentType("text/html");        ❶ View logic
  PrintWriter out = response.getWriter();
  out.println(                                  ❷ View
    "<!DOCTYPE HTML PUBLIC \"-//W3C//DTD "         logic
      + "HTML 4.0 Transitional//EN\">\n"
      + "<HTML>\n"
      + "<HEAD><TITLE>Message Board</TITLE></HEAD>\n"
      + "<BODY>\n");

  Class.forName("COM.ibm.db2.jdbc.app.DB2Driver") ❸ Model
    .newInstance();                                   logic
  Connection con = null;

  String url = "jdbc:db2:board";                 ❹ Model
                                                     logic
  con = DriverManager.getConnection(url);

  Statement stmt = con.createStatement();
  ResultSet rs =                                 ❺ Model
    stmt.executeQuery("SELECT subject, author, board" +  logic
                      " from posts");

  out.println("<h1>Message board posts</h1>");   ❻ View
  out.println("<TABLE border=\"1\">");              logic
  out.println("<TD><b>subject</b></TD>\n");
  out.println("<TD><b>author</b></TD>\n");
  out.println("<TD><b>board</b></TD>\n");
```

```
        while (rs.next()) {                          ❼ Model and
            out.println("<TR>");                        view logic
            String subject = rs.getString(1);
            String author = rs.getString(2);        ❼ Model and
            String board = rs.getString(3);            view logic

            out.println("<TD>" + subject + "</TD>\n"
            out.println("<TD>" + author + "</TD>\n");
            out.println("<TD>" + board + "</TD>\n");
            out.println("</TR>");
        }
        rs.close();                                  ❽ Model and view logic
        stmt.close();
        connection.close();                          ❽ Model and
        out.println("</TABLE>");                        view logic
        out.println("</body>");
    } catch (Throwable theException) {
    }

}
```

❶ The response writer is traditional view logic that establishes the result set and gets a writer to create the output result.

❷ This print statement contains traditional view logic that prints the HTML header to the output set.

❸ This database connection initialization is traditional model logic that initializes the class that establishes the connection to the database. Note that the database logic is right up against the view logic.

❹ In this traditional model logic, we establish the connection initialized earlier.

❺ Here we have more traditional model logic that runs the query and gets a result set.

❻ Once again, we switch back to view logic that prints table headings to the output result.

❼ Here, things actually get worse! We first start a result set, then print our HTML table headings, and then start to iterate through the result set.

❽ This model and view logic cleans up.

To continue with the listing, we will process the methods required to process the HTTP GET:

```
public void doGet(
    HttpServletRequest request,
```

```
        HttpServletResponse response)
        throws javax.servlet.ServletException, IOException {
        performTask(request, response);
    }
}
```

This method actually gets the HTTP request, which comes in the form of an HTTP GET. The method simply passes the request through to `performTask`, which we use as a consolidated service method.

The sample program returns a list of all posts on all bulletin boards. For our purposes, I stop there. The unabridged program was much longer. It also had to validate the input parameters; handle constraints for the post search; check for error conditions; manage user preferences like font, color, and viewing style; and count and process replies. The actual Perl script that formed the basis for the JSP rewrite was over 20 pages long! Table 3.1 shows the problems with this approach; a more detailed description follows.

Table 3.1 Common problems caused by the Magic Servlet. Most of these are project killers.

Problem	Discussion
No separation of concerns	The user interface and model are usually maintained by different people, but the view and model are integrated too tightly.
Difficult maintenance	Isolated changes in the model or view easily ripple out to force significant changes in other parts of the system.
Poor reliability	Since changes cannot be isolated, one change can break other parts of the system.
Little reuse	Because the application is not structured, there are no logical units for reuse beside the entire application. Instead, reuse will be limited to cut-and-paste programming.

- *No separation of concerns.* To efficiently maintain this system, your user interface design has to be maintained by your programmer. Ideally, we'd like the graphics designers to be working in an HTML editor and the programmer to be working in some programming environment. Since the HTML page only exists in the form of `print` statements in code, it's difficult for a graphics designer to edit effectively. It has been my experience that as a rule, great designers don't program well. Programmers usually can't design, and they generally know that they can't design. Unless you're building a team of one, it is usually more cost effective to split the workload between these groups. A clean delineation between the responsibilities of programmer and graphics designer is referred to as *separation of concerns.*

- *Difficult maintenance.* One result of this design is that making a change in the business process is difficult without a corresponding change in the code that returns the HTML to the client, the code that reads from the business model, the error-handling code, and the data-marshaling code. Bugs in both the presentation and the business logic must be maintained from the same place in the same way, even though the most efficient methods for each are very different.

- *Poor reliability.* This design makes it hard to spot bugs and easy to inject them. As a rule, the brain does a much better job grasping smaller scripts and scripts with a much more limited purpose.

- *Little reuse.* Because there are no business objects and no user interface templates, the most common reuse mechanism in this environment is cut and paste, which leads to dual maintenance and the proliferation of bugs throughout the system. In most organizations, cut-and-paste programming is responsible for more bugs than the next two problems combined. Y2K might be the best example. In this Y2K joke, the consultant says, "I have good news and bad news. The good news is that you only have three Y2K bugs. The bad news is that they have been proliferated through your enterprise 250,000 times." Cut and paste kills.

3.2.3   *Causes of the Magic Servlet*

The Magic Servlet can be found just about anywhere these days. The dominant feature is the encapsulation of model, view, and controller in a single method. This antipattern takes many forms. None of the intermediate refactoring steps that we will take goes quite far enough. Table 3.2 shows the causes of the Magic Servlet.

A servlet architecture can easily become the dominant organization for a program. The servlet alone is not enough. For all but the simplest applications, the servlet should only be the controller, and it should marshal view and model logic. Discipline is the best weapon against the Magic Servlet antipattern. Clear and concise design on each project doesn't cost time—it saves time. If you do find yourself looking down the barrel of a 10 KB servlet, don't panic. Refactor.

Table 3.2 The problems that cause the Magic Servlet. The most common causes are poor experience and porting. Perl is a particularly common port leading to this antipattern, exacerbated by many poor conversion guides on the Internet and other places showing how to do straight ports without redesign.

Cause	Description
Inexperience	Inexperienced Java programmers will use the design patterns that they have used the most. Programmers from scripting or procedural backgrounds are risks.
Perl rewrites	Most Perl programs are not well organized, and porting guides on the Internet do not preach restructuring the applications.
General porting	Porting a bad design to Java will lead to a Java program with a bad design.
Poor tools	Good design is easier with better tools. Some wizards create poorly structured code.

3.3 Solution: Refactor using commands

In the late 1990s, an IBM team led by Dr. Mike Conner did significant and powerful research on design patterns that could ease the adoption of Internet standards such as servlets and Java. This team was a key early collaborator for the creation of JSP and was also instrumental in the production of the early EJB specifications. To my knowledge, they were among the first to recognize the power of this family of design patterns. Many of those ideas are captured simply and effectively in a practical book called *Design and Implement Servlets, JSPs and EJBs for WebSphere*. Though it is written with WebSphere in mind, the concepts commute to other platforms as well. Similar models, like Model 2 in the Jakarta Struts framework, also support this type of model-view-controller separation.

The hard part of antipatterns is often recognizing them. Once we've identified an antipattern, we can take steps to refactor it or apply an existing design pattern. In this section, we will refactor our bulletin board listing servlet. Each step will get us closer to a Model-View-Controller design pattern. Settling for any of the intermediate steps of our refactored solution is not wise. The process should be followed all of the way to the model-view-controller conclusion. Our solution will deviate slightly, but the finished product will be easily recognizable as a model-view-controller architecture.

3.3.1 Break out the model

The 10 KB servlet is performing several functions that can be cleanly separated:

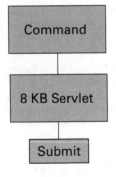

Figure 3.5
Breaking out the command is the first step in refactoring the Magic Servlet. The *Command* is a design pattern that allows clean wrapping of the business logic, or model. Later steps will break out the return-trip view.

- It is serving as the model for the program. The business logic is entirely or partially included in the servlet.
- It is serving as the controller for the program. It is handling the input form.
- It is performing the validation of the input data.

As we mentioned earlier, this design makes it difficult to make changes in business process without corresponding changes in the code that returns the HTML to the server, the code that reads from the business model, the error-handling code, and the code that marshals data between the user interface and the business logic. Changes in the returning HTML are code changes instead of simple editor changes. Validation and marshaling changes are similarly intrusive.

Figure 3.5 shows how we should begin to refactor this solution. We should break out the model for the program into a distinct component. Fortunately, several design patterns exist that do just that. We could create an object model to handle the back-end logic. We could package the components of this model as EJBs, a solution explored in chapter 8. Or, we could explore a command object instead.

3.3.2 *Wrapping the model with command objects*

Several design patterns place a thin wrapper of code around the business logic, or model, for convenience. The Facade design pattern in chapter 8 is essentially a thin wrapper with a different interface. The Jakarta Struts framework uses a similar wrapping concept, called *actions*. A third alternative is the *Command* design pattern, which has been around since the early days of Smalltalk. Internet search engines provide a wealth of information about commands.

Commands are convenient because the implementation behind the command layer does not matter. The interface is the same whether the command is accessing a full object-oriented model, a legacy COBOL application, messaging-oriented middleware, a transaction, or a database, as in our example. A command is a thin layer around the model, sometimes called the *command bean*. The command bean's interface consists of a series of sets representing input parameters, a validation to check the input parameters, an execute to access some aspect of the business model, and a series of gets to access the results of the execution. The command architecture does not make any assumptions about the structure of the model, giving the command bean many advantages:

- It can be tooled or generated by a wizard. Many tools already generate command beans, and a simple generator for them is easy to create.
- A generic command can be subclassed to encapsulate remote procedure calls (RPC). The APIs for commands and RPCs are remarkably similar.
- It is a convenient architecture for encapsulating undo/redo architectures. With the simple addition of an undo method, commands can be saved and undone or redone.
- It can package multiple requests to save round trips.
- The interface is always the same, making our code much easier to maintain and read.

Think of the command bean as a simple interface to an RPC. The interface sets a series of input parameters for the execution of the call. Then, the command validates the request, executes it, and returns the results. The results are achieved through a series of gets.

3.3.3 Separating the model logic

The following program shows a command object that returns the database records from a table called posts. The basic form of a command is a set of set methods for input parameters, an optional initialize method, and an execute method, as well as a series of get methods for output parameters. You may include additional private methods to handle such tasks as database connections, but the basic form for all commands is the same.

```
package bbs;

import java.io.*;
import java.sql.*;
import COM.ibm.db2.*;
import java.util.*;
```

For the commands, we have removed the imports for `javax.servlet.*` and `javax.servlet.http.*`. The servlet will house the controller, and command objects are used only for the model:

```
/**
 * PostListCommand
 * This class returns all posts from a database.
 * There are no input parameters. There is one output parameter.
 */
public class PostListCommand {

  // Field indexes for command properties
  private static final int SUBJECT_COLUMN = 1;
  private static final int AUTHOR_COLUMN = 2;
  private static final int BOARD_COLUMN = 3;
  protected Vector author = new Vector();
  protected Vector subject = new Vector();
  protected Vector board = new Vector();

  // SQL result set
  protected ResultSet result;
  protected Connection connection = null;
```

Now, we move on to the instance variables. Commands will frequently have private instance variables that mirror the state of the underlying model. In this case, since we copy an entire database result set into vectors instead of using the result sets directly, we have instance variables that map our model abstraction nicely. We have some implementation artifacts as well: the column variables map onto database columns, and we have declared our JDBC result set and connection here.

Listing 3.5 shows the primary methods in the command architecture: `initialize` and `execute`. In our case, they wrap simple database logic. They can also be used to provide a simple wrapper around a complex object-oriented model. With `execute` and `init` methods, we can begin to see the benefits of this design pattern. This entire `execute` method is dedicated to the execution of our query. Contrast this with the previous example where we were also printing the HTML result set. We have begun to break the tight coupling between user interface and model.

Listing 3.5   Wrapping the model logic with commands

```
public void initialize()                         ❶ Initialize connects and validates.
    throws IOException, DataException {

    try {
    Class.forName ("COM.ibm.db2.jdbc.app.DB2Driver")         ❷ Establish a
        .newInstance();                                          connection.
      String url = "jdbc:db2:board";
      connection = DriverManager.getConnection (url);
    } catch (Throwable theException) {
      theException.printStackTrace();
    }
}
public void execute()                    ❸ Execute fires the business logic.
    throws
      IOException,
      DataException {

    try {
      Statement statement = connection.createStatement();    ❹
      result =                                               Execute
        statement.executeQuery("SELECT subject, author, board" +   query
                              " from posts");                and get
      while (result.next()) {                                results.
        subject.addElement(result.getString(SUBJECT_COLUMN));
        author.addElement(result.getString(AUTHOR_COLUMN));
        board.addElement(result.getString(BOARD_COLUMN));
      }
      result.close();
      statement.close();
      connection.close();
    } catch (Throwable theException) {
      theException.printStackTrace();
    }

  }
```

❶ The initialize method is used to establish connections and handle early validation of input parameters. Our command simply establishes the connection.

❷ For our example, we have no input parameters to validate, so we simply get our
database connection. In chapter 8, we will discuss connection pooling, which can
yield a significant performance boost.

❸ The execute method is next. The generic trigger to the command, this method is used to fire business logic that will execute a query, fire a message or transaction, or perform any kind of local or remote activity.

❹ For this program, we simply set the query, execute it, and retrieve the results into our vector instance variables. The logic could not be simpler. In chapter 8, we discuss ways to distribute commands with stateless session EJBs.

Some command patterns tend to combine the initialize and execute methods into a single execute method. I tend to keep them separated because it gives me additional flexibility. I can add some validation here to make sure that my command was set up properly. This validation is especially important when I am counting on user input to populate my commands.

```java
public String getAuthor(int index)
  throws
    IndexOutOfBoundsException,
    ArrayIndexOutOfBoundsException {
  return (String) author.elementAt(index);
}

public String getBoard(int index)
  throws
    IndexOutOfBoundsException,
    ArrayIndexOutOfBoundsException {
  return (String) board.elementAt(index);
}

public String getSubject(int index)
  throws
    IndexOutOfBoundsException,
    ArrayIndexOutOfBoundsException {
  return (String) subject.elementAt(index);
  ;
}

public int getSize() {
  return author.size();
}
}
```

These methods are at the heart of the command API. You can think of them as input and output parameters for an RPC. Before the execute method, a series of set methods are called. Then, initialize and execute are called. After the execute method, a series of get methods are called.

I created this class manually, but it could have easily been created from a wizard. Outstanding characteristics are the generic interface and simplicity, which makes them easily adapted to development tools. The standard design pattern allows the other elements of the architecture to handle commands generically. In short, we let the computer do the work.

The interface for a command does conform to a well-known design pattern. There are getters for output parameters, setters for input parameters, an `initialize` method, and an `execute` method. Some architectures choose not to implement an `initialize` method, and some use a method called `prepareToCommit`. Given a list of parameters, it is easy to create a wizard or super class to build the base commands. The commands can then be invoked and accessed by other servlets.

In this example, I have left the Structured Query Language (SQL) in the commands, but it would be just as easy to express this architecture with stateless session beans wrapping an EJB. The difference between the business model in this example and the one in the previous servlet is tremendous. In our case, the wizard will probably maintain the command beans. Changes in the user interface will no longer affect the model.

Our servlet is getting much simpler, too. Here is the `performTask` method for the servlet that calls our command:

```
public void performTask(
  HttpServletRequest request,
  HttpServletResponse response) {

  try {
    PostListCommand postList = new PostListCommand();
    postList.initialize();
    postList.execute();
```

`performTask` is getting smaller. First, we need to allocate our `PostListCommand` object, which is performing our database access. Then, we initialize and load it:

```
    response.setContentType("text/html");
    PrintWriter out = response.getWriter();
    out.println(
      "<!DOCTYPE HTML PUBLIC \"-//W3C//DTD "
        + "HTML 4.0 Transitional//EN\">\n"
        + "<HTML>\n"
        + "<HEAD><TITLE>Message Board</TITLE></HEAD>\n"
        + "<BODY>\n");

    // display the commands results
    out.println("<h1>Message board posts</h1>");
    out.println("<TABLE border=\"1\">");
    out.println("<TD><b>subject</b></TD>\n");
    out.println("<TD><b>author</b></TD>\n");
    out.println("<TD><b>board</b></TD>\n");

    for (int i=0; i<postList.getSize(); i++) {
```

```
        out.println("<TR>");
        String subject = postList.getSubject(i);
        String author = postList.getAuthor(i);
        String board = postList.getBoard(i);

        out.println("<TD>" + subject + "</TD>\n");
        out.println("<TD>" + author + "</TD>\n");
        out.println("<TD>" + board + "</TD>\n");
        out.println("</TR>");
    }
```

Notice the loop that generates our dynamic content. The database origins of our data are no longer visible at all. The Command pattern has effectively isolated the model so that the implementation can change unencumbered.

```
        out.println("</TABLE>");
        out.println("</BODY>");
    } catch (Throwable theException) {
        theException.printStackTrace();
    }
    }
}
```

The remainder of the method simply closes our HTML constructs and catches the exception. Overall, this example is simpler and more direct than its counterpart.

Now, our program has a basic model, an HTML view on the client, and a servlet that has some "view" logic in the form of print statements, as well as some "controller" logic that takes a request, invokes our command, and gets the result. To clean up our implementation, we need to take the print statements out of the servlet. We will do this with a mechanism known as the JSP.

3.3.4 *Separating the return trip*

At this point, we will deviate slightly from the traditional model-view-controller architectures. Internet-related user interfaces are batch oriented. Model-view-controller user interfaces are interactive. We have two distinct communications in our model: the initial request and the return trip. Because we dynamically build our return page, it needs to be explicitly represented in our architecture. This is exactly what we have done in figure 3.6.

To continue to refactor this solution, we will next break out the return trip. This portion of code builds the HTML page that is returned to the user. To do this, we are going to use a JSP.

A JSP is a server-side derivative of HTML. JSPs allow Java code and pointers to dynamic content to be added to a server-side page, in addition to all of the

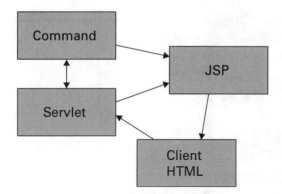

Figure 3.6   The completed Triangle design pattern. This is a modified form of Model-View-Controller. Because this technology is batch oriented, we have two views. The Client HTML is the input view, and the JSP is the output view.

existing HTML tags. The JSP is then compiled and executed on the server. The output of the executed JSP is a page of HTML. This HTML page is then returned to the client.

This architecture offers many advantages:

- *JSPs allow dynamic content.* Since HTML scripts like JavaScript execute on the client, dynamic content that exists on the server is not available. Since the JSP is compiled and run on the server, it is not limited like JavaScript.

- *Separation of concerns.* JSPs can be created and maintained in an editor. Many editors explicitly accept JSP tags and extensions. Almost all HTML editors allow HTML tags to be passed through. Using this design, a graphics designer can be deployed to build web pages even if dynamic content is involved with a minimum amount of scripting.

- *JSPs can be used to isolate the view from the controller and the model.* This advantage is academic, but since it applies to one of the oldest and most studied design pattern in modern history, it cannot be ignored. Years of practical experience have shown that the Model-View-Controller design pattern has improved readability, increased reliability, and reduced the disadvantages of change.

- *JSPs are an open standard.* Unlike many techniques for creating dynamic content, JSPs are based on collaborative standards. All of the techniques in this book are compatible with JSP designs. JSPs permit connection pooling, are compiled to long-running servlets, and handle dynamic content without the need of a full applet on the client.

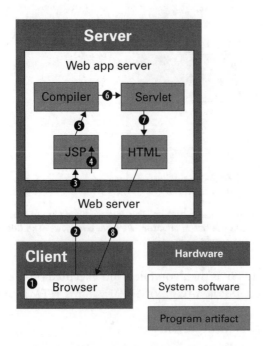

Figure 3.7 ❶ The user requests a JSP. ❷ The browser issues a GET or POST. ❸ The web server passes the JSP request through to the application server, probably installed as a plug-in. ❹ The web application server begins to process the JSP. ❺ The first time a JSP request is made, the JSP is compiled. ❻ The compiled JSP is a servlet. Text lines are compiled into print statements, and Java code is passed through. ❼ The web application server executes the JSP, producing an HTML page, which ❽ is returned to the user.

- *JSPs support tooling and generators.* Because they are based on open standards and serve a large marketplace, many programming tools support the JSP model. The interface is standard, which means it is easy to create a JSP from HTML editors. Generators or tools can generate the command bean templates and interaction controller templates. Many wizards create command, JSP, and interaction controller templates. Some of the examples in this book were created with wizards and simplified. allmystuff created a proprietary framework to automatically generate this triangle.

Figure 3.7 shows a request for a JSP on typical commercial web application servers. We will assume that the JSP has not yet been compiled, and that the web application server is deployed as a web server plug-in.

3.3.5   *Using a JSP for the return trip*

Here are the new elements to our refactored solution. First, let's take a look at the performTask method in our servlet, which is now a true controller. It is much simpler. A controller's job in Smalltalk is to handle the input and output streams. Our controller is doing exactly that:

```
public void performTask(
  HttpServletRequest request,
  HttpServletResponse response) {

  try {
    PostListCommand postList = new PostListCommand();
```

Here, we are using the class loader to instantiate our bean. This bean will be accessed by our JSP to print the results of the command's query that we'll execute next:

```
    postList.initialize();
    postList.execute();

    request.setAttribute("PostListCommand", postList);

    ServletContext servletContext = getServletContext();
    RequestDispatcher dispatcher =
      servletContext.getRequestDispatcher("/JSP/PostListResults.jsp");
    dispatcher.forward(request, response);
  } catch (Throwable exception) {
    exception.printStackTrace();
  }
}
```

These lines load the target JSP, which will use our executed command to print the result set. They do three significant things. First, they put a reference to our bean where our JSP can find it. Next, they get a dispatcher from the servlet context, which is used to call our JSP request page. Finally, they call the target result set JSP. (For a more robust application, we'd have pages for expected error conditions as well.) We then catch our exceptions and go home.

Listing 3.6 contains the return trip, in the form of a JSP. Note that there is no Java inline, except for a small amount to place dynamic content and to create our table. That is intentional. For a good separation of concerns, we want as little Java as possible.

Listing 3.6   Wrapping the model logic with commands

```
<HTML>

<HEAD>
<TITLE>Message Board Posts</TITLE>
</HEAD>

<H1>All Messages</H1>
<P>
<jsp:useBean id="postListCommand"  class="bbs.PostListCommand"
   scope="request"></jsp:useBean>

<TABLE border="1">

<TR>
  <TD>Subject</TD>
  <TD>Author</TD>
  <TD>Board</TD>
</TR>
  <% for (int _i=0; _i < postListCommand.getSize(); _i++) { %>
    <TR> <TD><%=postListCommand.getSubject(_i) %></TD>
    <TD><%=postListCommand.getAuthor(_i) %></TD>
    <TD><%=postListCommand.getBoard(_i) %></TD>
    </TR>
  <% } %>
</TABLE>
<P>
</BODY>

</HTML>
```

● JSPs mix HTML
with inline Java
content.

The `<jsp:usebean>` ●
tag identifies beans
we pass in.

The `<% %>` tags
bracket Java code.

This program is almost pure HTML, with very few exceptions. One JSP tag references the bean, and five process the loop that prints the table rows. That's it. A good web designer would have no problem writing the short looping code, and the programmer needs to know next to nothing about the web page designs. The JSP will be compiled to servlet form and will look very similar to our BreakOutCommand servlet.

With this last change, we have refactored our original solution to adapt it to the Triangle design pattern. The solution closely resembles the reliable model-view-controller architecture, with a full interaction controller, a command that wraps the model, an HTML page for the input view, and a JSP page for the output view. We will be able to change our model and view independently.

3.4   Summary

In this chapter, we have explored a relic from the bio labs of the past in which a single 10 KB script is attached to the Magic Pushbutton. Alas, the disease has escaped again. These days, a 10 KB *servlet* is attached to the magic Submit pushbutton. We have the antibiotic to kill this bug. We have applied the old Model-View-Controller command pattern to this new technology to form the *Triangle*. This design pattern uses HTML as the incoming view, which calls a servlet called the *interaction controller* to get incoming requests, call the corresponding models, and return pages. The interaction controller calls the *command bean* or stateless session bean to access the model, and returns one of several JSP pages as the outgoing view. This design pattern greatly simplifies maintenance for Java server-side programs, and it provides the foundation for J2EE architectures.

3.5   Antipattern in this chapter

This is the template for the antipattern that appears in this chapter. It provides an excellent summary format and forms the basis of the cross-references in appendix A.

The Magic Servlet

> RELATED ANTIPATTERNS: Spaghetti Code, Monolithic Servlet. This antipattern is the servlet-based version of Spaghetti Code. The JSP version of this antipattern is the Monolithic Servlet.
>
> DESCRIPTION: The Magic Servlet is a Java servlet that does all of the work itself. The servlet has elements of model, view, and controller. Servlets created in this form should be approached with extreme prejudice: they are simply evil.
>
> MOST FREQUENT SCALE: Application to enterprise. In most cases, this antipattern will be developed in more than one application, because one application is used as a template for others.
>
> REFACTORED SOLUTION NAME: The Triangle.
>
> SOLUTION ALSO KNOWN AS: Model 2, Modified Model-View-Controller.
>
> REFACTORED SOLUTION TYPE: Software.
>
> REFACTORED SOLUTION DESCRIPTION: The solution for this problem is a version of Model-View-Controller known as the Triangle design pattern. Because web applications are batch oriented instead of interactive, we

must modify Model-View-Controller to deal with upstream and downstream user interfaces. The upstream user interface is served as HTML. We break out model logic as a command (or see the alternative below) and the return-trip logic as a JSP. We service each with a servlet, called our controller.

TYPICAL CAUSES: This antipattern is usually caused when a programmer assumes that programming with servlets and HTML automatically separates the model and view. Another common cause are ports of poorly written scripting programs from Perl or ColdFusion. The bad design comes along with the code.

ANECDOTAL EVIDENCE: "Servlets are neat because they force us to separate the model and view." "I found this table on the Internet that shows me how to port Perl applications." "This servlet is a beast."

SYMPTOMS, CONSEQUENCES: Code is difficult to maintain, difficult to refactor, prone to errors, and difficult to read. Cycle times are longer. Applications are prone to round-tripping. Extensions such as distribution and adaptation of undo/redo models take longer than they should.

ALTERNATIVE SOLUTIONS: Many versions of command design patterns exist, dating back to early Smalltalk programming. These are some popular alternatives:

- In Jakarta Struts, *actions* essentially follow the Command pattern.
- Stateless-session beans can be used to wrap model logic if the command needs to be distributed.
- Distributed commands have been used successfully since the mid-1980s within the Smalltalk community, and again in many CORBA communities.

Bitter JSPs

4

When you're flying at 1,000 feet, suburban Dallas looks surprisingly different. Even at that altitude, you can hear the sounds of the City. It is early. Hot-air bal-loonists favor the windless hours right at sunrise. This is my second ride, and the morning is calm and beautiful. The pilot, Dee Crabtree, and I plan strategy with our chase crew by radio. We are now directly over our target, but the competition guidelines clearly state that we must drop our marker from below 100 feet to score. Just for kicks, we drop it anyway. We watch in horror as the streamer stretches out sideways, indicating screaming ground winds we cannot see. We need to land-now.

The City looms near, with high-rises, airports, and power lines. We swoop down, scanning for a landing zone among the ever denser artifacts and trees. The ground is flashing by much too quickly. Out of nowhere appears a perfect field with no live-stock. We drop so fast my stomach is in my throat. As the ground rushes toward us I pray that Dee will know how to save us. As he yells his instruc-tions, I crouch down in the bottom of the basket and wedge myself between the pro-pane tanks, preparing for impact.

4.1   Getting only halfway home

After making many smart choices on the front end of a project, many a pro-grammer stumbles on one of the secondary antipatterns we'll describe in this chapter. In some cases—for instance, with Compound JSPs—the problems are relatively minor, with mild consequences, and you can easily refactor. But occasionally, the antipatterns grow in severity over time and block you from enjoying many of the advantages of the base Triangle design pattern. In each case, we can soften our landings with some advanced knowledge about our landing zone—the intricacies of the design patterns that we employ. In this chapter, we will explore some danger signs and then work through several antipatterns and their refactored solutions.

4.1.1   Recognizing the danger signs

A common class of Internet development environments uses various tag lan-guages to create server-side Internet applications. ColdFusion and ActiveX are classic examples. These programs are popular because they capture the spirit of HTML scripting, a familiar and efficient choice for many users. These applica-tions encourage robust user interfaces, because the server-side scripting envi-ronments are similar to HTML tools. However, danger lurks here. Many applications using these technologies have the same characteristics of the Magic Servlet, with a massive server-side tag-language script instead of a Java servlet. Table 4.1 shows some of the key disadvantages to such a design.

Table 4.1 Here are some of the disadvantages of tag-language development on the server when it is used as a replacement for the model-view-controller architecture.

Characteristic	Disadvantage
Model logic is tightly coupled with view.	Extension and maintenance are difficult because changes cannot be isolated to the model or view.
Model logic is handled in a tag language or script.	Many times, a language like Java is superior to tag languages for models, because high-level languages are more flexible and robust for this task. Tag languages are better suited for the interface.
Concerns are not separated.	Programmers must be good designers and designers must be good programmers, leading to more expensive staffing.
Communications are proprietary.	After the initial implementation, choices for model implementation architectures are limited.
Tags are proprietary.	Choices for the user interface development are limited, because the proprietary tags make basic HTML editor integration difficult.

Lacking a clean delineation between model, view, and controller, we simply have another version of the antipattern created in chapter 3. Intuitively, this antipattern "feels" slightly different; you're dealing with a tag language rather than procedural or object-oriented development. In general, environments based primarily on server-side tag languages will tend to break down as entropy increases over time because they don't have a rich enough language to express a clean model-view-controller architecture. These are the symptoms: the efficiency of the environment begins to slip. The return page becomes progressively more difficult to edit. Since the coupling between the user interface and model is tight and difficult to break, it grows increasingly complex with each revision and cannot be refactored easily.

User interface redesigns take much longer than expected. Again, tight coupling forces too much model and controller logic into the view. Redesigning such logic is difficult, and attempts to refactor to a more scalable architecture fail. New programmers resist using the scalable architecture. This happens because the toolset expresses tagged user interfaces well but is more limited for true object-oriented development. Most programmers under these circumstances will try to stay in the most efficient realm, which in this case is the tagged user interface development environment.

4.2   Antipattern: Monolithic JSPs

Faced with such a daunting list of problems, a programmer may choose to rewrite a poorly designed, pure tag-language application using a more robust development language, such as JSPs. The temptation to build the same flawed architecture with the new technology can be overwhelming. After all, the JSP specification includes a tag language. This antipattern is not limited to application rewrites. The community of Java programmers has diverse roots, and some are bound to come from tag-language backgrounds. Given this experience base, writing programs in this style seems natural.

Even if we don't have a tag-language background and are armed with the proper knowledge, sometimes we just get lazy. If we plan to build a JSP by hand, then making one scripted JSP page with no method or class definitions and inline print statements is easier than taking the time to build a command bean, an interaction controller, and a JSP. However, keep in mind that the extra effort will be paid back with interest over time. Maintenance and user interface design are dramatically improved with a clean separation of concerns.

4.2.1   This program lacks model-view separation

Let's revisit our bulletin board example from chapter 3. This time, I've refactored it in the wrong direction in order to show the prototypical monolithic JSP. The antipattern is similar, but the "feel" of the application is different. In this case, it is easy to see the flow of the user interface. The model, however, is poorly defined and awkward. The tag-language environment simply does not allow the model's design to be cleanly partitioned in the way pure Java would. Consider the program in listing 4.1. This antipattern is really just another version of the Magic Servlet, but many programmers who would never even think of building something so ugly will choose to build monolithic JSPs with no reservations. I found three different JSP tutorials on the Internet that basically taught this model!

> **Listing 4.1   An example of the Monolithic JSP**

```
<%@ page import="java.sql.*" %>    ❶ Model specific initialization
<%

    // instance variables for connection
    ResultSet result;
    Connection connection = null;
    Statement statement = null;
    String url = "jdbc:db2:board";

%>
```

```
<HTML>       ❷  View specific HTML

<HEAD>
<TITLE>Message Board Posts</TITLE>
</HEAD>

<BODY BGCOLOR=#C0C0C0>

<H1>All Messages</H1>
<P>

<TABLE border="1">

<TR>
  <TD>Subject</TD>
  <TD>Author</TD>
  <TD>Board</TD>
</TR>
<%       ❸  Model specific database access
  // Establish a connection
  try {
    Class.forName ("COM.ibm.db2.jdbc.app.DB2Driver").newInstance();

    // connect with default id/password
    connection = DriverManager.getConnection (url);

    // set and execute SQL statement
    statement = connection.createStatement();
    result = statement.executeQuery
               ("SELECT subject, author, board from posts");

    // print the results
    // retrieve data from the database and print on the result page

    while (result.next()) {
        out.println("<TR> <TD>" + result.getString(1) + "</TD>");
        out.println("<TD>" + result.getString(2) + "</TD>");
        out.println("<TD>" + result.getString(1) + "</TD></TR>");
    }
    result.close();
    statement.close();
    connection.close();
  } catch (Throwable theException) {
    out.println("Connection or output print failed.");
  }

%>
</TABLE>       ❹  View specific HTML
<P>
</BODY>
</HTML>
```

❶ In this program, we will switch back and forth between model and view logic. This block of code, enclosed within the `<% %>` brackets, contains the initialization for the model language. It declares the variables and imports that will be used to handle the database logic.

❷ We switch to view logic. This is HTML-tagged text, and it handles the formatting of the entire page, up to the table headers.

❸ We switch, once again, back to the model language. Each switch is distracting to the overall flow of the application. This model logic is Java code that prints the individual rows of the table.

❹ With one final switch back to view logic, we clean up by closing the table, body, and HTML sections.

This application is only marginally better than the initial Magic Servlet. It has many of the same troublesome characteristics, including poor separation of concerns and difficult maintenance. Many readers of this book will open the third chapter, skim it, and see "... *some irrelevant text* ... Magic Servlet ... *still more irrelevant text* ... solution: refactor ... *blah, blah, blah* ... JSP." A JSP, by itself, is not a complete architecture; it is merely one of many tools in our bag of tricks that can be used to craft a complete architecture. We must also define how it interacts with the rest of the application and how external data is incorporated, and we must determine the scope of its responsibility.

4.2.2 *Solution: Refactor to Model-View-Controller*

It should be fairly obvious by now that the refactored solution is the refactored solution from the previous chapter. In general, this procedure can be used to methodically refactor these beasts:

▶ **Steps to refactor a monolithic JSP**

A poorly structured JSP is every bit as damaging as a servlet without good structure. These steps can be used to refactor the solution.

1 Create a template for a controller object. This should be a generic `HTTPServlet`, with the `performTask` similar to the one in listing 3.4.

2 Identify all major areas that build dynamic content. These will be the commands. Create a command template for each major area of dynamic content.

3 Within the JSP, for each command, create a bean tag in the JSP, within the body, that looks like this:

```
<jsp:useBean id="beanName" class="package.beanClass"
  scope="request"></jsp:useBean>
```

In most of my examples, the bean name and the class name are the same.

4 Identify the required attributes for each command. These will usually be defined as database fields, transaction fields, or something similar. You must define `set` methods for fields used to update the model and `get` methods for fields used to display the model. Create attributes in the commands as required and implement them.

5 Identify the core logic that will initialize and trigger the model's update or query. Move these Java statements to the model's `initialize` and `execute` methods, as in listing 3.4.

6 In the controller object, instantiate the command. This can either be done with a basic constructor (`command = new CommandClass()`), or if the class object needs special consideration, use the code that follows. Assume your command's variable name is `command` and that your command's class is of type `CommandClass`:

```
CommandClass command =
      (packagePath.CommandClass) java.beans.Beans.instantiate(
         getClass().getClassLoader(),
         "packagePath.CommandClass");
```

7 Then, initialize and execute the command:

```
command.initialize();
command.execute();

request.setAttribute("YourCommand", command);
```

8 Forward the response object to the JSP with the following call:

```
ServletContext servletContext = getServletContext ();
RequestDispatcher dispatcher =
   servletContext.getRequestDispatcher("theJSPResultsPage");
dispatcher.forward(request, response);
```

9 Replace the code that prints dynamic content in the original JSP with command bean references instead, as in the JSP in listing 3.4.

Using this method, we can take a monolithic JSP and refactor it to the coveted Triangle design pattern. In general, we are stripping out the code into three pieces: the JSP (encapsulating the return-trip view), the command (encapsulating the model), and the servlet (encapsulating the controller). For teams building many user interfaces, it may help to build a sample and a template that can be used for these types of user interfaces.

4.3   *Antipattern: Compound JSPs*

The basket is swinging wildly. Dee delicately brushes against a bush to dampen the swinging, and then slams us down. The bone-jarring impact throws Dee forward into the tanks. Ribs crack. With Dee's instructions, I am able to pull a rope that lowers the balloon's top panel, letting the hot air escape and bringing us finally to a standstill. We cannot believe that the riskiness of the operation was so well hidden from us at higher altitudes. We lick our wounds and wait for the ground crew to come and help pick up the pieces.

The Monolithic JSP is not the only JSP antipattern you could encounter. In the next antipattern, we have a model-view-controller-compliant architecture that falls short in other ways. On my fateful balloon trip, the calm air at higher altitudes lured us into a false sense of security. Only when we closely examined conditions at lower altitudes did we fully appreciate our danger. Confidence in the Triangle design pattern can also lure us into complacency. Choosing a higher level design does not mean you no longer have to worry about properly implementing the architecture. Closer to the ground-level details, we must also be alert to danger. In this antipattern, we will examine one such detail: should we force decisions into the JSP or the controller? Consider a case where the results of a command execution will determine which page, or page fragment, is returned to the user. The logical place for such a check might seem to be the JSP, as in figure 4.1.

4.3.1   *Should we combine multiple JSPs?*

This antipattern is known as the Compound JSP, in which a single JSP is used to return one of many result sets, leading to too much logic in our JSP. Severe error conditions and routine errors, such as not-found errors and validation-failed conditions, are common places to find this antipattern. Table 4.2 shows the problems with the Compound JSP approach.

In general, although Compound JSPs may be slightly easier to create, they make maintenance, reuse, design through common tools, and project management much more difficult. As antipatterns go, this one has relatively minor side effects. Still, the ease of refactoring and the ease of doing it right the first time make this an attractive refactoring target.

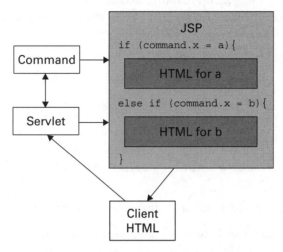

Figure 4.1 One solution to handling multiple conditions for a servlet is to process the decision in the JSP. The result is the antipattern called the *Compound JSP*. Some problems are poor separation of concerns and limited reuse.

4.3.2 An example combining two interfaces

In the following example, we have a Compound JSP that stems from an error condition. We will take our bulletin board example and modify it to return only the posts for a user-specified board. We will need to add an input HTML form so that the user can enter the name of the board, modify the command to

Table 4.2 Problems created by combining multiple user interfaces in a single JSP, called the Compound JSP antipattern.

Problems with Compound JSPs	Description
No separation of concerns	Combining code and HTML script makes it necessary to find people with programming and designing skill. This is expensive and difficult.
Poor reuse	It is harder to reuse a compound view with built-in control logic.
Harder use of tools	Tools handle single-user interface screens better than multiple screens.
Lack of common error treatments	Users like common error windows and treatments. This design makes it more difficult to include these.

set (rather than get) the board attribute, and add a check so that if the user specifies the name of a board with no posts, he or she can make another choice.

First, the input form:

```
<!DOCTYPE HTML PUBLIC "-//W3C//DTD HTML 4.0//EN">

<HTML>
<BODY>
  <FORM METHOD="post" ACTION="/servlet/bbs.CompoundJSPController">
  <P>Please complete the form.</P>
  <P>board
   <BR>

   <INPUT TYPE="text" NAME="board" ID="board" SIZE="20"
      MAXLENGTH="20">
  </P>
  <INPUT TYPE="hidden" NAME="mlname" ID="mlname" VALUE="HTML">
  <P>
  <INPUT TYPE="submit" NAME="Submit" ID="Submit" VALUE="Submit">

    

  <INPUT TYPE="reset" NAME="Reset" ID="Reset" VALUE="Reset">

    
  </P>
  </FORM>
</BODY>
</HTML>
```

There is no magic here. This input form will collect a board name and invoke our controller. The "action" tag specifies our interaction controller. In this case, it will be invoked with an HTTP POST that will call our doPost method instead of the doGet method from our previous example. Next, we have our interaction controller:

```
package bbs;

// Imports
import java.io.*;
import javax.servlet.*;
import javax.servlet.http.*;

// Import for commands used by this class
import bbs.CompoundJSPCommand;
```

We will import the command for this example. We are using the Triangle design pattern outlined in chapter 3.

```
public class CompoundJSPController
  extends javax.servlet.http.HttpServlet
  implements Serializable {
```

```
/**
 * DoPost
 * Pass post requests through to performTask
 */
public void doPost(
  HttpServletRequest request,
  HttpServletResponse response)
  throws ServletException, IOException {
    performTask(request, response);
}
```

This example is initiated from an input form, which calls doPost instead of doGet as in our previous example. We simply pass the response and result through to the performTask method.

```
/*************************************************************
 * Process incoming requests for information
 *
 * @param request encapsulates the request to the servlet
 * @param response encapsulates the response from the servlet
 */
public void performTask(
  HttpServletRequest request,
  HttpServletResponse response) {

  try {
    String board=request.getParameter("board");
    CompoundJSPCommand postList = new CompoundJSPCommand();
    postList.setBoard(board);
    postList.initialize();
    postList.execute();
```

Here, we parse the single input parameter provided by the form, and follow our design pattern by issuing sets, initialize, execute, and gets (in our controller and our JSP output page):

```
    request.setAttribute("CompoundJSPCommand", postList);

    ServletContext servletContext = getServletContext ();
    RequestDispatcher dispatcher =
      servletContext.getRequestDispatcher("/JSP/CompoundJSPResults.jsp");
    dispatcher.forward(request, response);

  } catch (Throwable theException) {
    theException.printStackTrace();
  }
}

/**
 * DoGet
 * Pass get requests through to performTask
 */
```

```
public void doGet(
  HttpServletRequest request,
  HttpServletResponse response)
  throws ServletException, IOException {
    performTask(request, response);
  }
}
```

The rest of the controller is just like our previous examples. Our command bean has changed slightly. Our `board` attribute is a single string instead of a vector, with a new `set` method and a revised `get`:

```
protected String board = null;

public String getBoard() {
  return board;
}
```

The `execute` must change to reflect the modified query and the revised attribute type. Only the differences are shown here:

```
public void execute() {

...

  result =
    statement.executeQuery(
      "SELECT subject, author, board from posts where board = '"
      + getBoard() + "'");
  while (result.next()) {
    subject.addElement(result.getString(SUBJECT_COLUMN));
    author.addElement(result.getString(AUTHOR_COLUMN));
  }
...
```

So far, this balloon is flying smoothly. We have addressed our separation of concerns and stayed true to our base design pattern. Listing 4.2 contains the revised JSP. Unfortunately, we are in for a hard landing. This response set is just like our last, with an additional page for a not-found condition.

Listing 4.2   The compound JSP processes decisions in the JSP

```
<HTML>

<jsp:useBean id="CompoundJSPCommand"  class="bbs.CompoundJSPCommand"
  scope="request"></jsp:useBean>

<% if (CompoundJSPCommand.getSize() == 0) { %>         ❶ Decision 1
<HEAD>
<TITLE>Choose another board! </TITLE>
</HEAD>
<p>
```

```
There were no posts for board <%=CompoundJSPCommand.getBoard()%>

<BODY BGCOLOR=#C0C0C0>
  <FORM METHOD="post" ACTION="/servlet/bbs.CompoundJSPController">
<P>Please complete the form.</P>
<P>board
      <BR>

  <INPUT TYPE="text" NAME="board" ID="board" SIZE="20" MAXLENGTH="20" >
</P>
<INPUT TYPE="hidden" NAME="mlname" ID="mlname" VALUE="HTML">
<P>
  <INPUT TYPE="submit" NAME="Submit" ID="Submit" VALUE="Submit">

    

  <INPUT TYPE="reset" NAME="Reset" ID="Reset" VALUE="Reset">

    
</P>
</FORM>
<% } else { %>
```

❷ **Decision 2**

```
<HEAD>
<TITLE>Message Board Posts</TITLE>
</HEAD>

<BODY BGCOLOR=#C0C0C0>
<H1>All Messages</H1>
<P>

<p>
Board: <%=CompoundJSPCommand.getBoard()%>
<TABLE border="1">

<TR>
  <TD>Subject</TD>
  <TD>Author</TD>
</TR>
      <% for (int _i=0; _i < CompoundJSPCommand.getSize(); _i++) { %>
      <TR> <TD><%=CompoundJSPCommand.getSubject(_i) %></TD>
      <TD><%=CompoundJSPCommand.getAuthor(_i) %></TD>
      </TR>
      <% } %>
</TABLE>
<P>
<% } %>

</BODY>
</HTML>
```

❶ This section handles the classic not-found condition. We drop into Java to make a decision and specify which interface to present.

❷ This section handles the mainline condition. The conditional logic is very distracting to the mainline processing.

The readability is diminished. None of the HTML editors that I used liked the structure. My intuition says that many designers would not have a problem understanding our structure, but each additional enhancement would continue to break down our separation of concerns. In general, Java code in a JSP should be used only for:

- Accessing commands
- Basic looping
- Handling simple cosmetic output conditions, like adding an "s" to make words plural

That's it. If you need convincing, find a ColdFusion shop that has had to maintain a complex site for two years. You'll be scared straight. I was.

4.3.3 Solution: Split the JSP

In our revised solution, we'll split the Compound JSP into two files and move the decision point into the controller. Our command will not change. Figure 4.2 shows a solution that improves readability, preserves our separation of concerns, and is infinitely more *toolable* (easily supported by development products and tools).

4.3.4 Making decisions in the controller servlet

In our updated example, the command does not change. Listing 4.3 contains the updated method in our controller. The last seven lines now process the decision that was previously handled in our JSP. We lose very little readability, in spite of the additional complexity.

Listing 4.3 Decisions are moved to the controller servlet

```
public void performTask(
  HttpServletRequest request,
  HttpServletResponse response) {

  try {
    String board=request.getParameter ("board");
    CompoundJSPCommand postList = new CompoundJSPCommand();
    postList.setBoard(board);
    postList.initialize();
```

```
      postList.execute();

      request.setAttribute("CompoundJSPCommand", postList);

      ServletContext servletContext = getServletContext ();

      String resultsPage;
      if (postList.getSize() > 0) {
        resultsPage = "/JSP/BoardResults.jsp";
      } else {
        resultsPage = "/JSP/NotFoundResults.jsp";
      }
      RequestDispatcher dispatcher =
      servletContext.getRequestDispatcher (resultsPage);

      dispatcher.forward(request, response);
    } catch (Throwable theException) {
      theException.printStackTrace();
    }

}
```

❶ Decision 1

❷ Decision 2

❶ The first decision processes the expected case. Note that in the same section of code we are able to determine what triggered the condition and the actions that can occur.

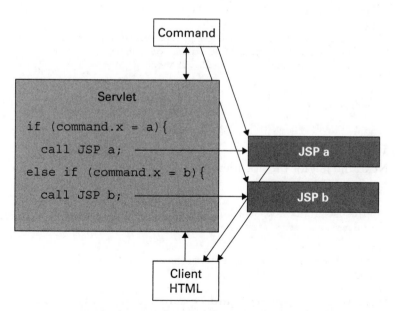

Figure 4.2 It is better to process decisions in the controller servlet than within the JSP. Simplicity and better tool integration are goals of JSP design.

❷ The next decision processes the not-found condition. We do not want to dedicate too much screen real estate to conditions outside our main processing. We conveniently transfer execution to a dedicated exception processor: Not-FoundResults.jsp.

Next, we'll have two JSPs instead of one. Each is infinitely more readable than listing 4.2. First, the expected case, returning all posts for a board:

```
<HTML>

<jsp:useBean id="CompoundJSPCommand"  class="bbs.CompoundJSPCommand"
  scope="request"></jsp:useBean>

<HEAD>
<TITLE>Message Board Posts</TITLE>
</HEAD>

<BODY BGCOLOR=#C0C0C0>
<H1>All Messages</H1>
<P>

<p>
Board: <%=CompoundJSPCommand.getBoard()%>
<TABLE border="1">

<TR>
  <TD>Subject</TD>
  <TD>Author</TD>
</TR>
      <% for (int _i=0; _i < CompoundJSPCommand.getSize(); _i++) { %>
      <TR> <TD><%=CompoundJSPCommand.getSubject(_i) %></TD>
      <TD><%=CompoundJSPCommand.getAuthor(_i) %></TD>
      </TR>
      <% } %>
</TABLE>
<P>
</BODY>
</HTML>
```

Next, the JSP for the not-found condition:

```
<HTML>

<jsp:useBean id="CompoundJSPCommand"  class="bbs.CompoundJSPCommand"
  scope="request"></jsp:useBean>

<HEAD>
<TITLE>Choose another board! </TITLE>
</HEAD>
<p>
There were no posts for board <%=CompoundJSPCommand.getBoard()%>

<BODY BGCOLOR=#C0C0C0>
```

```
<FORM METHOD="post" ACTION="/servlet/bbs.CompoundJSPController">
<P>Please complete the form.</P>
<P>board
        <BR>

  <INPUT TYPE="text" NAME="board" ID="board" SIZE="20" MAXLENGTH="20" >
</P>
<INPUT TYPE="hidden" NAME="mlname" ID="mlname" VALUE="HTML">
<P>
  <INPUT TYPE="submit" NAME="Submit" ID="Submit" VALUE="Submit">

   

  <INPUT TYPE="reset" NAME="Reset" ID="Reset" VALUE="Reset">

   
</P>
</FORM>

</BODY>
</HTML>
```

Aside from the board name, this page could have been pure HTML, but it's returned as a JSP. Especially for error conditions that typically don't have a significant performance impact, it often makes sense to bite the bullet and deliver them as JSPs even when HTML would suffice to keep the overall code more readable and the tooling more uniform. Many development shops opt for a uniform delivery of JSPs. Those that do usually precompile them.

Our refactoring steps for Compound JSPs are straightforward:

▶ **Steps to refactor compound JSPs**

Compound JSPs have too much decision logic. While the problems caused are relatively minor, the simplicity of refactoring can make them an effective target. To refactor, move the decision logic to the controller.

1. We broke the JSPs into distinct pages, with no more Java in each than necessary.

2. We moved the decision point into the controller.

3. We located the decision after the execution of our commands and before dispatching the result.

4. We dispatched the result to the appropriate JSP.

If the Compound JSP is simple and based on decisions made at the command level, the refactoring in this case should be painless. This example took 10 minutes to refactor and another 10 minutes to test.

4.4   *Mini-antipatterns: Coarse and Fine Commands*

One of the primary benefits of commands is the convenient organization of model interface points that they can provide. Commands make an easy point of reuse for applications. With them, we can wrap a variety of different technologies. allmystuff used commands as the exclusive interface points to its EJB-based architecture. Its API literally consisted of a set of commands.

New users of the Command design pattern frequently struggle with the appropriate granularity for commands. It's not surprising—partitioning a model into commands takes experience. If command granularity is too coarse, no reuse is possible; if it's too fine, some benefits, such as a reduction in round-tripping (see chapter 8), are diminished.

Consider an auto insurance application. Figure 4.3 shows a user interface for the display of information on the customer and policy.

As usual, we will implement the Triangle pattern. We can decide to divide the commands in several different ways.

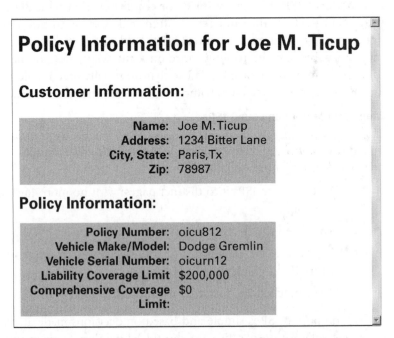

Figure 4.3   This is a simplified user interface for a display of information on a customer's insurance policy. The user interface will allow us to make several possible choices regarding command granularity.

4.4.1 *Too many commands in a group*

The most common mistake made in choosing command granularity is to package all the fields on a page in a single command, regardless of the organization of the data on the page. For our example, we could choose to use a single command to collect all of the information in the insurance policy along with some additional customer-level data. In practice, that decision might not be all bad, if the expectation is that all of the customer information will be needed every time a policy is retrieved. In our case, let's suppose that we know that our policy data will need to be retrieved independently. This decomposition, called *page-level granularity*, would be too coarse. The problems with page-level command granularity include:

- *Reuse is damaged.* To reuse a command (which is essentially a wrapper around a model), our units must be based on granularities that make sense for the model, not the user interface.

- *User interface redesigns are more difficult, because the command layer is organized around the user interface.* The command layer loses much of its promise. Instead, if our commands are grouped logically, we can expect them to be applicable across many different solutions.

- *Commands are not in logical units for other purposes, such as undo/redo.* In a user interface, it would not make sense to "Undo customer and policy change." (This is applicable only to update commands.) Logical groupings would allow better packaging for undo/redo functions.

Essentially, though our application's model and view are physically decoupled, we have built a logical coupling based on our granularity decision. In the next section, we will explore the characteristics of a better grouping.

4.4.2 *Solution: Refactor to appropriate granularity*

So far, the examples in this book have used a single command per page. That's due to the simplicity of the examples that we have chosen. Multiple commands per controller and output page are relatively common and can be good designs, especially when user interfaces get complex. Figure 4.4 shows this architecture with our latest example, refactored.

In most cases, refactoring this antipattern is straightforward. We'll borrow a couple of ideas from relational database theory. Here are the steps for refactoring coarse commands.

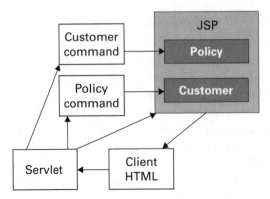

Figure 4.4 **This version of the Coarse Command antipattern has been refactored. Commands of page-level granularity can be factored into logical groups, yielding better readability and reuse at a slight performance cost.**

► Steps to refactor coarse or fine commands

Coarse commands place too much code in a single command, impairing reuse. Fine commands place too little code in each command, forcing too many round-trip communications, harming performance.

1   First, identify the correct granularity for the command set. Optimally, the fields that logically belong together and that will usually be used as a unit should be coupled in a single command.

2   Create a new set of command templates for each new command in the refactored scheme.

3   Move the appropriate `execute` and `initialize` methods from the old command to each of the new ones for the new organization. Move applicable instance variables and access methods for the new command granularity. Delete unused code.

4   Identify primary key relationships for the new model. For example, though customer-name is customer data, it is necessary to establish a relationship between a customer and an auto policy. Using key relationships, it is possible to reduce the size of a command because it is not necessary to have all of the related fields of a related command.

Granularities can also be too fine. In our example, field-level granularity would be too fine. This antipattern is common for the automation of a command framework. The three easiest ways to automate commands are based on a model object, model fields, and pages. In general, object level is best but may not be coarse enough.

4.4.3 *Tips for granularity*

When we're deciding how to partition a set of commands, we must consider a number of clues. We should start by looking at the entities and attributes in our model. For an object-oriented application, this exercise is relatively simple. If the model is data driven, it may be more complex, especially if the database tables are not normalized to interesting entities and relationships. Transaction and messaging models may be similarly difficult.

After identifying the entities and attributes, we should look for groupings that appear to be natural, intuitive, and logical. We should also examine usage in our current interface and determine what entities are being used. What are the usage patterns? Are there natural groupings? If we have any use cases available, they may also suggest groupings. Who are the users of the system? Will our command layer be exposed as an API? If so, how are interfaces in our domain usually organized? Finally, based on domain knowledge, we should anticipate how the commands are likely to be used.

The answers to all of these questions can be used to partition the command set. The first iteration is not necessarily set in stone. In the early stages of development, refactoring is easy. Several rules of thumb are helpful:

- If logical groupings and usage patterns conflict, choose the logical grouping. Also, look harder because sometimes entities are related in unusual ways.

- If a group of commands are used both individually and together, package them individually.

- It is okay to use a command that returns slightly more than you need. If you find yourself using a small fraction of the fields in a command on a regular basis, then it's time to refactor.

- If the same combination of logically similar commands is used frequently, consider refactoring to combine the group.

- Read good code. Find a mentor whom you trust, and read that person's code. Even if the code does not explicitly use the command pattern, many of the concepts of good object-oriented design translate.

4.5 *Mini-antipattern: Fat Commands*

In our Java "flights," we must pay attention to other low-altitude details. One of these is the composition of our command layer. The command architecture is powerful because the small, lightweight command is easy to code and maintain. Those characteristics make it a convenient place to tack on additional model logic. If the model is a legacy database or transaction code, we might not have an alternative. If a fully functional object model powers the command, it pays to carefully consider alternatives before attaching extra functionality to the command layer. Otherwise, functionality will leak into increasingly bloated commands, and that increasing layer will become more difficult to manage, as in figure 4.5.

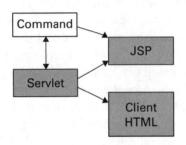

Figure 4.5
The Fat Command antipattern occurs when functionality belonging in the model, JSP, or servlet creeps into the command. The design pattern is indistinguishable from a proper Model-View-Controller pattern, but code belonging in the controller, JSP, or model sneaks into the command.

It is also possible for commands to take more of a controller role in some situations. Some architectures provide a JSP and command layer, without the benefit of an interaction controller. When this occurs, the command will often take on the role of the controller. Problems with this approach include a tighter coupling than necessary between the user interface and model and more complex JSPs, both of which reduce readability and increase the complexity of user interface revision.

4.6 *Reviewing the JSP antipatterns*

In this chapter, we have taken the Triangle design pattern and worked through some antipatterns that plague it. Most of these patterns deal with keeping the roles of the base model-view-controller architecture sound. The JSP layer should only include user interface scripting, and as little Java as it takes to include the dynamic content. The controller should be used exclusively to control the information flow between client and server. The command layer should serve as a thin and efficient layer around the model, and should not be used as a substitute for the model.

Java can still be bitter, and when it is, you know the steps to take to refactor the antipattern variations of the Triangle. The next chapter will begin a series of refactoring steps that will make our bulletin board more scalable and efficient. We will look at the approaches and impact of caching on applications that use dynamic content.

4.7   Antipatterns in this chapter

These are the templates for the antipatterns that appear in this chapter. They provide an excellent summary format and form the basis of the cross-references in appendix A.

Monolithic JSPs

ALSO KNOWN AS: The Magic Pushbutton, the Magic JSP. The Magic Pushbutton and Spaghetti Code are generic forms of this antipattern.

RELATED ANTIPATTERNS: The Magic Servlet.

DESCRIPTION: Like the Monolithic Servlet, the Monolithic JSPs antipattern shows a complete absence of any trace of model-view-controller separation. In this case, all of the code is in a tag language.

MOST FREQUENT SCALE: Application.

REFACTORED SOLUTION NAME: The Triangle.

SOLUTION ALSO KNOWN AS: Model 2, Modified Model-View-Controller.

REFACTORED SOLUTION TYPE: Software.

REFACTORED SOLUTION DESCRIPTION: The solution for this problem is a version of Model-View-Controller known as the Triangle design pattern. Since web applications are batch oriented instead of interactive, we must modify Model-View-Controller to deal with upstream and downstream user interfaces. The upstream user interface is served as HTML. We break out model logic as a command (or see the alternative solutions below) and the return-trip logic as a JSP. We service each with a servlet, called the controller.

TYPICAL CAUSES: Many of these come from tag-language development environment rewrites (like ColdFusion), or first-time creations from those who have tag-language experience and little else.

ANECDOTAL EVIDENCE: "That is one big JSP." "Don't get too close to it."

SYMPTOMS, CONSEQUENCES: View redesigns, no matter how small, ripple into other places of the JSP and into other parts of the system. The code is very difficult to read.

ALTERNATIVE SOLUTIONS: Many versions of command design patterns exist, dating back to early Smalltalk programming. These are some popular alternatives:

- The Jakarta Struts framework is similar to this design pattern. The *actions* are essentially a *command* treatment.
- Stateless session beans can be used to wrap model logic if the command needs to be distributed.
- Distributed commands have been used successfully since the mid-1980s within the Smalltalk community, and again in many CORBA communities.

Compound JSPs

DESCRIPTION: When a command's execution can lead to one of many pages being returned to the user, sometimes a programmer will express this decision logic in a JSP.

MOST FREQUENT SCALE: Application.

REFACTORED SOLUTION NAME: Push decision-making into controllers.

REFACTORED SOLUTION TYPE: Software.

REFACTORED SOLUTION DESCRIPTION: The solution is to split the JSP along the decision lines and branch to separate JSPs in the interaction controller.

ROOT CAUSES: Ignorance.

SYMPTOMS, CONSEQUENCES: The primary consequence is poor separation of concerns. JSP code that is difficult to read because of too much Java can be a symptom of this problem. More than one HTML body or head tags can be symptomatic of this problem as well. Tools will not always view Compound JSPs well.

Coarse or Fine Commands

DESCRIPTION: Commands can be divided too coarsely or finely for optimal performance, readability, or reuse.

MOST FREQUENT SCALE: Application.

REFACTORED SOLUTION NAME: Optimal command granularity.

REFACTORED SOLUTION TYPE: Software.

REFACTORED SOLUTION DESCRIPTION: Command granularity should be based on the model, not the view. Commands should contain fields that are logically grouped and frequently used as a unit by clients of the command.

TYPICAL CAUSES: New programmers tend to make command granularity match the user interface so that there is one command for every page, defeating reuse. Lazy programmers might make a command for each method in a model, defeating the purpose of logical grouping.

SYMPTOMS, CONSEQUENCES: If the granularity is too coarse, commands must be created for every user interface regardless of which model parts are being reused. User interface redesigns significantly change the command architecture. If the granularity is too fine, commands are always used in the same groups, and the solution is susceptible to the Round-tripping antipattern.

Fat Commands

DESCRIPTION: Functionality that belongs in the model or controller can creep into the command layer.

MOST FREQUENT SCALE: Application.

REFACTORED SOLUTION NAME: Model-based commands.

REFACTORED SOLUTION TYPE: Software.

REFACTORED SOLUTION DESCRIPTION: Commands should contain only a thin wrapper around the model. The command layer is not the place for general-purpose utilities or view logic.

TYPICAL CAUSES: The command layer is lightweight, and it's easy to implement and use. Consequently, lazy or ignorant programmers might use this layer as the default dumping ground for new functionalities.

SYMPTOMS, CONSEQUENCES: The base command methods contain public methods beyond `get`, `set`, `init`, and `execute`. Command layers significantly change with every model revision. The command layer looks like a utility collection. The design is difficult to read.

Bitter cache management

This chapter covers

- Strategies for implementing a cache
- Antipatterns related to caching
- Descriptions of products that cache

On a business trip, a friend and I make a side visit to Salt Lake City, to work in some downhill skiing. Three weeks before, I had sprained my ankle but it's start-ing to recover. The high ski boots, I am thinking, will brace my ankle enough to avoid pain. We wake up to 8 inches of fresh powder and not a cloud in sight. My ankle throbs, but I know those ski boots are stiffer than any plaster cast. I am con-vinced the ankle will be fine. As we try on our boots mine feel like ... well ... like they might just hold my ankle together if I can endure the gathering pain. I crank them still tighter.

One look down the slopes shatters my illusions. Ed Elze, my ski partner, is a member of a volunteer ski patrol at home, while I've recently graduated from reckless beginner to aggressive intermediate. Most skiers love new snow. I learned to ski in poor conditions and powder scares me to death. I let Ed, and the reassur-ing firmness of my boots, convince me that turns in powder will be easier to make if we're skiing in steeper terrain. Without waiting for objections, he speeds down an unmarked, isolated canyon. I follow. At least no one will hear me scream.

5.1   *We need caches!*

A surprising number of system cycles are burned doing work that just does not need to be done. Most Internet sites that deploy database engines make expensive connections and close them instead of reusing them. Implementa-tions might rely on several small communications when one would do the trick. At the core of this chapter are *cache-related antipatterns*. In general, a cache is a solution to this basic problem: we are spending most of our process-ing time fetching data that we've already retrieved recently. We'll refactor our bulletin board system (BBS) servlet by creating a cache to hold that data in temporary storage.

Keep in mind that cache management introduces its own set of problems, however. Table 5.1 describes some of those issues.

In this chapter, I rely heavily on an article titled "Scaling Up E-business Applications with Caching," by Mike Conner, George Copeland, and Greg Flurry (you can read it at http://www6.software.ibm.com/devtools/news0800/art7.htm). The authors created a design for the Command design pattern defined in chapter 3. Their ideas about the command cache helped me to organize many of my thoughts in this chapter. Within the article, in three fig-ures, Dr. Conner illustrates the impact of an aggressive cache strategy on sys-tem performance. He presents three scenarios; I have condensed the two extremes and projected the impact of a command cache. Figure 5.1 shows Dr. Conner's first example. As you can see, nearly all of the requests make it far into our infrastructure. For common usage patterns, many of these requests may be unnecessary, because most of the requests are probably for data that has recently been retrieved.

Table 5.1 Caching has important benefits but requires an understanding of key issues for successful implementation. To cache Java applications, you must solve some or all of these basic problems.

Issue	Description
When should we cache?	Decision points are based on the operation cost, volatility of data store, access patterns of the data store, and size of data store.
How do we manage updated data?	Incorrect data must be invalidated and updated appropriately.
How do we manage old data?	Sometimes, stale data is acceptable, but often a strategy is required to flush it over time.
How do we manage concurrent access to our cache?	Concurrent access can be protected with synchronized methods, but this may be too restrictive.

Caching solutions for static content are well developed. Caching proxy servers can dramatically reduce load times near the client. Various nodes on the Internet network already cache. Edge servers, such as firewalls and hardware caches, are extremely efficient at serving static content, and they can handle most requests before they even reach our web and application server layers. Today's web servers also have strong caching extensions built in, but most caching servers so far have been dedicated to static content. Dynamic content also shows potential for caching.

5.2   *Antipattern: The Cacheless Cow*

Figure 5.2 shows the same example, with aggressive caching throughout the network. In addition to Dr. Conner's original assumptions, I've accounted for a 70 percent hit rate in our command cache. This number is fairly conservative for our message board application. Even so, the results are dramatic. Each layer makes a significant impact on the overall system performance. As we explained earlier, because several of the requests are for repeated content, most of the work that many applications do is unnecessary.

After I started my consulting company, I worked with a customer that served an extremely popular bulletin board. As is typical, hundreds of posts

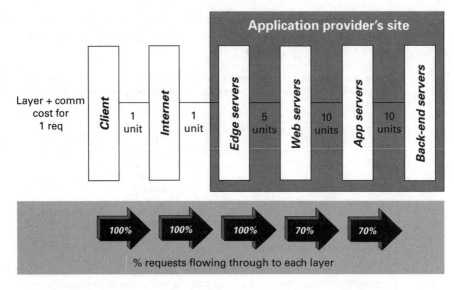

Figure 5.1   With this architecture, we show the total costs of each communication round-trip. The back-end calls are weighted more heavily because requests for front-end static content are inherently cheaper. Toward the right, content becomes more dynamic. We can assume that some requests will fail or be satisfied by the static web servers.

were read for each one created. The board's software was powered by wwwthreads, a Perl script–based message board package. wwwthreads is substantially more robust than most message board packages, and it can be attached to a database, instead of simply reading flat files. However, the package has at least one significant limitation: individual messages are not cached. (My customer's entire database would fit in memory!) Ninety percent of all of the communications between the database server and the application server were repeated message retrievals, and nearly all of that was overhead.

5.2.1   *Bitter BBS with no cache*

For the Cacheless Cow antipattern, we will continue to develop our message board. As with all of the "before" programming examples in this book, this one will have problems:

- It will have no cache.

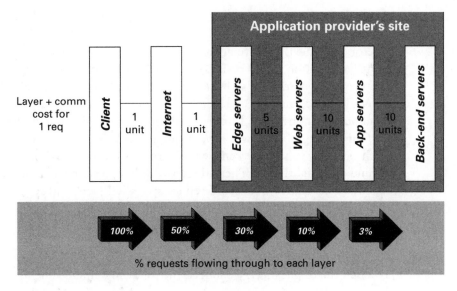

Average cost

Layer: *100%*1=1   50%*1=.5   30%*5=1.5   10%*10=1   3%*10=.3*

Total: *1+.5+1.5+1+.3=4.3*

Figure 5.2   Aggressive caching can result in improved performance on an e-business architecture, and will also significantly decrease the workload of nodes that are protected by earlier caches. This architecture implements caches at many different points, and the Internet has some built-in caches that we never see.

- It will have a memory leak in the cache (which may be acceptable if the database size is small).
- It will not clean connections in a `finally` block.
- It will not pool connections.

In the spirit of our continuous refactoring, these issues will all be addressed in successive refactoring steps. This example shows only one possible problem where a cache would make an extreme difference in performance. In our bulletin board, the content is dynamic, because the posts will change as people respond and the lists will change as new posts are added. This characteristic makes caching much more problematic than the caching of static content. The base web server's cache cannot handle dynamic data. Regardless, we expect to serve the same post many times between updates, which will place a significant drain on performance. E-commerce catalogs, content-publishing systems, and high-volume stock tickers are similar, because the ratio of reads to writes is very high.

For this and the more advanced topics in this book, we'll need a more robust application. We'll revise our example from chapter 4 to make a primitive message board. The style and structure is taken from the combination of two different consulting engagements. (They volunteered source code on the condition of anonymity.) I have already applied our Triangle design pattern.

Our message board will have a variety of discussion topics called *boards*. Each board will have *threads*, which are top-level discussions of the topics around a central theme. These threads will have a series of attached messages called *replies*. Both threads and replies are called *posts*, and they are stored in the same database table. Chapter 8 explains how to refactor this solution to form a persistent object model for this application.

BBS requirements

To build this application, we'll need the following enhancements:

- *Display a list of top-level posts for our bulletin board.* The subjects should be displayed as links so that when they are clicked, the replies to the post can be viewed. This list should include a link that can be used to post another main thread.
- *Display a full thread.* The thread should consist of a top-level post and all of the replies to the post.
- *Display a form to add a post.* The same form can be used to add both kinds of posts: top-level threads and low-level posts.

We'll provide the entire example to allow you to keep all of the code at your fingertips, and to serve as a refactoring foundation for the other examples in this book. If you'd like to skip ahead, see the section "Performance Problems," later in this chapter.

5.2.2 Building the model, view, and controller for ShowBoard

We'll have a triangle pattern for a board, thread, and post. ShowBoard is the prefix that we'll put in front of the controller, command, and JSP for the triangle that shows the contents of a message board. Where possible, we'll show only the refactored changes between the solution in chapter 4 and our new solution.

The model wrapper for ShowBoard

First, let's examine the changes to PostListCommand and PostListController. We renamed the class to ShowBoardCommand because it is now limited to a single board. Here are the changes:

```
private static final int NUMBER_COLUMN = 4;
protected Vector number = new Vector();
public String getNumber(int index)
    throws
      IndexOutOfBoundsException,
      ArrayIndexOutOfBoundsException {
    return (String) number.elementAt(index);
}
```

The command now supports getNumber so that the post number can be used when we make the subject line linkable. In our database and in most bulletin boards, the post.number attribute is the *key* on the table posts, meaning that it alone is enough to uniquely identify a database row. To list all replies, we'll look for all posts with the parent set to this number. To simplify the implementation, we'll pass this number field through in the link URL.

In execute, here are the changes (in bold):

```
result =
  statement.executeQuery(
  "SELECT subject, author, board, number from posts where board = '"
    + getBoard() + "' and parent=0");
while (result.next()) {
  subject.addElement(result.getString(SUBJECT_COLUMN));
  author.addElement(result.getString(AUTHOR_COLUMN));
  number.addElement(result.getString(NUMBER_COLUMN));
}
```

Our query is slightly different, because we are searching on a single board and looking only for the top-level posts where there is no parent (parent=0). We also had to add the code to populate the number vector. The rest of the command is the same.

The controller for ShowBoard

The controller is very similar. We changed only the names of the controller, the command, and the return JSP. Here is the meat of performTask:

```
String board=request.getParameter ("board");
ShowBoardCommand postList = new ShowBoardCommand();
postList.setBoard(board);
postList.initialize();
postList.execute();

request.setAttribute("ShowBoardCommand", postList);
```

```
ServletContext servletContext = getServletContext ();
RequestDispatcher dispatcher=null;
if (postList.getSize()>0) {
  dispatcher=
    servletContext.getRequestDispatcher(
    "/JSP/ShowBoardResults.jsp");
} else {
  dispatcher = servletContext.getRequestDispatcher("/JSP/
  NotFoundResults.jsp");
}
dispatcher.forward(request, response);
```

We can begin to see the benefits of chapter 4's refactored solution. Though we changed the class names in this example to make it easier for us (and you) to manage the many examples in the book, we probably wouldn't change them in a real-world revision. The model-view-controller architecture has effectively insulated different parts of the application from major change. We're adding significant new functionality, and yet the solution continues to flow easily.

The JSP for ShowBoard

Next, we'll look at the primary revisions in our JSP. We renamed PostList-Results.jsp to ShowBoardResults.jsp:

```
<TABLE border="1">

  <TR>
    <TD>Subject</TD>
    <TD>Author</TD>
    <TD>Number</TD>
  </TR>
    <% for (int i=0; i < ShowBoardCommand.getSize(); i++) { %>
    <TR> <TD>
      <A href=bbs.ShowThreadController?
        parent=<%=ShowBoardCommand.getNumber(_i) %>>
        <%=ShowBoardCommand.getSubject(_i) %></A></TD>
      <TD><%=ShowBoardCommand.getAuthor(_i) %></TD>
      <TD><%=ShowBoardCommand.getNumber(_i) %></TD>
    </TR>

      <% } %>
</TABLE>
<A href="../JSP/reply.jsp?parent=0&
board=<%=ShowBoardCommand.getBoard()%>" >
  Post a top level message</A>
```

We added a table column for the post number and a link for replies, and we linked the subject line to ShowThreadController, which retrieves a thread and all of its replies. This new link also passes through the parent so that the user will not need to type it.

5.2.3 *Building the model, view, and controller for ShowThread*

For our purposes, a board displays a collection of threads, and a thread displays a collection of posts. This controller will serve a list of posts. In the next listings, we establish a controller, command, and JSP triangle to show a thread. This triangle, given a parent ID, will display a post and all of its replies.

The model wrapper for ShowThread

First, here is the command:

```
package bbs;

import java.io.*;
import java.sql.*;
import COM.ibm.db2.*;
import java.util.*;

public class ShowThreadCommand {

    private static final int SUBJECT_COLUMN = 1;
    private static final int AUTHOR_COLUMN = 2;
    private static final int BOARD_COLUMN = 3;
    private static final int POSTTEXT_COLUMN = 4;
    private static final int NUMBER_COLUMN = 5;
```

The imports are the same as `postList`. We have column definitions for all of our main database columns so that we can descriptively refer to each of the columns in the `select` statement:

```
    protected Vector author = new Vector();
    protected Vector subject = new Vector();
    protected Vector board = new Vector();
    private Vector postText = new Vector();
    private String parent = "0";

    private String query = null;
    protected ResultSet result;
    protected Connection connection = null;

    public String getAuthor(int index) {
      return (String) author.elementAt(index);
    }

    public String getBoard(int index) {
      return (String) board.elementAt(index);
    }

    public String getParent() {
      return parent;
```

```
    }
    public String getPostText(int index) {
      return (String) postText.elementAt(index);
    }
    public String getQuery() {
      return query;
    }
    public int getSize() {
      return author.size();
    }
    public String getSubject(int index) {
      return (String) subject.elementAt(index);
    }
    public void setParent(String newParent) {
      parent = newParent;
    }
```

These are the attributes for our command, along with the get and set methods. Since we'll have a different value for every row, we'll allocate a vector to store the results.

```
public void initialize()
    throws IOException, com.ibm.db.DataException {

    try {
      Class.forName ("COM.ibm.db2.jdbc.app.DB2Driver").newInstance();

      String url = "jdbc:db2:board";

      // connect with default id/password
      connection = DriverManager.getConnection (url);
    } catch (Throwable theException) {
      theException.printStackTrace();
    }
}
```

As with the other commands, we initialize our database connection. In chapter 7, we'll pool these connections for performance.

```
public void execute ()
    throws
      SQLException,
      IOException,
      DataException {

    query =
      "select subject, author, board, postData, number "
        + "from posts where (number = "
        + getParent()
```

```
+ ") or"
+ " (parent = "
+ getParent()
+ ") order by number";
```

In this query, we'll retrieve the top-level thread and the replies. To do so, we'll retrieve a row from the database if the number of the specified top-level thread, called parent, is equal to the number of the primary post (number = getParent()) or the parent (parent = getParent ()). This is how we represent a top-level discussion, or thread:

```
Statement statement = connection.createStatement();
result = statement.executeQuery(query);
while (result.next()) {
  subject.addElement(result.getString(SUBJECT_COLUMN));
  author.addElement(result.getString(AUTHOR_COLUMN));
  board.addElement(result.getString(BOARD_COLUMN));
  postText.addElement(result.getString(POSTTEXT_COLUMN));
  }
result.close();
statement.close();
connection.close();
  }
}
```

We then execute the query. Next, we populate our attributes with a pass through the result sets. Finally, we clean up.

The controller for ShowThread

Our ShowThreadController is nearly identical to ShowBoardController. To save space, once again, we'll show only the interesting performTask method:

```
public void performTask(
  HttpServletRequest request,
  HttpServletResponse response) {

  try {
    String parent=request.getParameter ("parent");
    ShowThreadCommand fullThread = new ShowThreadCommand();
    fullThread.setParent(parent);
    fullThread.initialize();
    fullThread.execute();
```

In this case, we're showing all of the posts related to a thread. We want to set the top-level parent, which is passed into this method as a URL parameter. We then use our established protocol of create, set, initialize, and execute:

```
request.setAttribute("ShowThreadCommand", fullThread);

ServletContext servletContext = getServletContext ();
```

```
    RequestDispatcher dispatcher=null;
     if (fullThread.getSize()>0) {
        dispatcher = servletContext.getRequestDispatcher("/JSP/
   ShowThreadResults.jsp");
      } else {
        dispatcher = servletContext.getRequestDispatcher("/JSP/
   messageNotFound.jsp");
      }
      dispatcher.forward(request, response);
```

We then dispatch to the JSP, which will display the results:

```
   } catch (Throwable theException) {
     try {
       java.io.PrintWriter out = response.getWriter();
       out.println("<HTML>");
       out.println("<BODY BGCOLOR=#C0C0C0>");
       out.println("<H2>Exception Occurred</H2>");
       out.println(theException);
       out.println("</BODY></HTML>");
     } catch (Throwable exception) {
       theException.printStackTrace();
     }
   }
}
```

Finally, we clean up and catch our exceptions.

The view for ShowThread

This is ShowThreadResults.jsp, which displays the results:

```
<HTML>

<jsp:useBean id="ShowThreadCommand"  class="bbs.ShowThreadCommand"
   scope="request"></jsp:useBean>

<HEAD>
<TITLE>Message Board Posts</TITLE>
</HEAD>

<BODY BGCOLOR=#C0C0C0>
<H1>All Messages</H1>
<P>

<h3>
Board: <%=ShowThreadCommand.getBoard(0)%></h3>

<TABLE border="1">

<TR>
  <TD>Subject</TD>
  <TD>Author</TD>
  <TD>Post Text</TD>
```

```
</TR>
      <% for (int _i=0; _i < ShowThreadCommand.getSize(); _i++) { %>
      <TR> <TD><%=ShowThreadCommand.getSubject(_i) %></TD>
      <TD><%=ShowThreadCommand.getAuthor(_i) %></TD>
      <TD><%=ShowThreadCommand.getPostText(_i) %></TD>
      </TR>
      <% } %>
</TABLE>
<P>
<A href="../JSP/reply.jsp?parent=<%=ShowThreadCommand.getParent() %>&
board=<%=ShowThreadCommand.getBoard(0) %>&
subject=<%=ShowThreadCommand.getSubject(0)%>" >
Post a reply to this message</A>
</BODY>
</HTML>
```

This JSP is nearly identical to ShowBoardResults.jsp. We also provide a link to reply.jsp. To maintain the conversation state, we pass parameters for the board and subject.

5.2.4 *Building the model, view and controller for AddPost*

The final elements of our message board are the input form called reply.jsp and the AddPostCommand and AddPostController that we use to add a post.

The AddPost input view

Here is the input form reply.jsp:

```
<HTML>
<HEAD>
<META HTTP-EQUIV="Content-Type" content="text/html>
</HEAD>
<BODY>
<FORM METHOD="post" ACTION="/servlet/bbs.AddPostController">
<P>Please enter your post.</P>
<P>
<table>
  <tr>
  <td> Board: </td>
  <td> <b><%=request.getParameter ("board") %></b></td></tr>
  <tr>
    <td> Subject: </td>
    <td><INPUT TYPE="text" NAME="subject"
      value="<%=request.getParameter ("subject") %>" ID="subject"
      SIZE="50" MAXLENGTH="50" ></td></tr>
```

In this case, we are using the value parameter to prepopulate the subject field. This technique demonstrates the power of the JSP. We are easily parsing the input parameters without any complex code.

```
   <tr><td> Author: </td>
     <td><INPUT TYPE="text" NAME="author" ID="author"
       SIZE="20" MAXLENGTH="20" ></td></tr>
   <tr><td> Post text: </td>
     <td><textarea cols="50" rows="5" wrap="soft"
       name="postText"></textarea></td>
   </tr>
 <table>
 <INPUT TYPE="hidden" NAME="parent"
   value="<%=request.getParameter ("parent") %>" ID="parent" >
 <INPUT TYPE="hidden" NAME="board"
   value="<%=request.getParameter ("board") %>" ID="board" >
<INPUT TYPE="submit" NAME="Submit" ID="Submit" VALUE="Submit">
 <INPUT TYPE="reset" NAME="Reset" ID="Reset" VALUE="Reset">
</P>
</FORM>
</BODY>
</HTML>
```

In this example, we could have easily used HTML instead of this JSP page. We opted to use a JSP to assist with handling prepopulation of the form with input parameters. We were also able to dynamically create the text that showed the board. However, we have no controller or command, because this JSP data does not need any input from command beans.

The model for AddPost

The following classes will take the user's responses on the reply.jsp form and add them to the database. If we're successful, instead of returning a new JSP we'll return the user to the ShowBoardResults.jsp view via ShowBoardController. Here is the AddPostCommand:

```
package bbs;

import java.io.*;
import java.sql.*;
import COM.ibm.db2.*;
import java.util.*;

public class AddPostCommand {
```

Here are the usual imports that we use in the rest of our commands:

```
   private String author = null;
   private String subject = null;
   private String board = null;
   private String parent = "0";
   private String postText = null;
   private ResultSet result;
   private Connection connection = null;
   private String query = null;
```

```
public String getAuthor() {
  return (String) author;
}

public String getBoard() {
  return (String) board;
}

public String getParent() {
  return parent;
}

public String getPostText() {
  return postText;
}

public String getQuery() {
  return query;
}

public String getSubject() {
  return (String) subject;
}

public void setAuthor(String newAuthor) {
  author = newAuthor;
}

public void setBoard(String newBoard) {
  board = newBoard;
}

public void setParent(String newParent) {
  parent = newParent;
}

public void setPostText(String newPostText) {
  postText = newPostText;
}

public void setSubject(String newSubject) {
  subject = newSubject;
}
```

Listing 5.1 contains the attributes and the get and set methods. This list is fairly long, because we have an attribute for every database field.

Listing 5.1   Validation is a good reason to separate execute and initialize

```
public void initialize()
  throws
    AddPostValidationException,
    IOException,
    DataException {

    try {

      if (getAuthor() == null) {                        ●  Validate author
        throw new AddPostValidationException(
        "Author field is required.");
      }
      if (getSubject() == null) {                       ●  Validate subject
        throw new AddPostValidationException(
        "The Subject field is required.");
      }
      if (getPostText() == null) {                      ●  Validate postText
        throw new AddPostValidationException(
        "The post is empty.");
      }
      if (getBoard() == null) {                         ●  Validate board
        throw new AddPostValidationException(
        "The board is not valid.");
      }
      Class.forName("COM.ibm.db2.jdbc.app.DB2Driver").newInstance();

      String url = "jdbc:db2:board";

      // connect with default id/password
      connection = DriverManager.getConnection(url);

    } catch (Throwable theException) {
      theException.printStackTrace();
    }

}
```

In this initialize, we introduce validation. Here, we raise our own exception, called AddPostValidationException. If at all possible, we should keep from throwing a bare exception. This new exception serves as a collection point for information about the error condition. It also clearly communicates the problem with the exception name. The code annotations show the four points where we check the required fields, and if they haven't been set, we throw a specialized exception. In a more advanced implementation, our controller would use the information in the exception and populate a bean that could be used by our standard error JSP.

After the validation, we connect to the database and then clean up:

```
public void execute()
throws
  IOException,
  DataException {

try {
  query =
    "INSERT INTO POSTS values ('"
      + getSubject()
      + "', (select max(number) from posts) + 1, '"
      + getAuthor()
      + "', '"
      + getPostText()
      + "', current timestamp, "
      + getParent()
      + ", '"
      + getBoard()

      + "')";
```

In our `execute` method, we add a record to the database. The logic is noticeably simpler than usual because we have already done the validation of the elements and we catch the database exceptions elsewhere.

```
    Statement statement = connection.createStatement();
    result = statement.executeQuery(query);
    result.close();
    connection.close();
    statement.close();
  } catch (Throwable theException) {
    theException.printStackTrace();
  }

  }

}
```

We then execute the query, clean up, and catch exceptions.

The controller for AddPost

`AddPostController` is similar to the other commands, with a new twist: We will dispatch an existing servlet instead of a new JSP. As usual, we'll focus on the action in `performTask`:

```
public void performTask(
  HttpServletRequest request,
  HttpServletResponse response) {

  try {
    String board = request.getParameter ("board");
```

```
String subject = request.getParameter ("subject");
String author = request.getParameter ("author");
String postText = request.getParameter ("postText");
String parent = request.getParameter ("parent");
AddPostCommand addPost = new AddPostCommand();

try {
  addPost.setBoard(board);
  addPost.setSubject(subject);
  addPost.setAuthor(author);
  addPost.setPostText(postText);
  addPost.setParent(parent);
  addPost.initialize();
```

We are putting our add and initialize methods into their own try/catch
loop. This design will allow us to catch the exceptions that we raised for validation failures. In a more robust architecture, we'd create a bean from the
data in our custom exception and return an appropriate error JSP.

```
} catch (Throwable Exception) {
  try {
    ServletContext servletContext = getServletContext ();
    RequestDispatcher dispatcher =
      servletContext.getRequestDispatcher("/JSP/AddPostError.jsp");
    dispatcher.forward(request, response);
    return;
  } catch (Throwable exception) {
    exception.printStackTrace();
  }

}
addPost.execute();
request.setAttribute("AddPostCommand", addPost);

ServletContext servletContext = getServletContext ();
RequestDispatcher dispatcher =
  servletContext.getRequestDispatcher("/servlet/
bbs.ShowBoardController");
  dispatcher.forward(request, response);
```

In this case, no dynamic data is to be displayed beyond success or failure. For
the success case, users would probably prefer to continue browsing the board
from the ShowBoard view. Therefore, through our controller, we simply dispatch the user to ShowBoardController. Our request object already has the
requisite board parameter set, so there is no need to re-create one.

```
} catch (Throwable theException) {
  try {
    java.io.PrintWriter out = response.getWriter();
    out.println("<HTML>");
    out.println("<HEAD><TITLE>Post List Controller</TITLE></HEAD>");
```

```
        out.println("<BODY BGCOLOR=#C0C0C0>");
        out.println("<H2>Exception Occurred</H2>");
        out.println(theException);
        out.println("</BODY></HTML>");
    } catch (Throwable exception) {
        theException.printStackTrace();
    }
  }
}
```

The rest of the method catches our exceptions.

5.2.5   *Performance problems*

This solution has a critical flaw: Most of the cycles will be wasted fetching the same values. With caching, the customer realized an improvement from an average of 19 seconds to a subsecond average response time. This is not at all unusual. Notice the communication between our command object layer and the database. This communication represents most of the expense for the system. In this case, we've seen that five distinct communications, or round-trips, are necessary out of 20. Because a message board can usually fit entirely in memory, our application is especially sensitive to caching. Without a cache, it wouldn't be unusual for us to fetch a post hundreds of times, even though the value remains unchanged. For real-world high-volume Internet applications, cache solutions can be considerably faster.

5.3   *Solution: Cache*

With a sick feeling, I gaze down the near vertical trail. I then look down at my magic boots, but they're covered in snow. I make my first turn with no problem and start to relax. Halfway through the second turn, as I brace to finish rounding it off, my magic boots abandon me. I am pointed directly downhill, and I pick up too much speed before falling spectacularly, but softly, in the fresh powder. My poles and skis have abandoned me at various places along the trail. With great effort, I dig through the snow, gather my gear, and start down the hill once more. Turn. Brace. Poof. Yard sale. After collecting my gear—and what is left of my dignity—I try again. I crash again. My normally calm demeanor shattered, I let out a long string of profanities. When certain geologic conditions exist, echoes carry surprisingly well. I am certain that mine carry to all of the amused Utah residents around the easy slope that skirt my canyon.

I've never had a more acute sense of embarrassment than I did on that mountain slope in Utah. After I was back in the ski lodge and thinking more clearly,

I decided that my biggest mistake was making the trip in the first place. Sometimes, the best antidote for a bad trip is *not to go in the first place*. Poor-performing Java applications can make an incredible number of needless communication trips. Simply caching posts as we retrieve them will help us tremendously. Next up, we'll look at ways we can apply caching solutions to our problem.

5.3.1 Solution 1: Use a hardware cache

The first part of our refactored solution, called a *caching proxy*, deals with the static content and is completely independent of Java. This solution is a piece of inexpensive hardware placed between the web server and the clients, as shown in figure 5.2 on page 111. Because most of the HTTP requests are for images, they can be serviced without even consulting the server.

For taxed HTTP servers, this solution can make a tremendous difference. Each graphic, animation, or sound is retrieved independently. Good browsers optimize by grouping these requests in blocks of four, but caching the content in a proxy can insulate a majority of the requests from ever reaching a web server.

5.3.2 Solution 2: Cache commands

In general, a cache is simply a rapidly accessible place to store data that is expensive to retrieve. PCs generally have hardware caches on video cards so that the video processors have immediate access to video data. Most operating systems have disk caches for storing frequently accessed disk records (which is one of the reasons you have to shut down the Windows operating system instead of just turning it off). The data in these examples is fairly fluid, so we should be able to come up with a scheme for caching the commands that fetch our dynamic data.

In this example, we'll build a command cache. For simplicity, our example will build a hash table into our command layer. That way, our controllers won't need to change at all. In practice, it may be far more cost effective to build a single, systemwide command cache. Many vendors are already working on these types of technologies.

Instead of creating a new command from the class object each time, the controller will ask the cache manager for a command. If a command is in the cache, we'll return it to the requesting instance. In this case, there's no need to initialize or execute the command, because the get attributes are already populated. If the command isn't in the cache, the cache manager will create a new one as before, following the set, initialize, and execute protocol to prepare the command for use by the controller and JSP layers.

In general, in order for a cache strategy to be useful, our application should have several properties:

- Our solution should have a logical partitioning of cacheable units. Examples are URLs, documents, policies, customers, and pages. The command gives us an ideal partitioning of cacheable units.

- The units should have a value that's stable enough to make the cache worthwhile. We want to have a relatively high probability of finding data in the cache. Several factors come into play, including:

  - *The volatility of the data.* Higher volatility means that we are less likely to use the data before it changes. In such cases, we'll need a very high access frequency to make the cache worthwhile, but these cases do exist (for example, a popular stock price).

  - *The size of the database.* If a database is very large, it may be difficult to cache enough data to have repeat requests, unless the requests are not uniformly distributed.

  - *The distribution of data requests.* If a database is too large, a uniform distribution will inhibit caching.

  - *The size of the cache.* If we can cache more data, we have a higher likelihood of a hit for any individual request.

  - *The frequency of access.* If the data volatility is high and the frequency is low, a cache strategy may not be appropriate. If the database is very large, the resources for the cache are constrained, and the distribution of requests is spread uniformly across the data, then the cache would probably not provide meaningful benefit. In most cases, though, a cache can add exceptional value.

There should be a convenient way to handle cache data that has changed (referred to as *stale cache data*). One solution is to simply expire cache data after a certain period of time. We may instead explicitly invalidate cached data through the commands that change the data. Alternatively, we may use a publish/subscribe pattern to automatically notify the cache when a change occurs. Table 5.2 shows three requirements for caching to make sense.

Table 5.2 If data can be partitioned into cacheable units, values are reasonably stable, and detecting change and age is practical, then caching is a viable enhancement.

Requirement	Description
Data must have cacheable units.	The application must have a partitioning that lends itself well to caching. A partition of elements that are close to the same size and practical to store are keys for effective caching.
Values must be stable.	If a value does not stay stable long enough to be read more than once for the expected case, a cache is not practical. For example, a stock value may not be considered stable for a pool of 10 users who use a ticker occasionally, but it might be stable enough for thousands of interested traders on a single server.
Detecting change and age must be practical.	We need a convenient way to handle critical data changes that must be detectable, or some reasonable definition of what constitutes stale data.

Our example has cacheable units. Our database is small and the distribution far from uniform, because the most interesting posts will be viewed most frequently. It's likely that our entire database will fit in memory. Our invalidation is also simple; so far, we write posts to the database in only one place. For us, a cache makes sense.

5.3.3 Adding a cache to our BBS

In this example, we'll add a cache object for the `ShowBoardCommand` and `ShowThreadCommand` classes. We'll call them `BoardCacheCommand` and `ThreadCacheCommand`, respectively. The techniques for each are identical, so we'll show only the `BoardCacheCommand` in listing 5.2.

Listing 5.2 The BBS example with an added cache

```
package bbs;

import java.io.*;

import java.util.*;                                    ❶ Imports

import bbs.AddPostValidationException;

import bbs.ShowBoardCommand;

public class BoardCacheCommand {

    protected String board = null;        ❷ Cache key field
```

```
public boolean cached = false;
```
❸ Instructional field, true for cache hits

```
protected ShowBoardCommand boardCommand = null;
private static java.util.Hashtable boardCache = null;
```
❹ This is the cache. Note static.

```
public void initialize ()
  throws
    IOException,
    DataException {
```
❺ Initialize is lighter than usual.

```
  synchronized(boardCache) {
    if (boardCache == null) {
      boardCache = new Hashtable();
    }
  }
}
```
❻ Synchronization controls access.

```
public void invalidate(String key) {
  synchronized(boardCache) {
    getBoardCache().remove(key);
  }
}
```
❼ Invalidate handles changed data.

```
public void execute ()
  throws
    IOException,
    DataException {
 synchronized(boardCache) {
  try {
    // Cached is an instructional flag to show whether a
    // value was fetched from the cache.
    cached = true;
    Hashtable cache = getBoardCache();
    if (cache == null) {
      throw new Exception();
    }
    boardCommand = (ShowBoardCommand) cache.get(getBoard());
    if (boardCommand == null) {
      boardCommand = new ShowBoardCommand();
      boardCommand.setBoard(getBoard());
      boardCommand.initialize();
      boardCommand.execute();
      cache.put(getBoard(), boardCommand);

      cached = false;
    }
  } catch (Throwable theException) {
    theException.printStackTrace();
  }
 }
}
```
❽ Execute will try cache first.

❾ Synchronized to protect static cache

Cache missed, so ❿ fire a command.

```
public String getAuthor(int index)
  throws
    IndexOutOfBoundsException,
```
⓫ Most getters pass through.

```
          ArrayIndexOutOfBoundsException {
        return getBoardCommand().getAuthor(index);
      }
      public String getBoard() {
        return board;
      }

      protected static Hashtable getBoardCache() {
        return boardCache;
      }

      ShowBoardCommand getBoardCommand() {
        return boardCommand;
      }
      public boolean getCached() {
        return cached;
      }

      public String getNumber(int index)
        throws
          IndexOutOfBoundsException,
          ArrayIndexOutOfBoundsException {
        return getBoardCommand().getNumber(index);
      }

      public int getSize() {
        return getBoardCommand().getSize();
      }

      public String getSubject(int index)
        throws
          IndexOutOfBoundsException,
          ArrayIndexOutOfBoundsException {
        return getBoardCommand().getSubject(index);
      }

      public void setBoard(String name) {
        board = name;
      }

      void setBoardCommand(ShowBoardCommand newBoardCommand) {
        boardCommand = newBoardCommand;
      }
    }
}
```

⑫ Cache key is held locally.

❶ These imports get our usual Java utility classes and a couple of others. We'll use this command to actually create a ShowBoardCommand or retrieve it from our class. We'll also include a validation step to ensure that the key fields entered by the controller are valid.

❷ `board` is the unique identifier that we'll use for a key field in this example. Conceptually, we'll have a hash table entry for every board. Each hash table entry is an executed command that has the whole list of boards.

❸ `cached` is a variable that will tell us whether the command was retrieved from the cache, and we can display that status on the JSP. Of course, in practice, this attribute is not necessary.

❹ Danger! `boardCache` is declared as a static attribute. That means only one copy exists, attached to the class object. Whenever we access this attribute, we must do so in `synchronized` code, which means that only one method can use our hash table at a time. Later in the chapter, we'll introduce read-write locks, which will provide more concurrent access without the loss of thread safety.

❺ Next, we have the `initialize` method. We initialize and validate, as usual. We are slimmed down somewhat, because the database connections and validation are handled in the sister command.

❻ The first time any object uses the hash table, it will need to be initialized, but only the first time because it is a static variable.

❼ Next is the `invalidate` method. This method is used whenever the board's list of posts can change. In our case, we'll need to call `invalidate` whenever we add a new top-level post.

❽ Next is the `execute` method. We fire the logic wrapped by the command, as usual.

❾ This code section is synchronized because it writes to the hash table. If a command with our key is in the hash table, then we've just about completed this `execute` method. Compare that with the `intialize` and `execute` methods in the previous edition of `ShowBoardCommand`, which validated the input parameters, connected to a database, executed a query, and fetched the results of the query to populate the input variables. The system was also working hard, with several round-trip communications to the database server, an expensive database connection, and plenty of expensive string manipulation.

❿ We check to see if we found the requested board in the cache, also called a *cache hit*. If not, we simply create the command, process the sets, initialize, and execute, just like before. We've added a layer of complexity in front of our regular command in case our cache doesn't get a hit. Remember that this case is the exception. For most applications, hits of 90 percent or more in the cache are not out of the ordinary. For our bulletin board example, the entire message board might fit into memory, so we can probably expect to see much higher hit rates. As long as our system stays up, we'll retrieve a row once for every new post or update, per server, resulting in tremendous savings.

⓫ These are our `get` and `set` methods. The value of encapsulating them is clear: We won't have to change the interface for the command even though we've changed the implementation of our instance variables. For the most part, for the interface attributes for `ShowBoardCommand` we simply pass through to the `get` and `set` methods of the imbedded commands.

⓬ Because `board` is the key, we have that one on hand and pass it back directly.

Continuing with the next part of our program, we need to modify `AddPost-Command` to invalidate the appropriate cache when a new post is added. Here are the changes, which are added to the `execute` method in our new class, called `FastAddPostCommand`:

```
query =
  "INSERT INTO POSTS values ('"
    + getSubject()
    + "', (select max(number) from posts) + 1, '"
    + getAuthor()
    + "', '"
    + getPostText()
    + "', current timestamp, "
    + getParent()
    + ", '"
    + getBoard()
    + "')";
Statement statement = connection.createStatement();
result = statement.executeQuery(query);
result.close();
statement.close();
connection.close();
```

The query and its execution remain unchanged:

```
// If it's a top-level post, we must invalidate the board cache
// because the board list will be different.
if(getParent()=="0") {
  BoardCacheCommand boardCache = new BoardCacheCommand();
  boardCache.invalidate(getBoard());
} else {
// otherwise, we must invalidate the thread cache
  // because the message content has changed.
  ThreadCacheCommand threadCache = new ThreadCacheCommand();
  threadCache.invalidate(getParent());
}
```

We then check to see if we're adding a top-level post or a reply to an existing thread. If it is a top-level thread, we need to invalidate the cache for board-Cache. If it's a reply to a thread, we have to invalidate the cache for the thread. In either case, we won't write the new value to the cache until it's fetched again. The slight performance penalty is more than compensated for by the improvement in readability.

The usage of these commands is identical; only the name of the command is different. Here, we show the revised controller statements in our new controller, FastShowBoardController:

```
String board=request.getParameter ("board");
BoardCacheCommand postList = new BoardCacheCommand();
postList.setBoard(board);
postList.initialize();
postList.execute();
```

The changes in FastShowThreadController are identical.

5.3.4 *Possible enhancements to cached commands*

In "Scaling Up E-business Applications with Caching," the authors define a dynamic cache manager. This section describes some natural extensions to our cache example. The following list represents the enhancements that we'd likely want to make for a robust cache manager:

- Refactor. First, the generic command methods should be promoted to an interface. This would give us flexibility in initializing and executing our commands.
- Extend our commands to have a generic key attribute.
- Add a time stamp and timeout to our commands, to allow us to periodically expire old cache items.
- Record the key values for any command dependencies that we might have (to use in invalidation schemes).
- Generalize the cache management functions in BoardCacheCommand and ThreadCacheCommand to a general CommandCache class. This class would handle caching of systemwide commands and invalidation.
- Establish various levels of validation and the protocols that application developers might use to support them. Some elements would be fully automatic, such as a timeout mechanism. Some would be more advanced—an automatic notification scheme, for example. Some would be simple but tedious and bug prone, such as the manual invalidation scheme we used in this example.

- Cache JSP fragments, so that dynamic pages could be built once and retrieved intact.

Products that cache full servlets

Some servlets generate pages that change only every 15 minutes or so. With supporting software, these can be cached much like static pages. Caucho's Resin, which has a very fast servlet container, caches servlets and JSPs in this way. To do so, the page sets up a caching header, which marks the page as cacheable and sets the appropriate parameters for timeout and the like. BEA Systems and IBM have similar solutions.

Keep in mind that with these products, you're addressing only the first and most basic type of JSP caching. You should also consider solutions that cache dynamic content at various points of the architecture and various levels of granularity.

Caching JSP fragments

There are many solutions calling for complex user interfaces to compose dynamic web pages from smaller JSPs called *fragments*. If a given fragment is based on a command or similar construct and the command can be cached, it may make more sense to cache the HTML generated from the compiled and executed JSP fragment. This practice is known as *JSP fragment caching*. The cache is maintained the same way: through the keys generated from the combination of input parameters from the command object. Instead of caching the output parameters, we cache the executed JSP. IBM has submitted a request (JSR 126) to the Java Community Process to propose a uniform implementation of JSP fragment caching.

Buying a full cache manager

It would require too many pages for us to build all of the previously suggested enhancements into our example. We should point out that many vendors are working on robust cache managers for command frameworks similar to this one. For example, BEA has an alliance with TimesTen, who builds FrontTier, a dynamic data cache for WebLogic. IBM's edge server has a cache that stores dynamic JSP fragments. The capability to cache JSP fragments offers a significant performance boost; it eliminates communication and processing by the web server and web application server layers for a cache hit, even for dynamic content.

By the time this book is published, it's likely that most of the major web application server vendors will have some form of dynamic cache. Still, you can use the techniques in this chapter wherever round-tripping is a concern and the back-end services lend themselves to caching architectures.

Vignette's fast portal solutions

Vignette takes caching a step further: it offers highly personalized content-management solutions for the development of portals and other Internet software. With the Vignette system, templates (using JSPs and JSP fragments) make it possible to publish dynamic content. The architecture performs well, partially because of a good caching solution. A template manager helps to maintain a template cache and flushes an entry whenever a template is added, deleted, or modified. An additional manager, the Docroot Manager, works with the web server to ensure that outdated files are completely purged from the server's document root. This combination makes it easy for the web server and application server to work together and maintain an efficient and effective cache, with little management overhead for the user. You can read more about these content-management solutions at http://www.vignette.com.

5.4   *Cache-related mini-antipatterns*

By far the biggest problem related to caches is the failure to use one where appropriate. We should be aware of a few additional issues as we implement caches. Within Java, two common antipatterns are related to concurrent programming. In addition, we need to carefully manage our memory: we should have a firm strategy for removing stale elements from the cache, and for capping the size, or at least doing some garbage collection if memory becomes constrained.

5.4.1   *Concurrent access to static cache*

Trying to access static class-level variables concurrently is a common problem. We must synchronize access to these variables in order to make them thread-safe. You can't have more than one instance writing to the hash table at the same time and expect correct results. Note that synchronizing on the method level won't work unless the method is static, because although there could be several commands, there's only one hash table. Synchronizing at the method level will merely prevent several threads in the same instance from using the same method concurrently. The synchronize keyword will lock only a single object. Since all of the execute methods in our command objects could try to concurrently access our boardCache object, we need to lock it with a critical section. By synchronizing on the boardCache object, we ensure that all threads accessing it need to first obtain a lock. We effectively lock the critical resource instead of the methods accessing it.

5.4.2   *The ever-growing cache*

If we were to implement this solution in front of a database with significant size, our cache would steadily grow until we ran out of memory; we simply have no mechanism for cleaning the cache. A surprising number of commercial applications have this characteristic. Here are some strategies for cleaning the cache periodically:

- For caches of user-related data, either cache user data in the session or flush the session data when sessions expire. Since most web servers allow for notification when a session expires, you can use this event to clean up a command cache as well as session data.

- Time stamp elements of the cache. When a cached item is accessed, update the time stamp. Use a maximum-limit-exceeded exception to trigger a garbage-collection process. This process iterates through the cache, expiring a specified number of the oldest items.

- Instead of an event-driven garbage collector, have a timed garbage collector that periodically expires elements in the cache. This approach also requires the addition of a time stamp to cached entries.

5.5   *Antipattern: Synchronized Read/Write Bottlenecks*

Mark Wells, a former vice president of engineering at Agillion, suggested this antipattern. In the previous example, our synchronization scheme required us to lock the hash table objects for every hash table access. This lock is necessary so that the results of the execution are correct, even if there are multiple threads. Consider the following class:

```
class counter {
public static Integer count=0;
public void count() {
  Integer temp = count;
  temp = temp + 1;
  count = temp;
}
```

Table 5.3 shows a possible timeline for the program with two threads of execution. Two threads are running the same program.

Table 5.3 Executing parallel threads can have many different results. This shows the possible results of executing our program with inadequate protection. While we should increment our counter twice, we come out with a total of one.

Value of count	Value of temp	Thread 1	Thread 2
0	0	Integer temp = count;	
0	1	temp = temp + 1	
0	0		Integer temp = count;
0	1		temp = temp + 1
1	1	count = temp	
1?	1		count = temp

We can protect execution from simultaneous access by adding the synchronized keyword to the method:

```
public synchronized void count() {
```

For synchronized code, when a thread enters a method it locks the instance's object so that other threads of the same instance cannot enter the method at the same time. Here's the key: The Java synchronized keyword locks on the object level. For Listing 5.2, a synchronized method would not have been strong enough, because many commands could exist and write to the hash table at the same time. Therefore, we must lock the cache object.

5.5.1 *Collisions between readers can hurt performance*

For cache applications, you should have far more reads *from* the cache than writes *to* the cache. If this were not true, you'd be adding overhead without getting much value. You don't need to protect simultaneous reads from the cache, because reads are not destructive. However, a writer and a reader using the cache at the same time would possibly generate unpredictable results. The problem is that writing applications need exclusive access, so to keep the reading applications out, both readers and writers must obtain a lock. Because the locks are exclusive, readers are also reduced to sequential access. This is a classic case of the Read/Write Bottleneck antipattern.

Consider a bathroom that's located between two important rooms of a house. It should be acceptable for many people to walk through the bathroom, as long as no one is using it. Once someone is using the bathroom, those passing through must clear out and the doors on either side must be locked. The readers share the bathroom, passing through concurrently. Writers use the bathroom exclusively. We should not force people simply passing through to wait, but that's precisely what our sample application does. We allow only one user of the bathroom, analogous to our cache objects, to pass through at any given time, regardless of the use. I'm reasonably certain that I have seen bathroom lines at many parties that indicated use of this algorithm. If the read/write ratio is very high, then the penalty can be significant.

5.5.2   *Read/write locks allow correct shared access*

Database systems solve this problem with a multilevel locking system. In this case, obtaining a read lock on a database object allows multiple users to read the same data. A write lock is not compatible with a read lock. An application requesting a write lock must wait for all readers to clear. Java has no native support for read/write locks, but creating an object to provide this functionality is straightforward. To see how a read/write lock works, we present an example provided by Amandeep Singh, from a self-published article titled "Implementing Read-Write Locks in Java":

```
class RWLock
{
  private int givenLocks;
  private int waitingWriters;
  private int waitingReaders;
  private Object mutex;
  :
  :
  public void getReadLock()
  {
    synchronized(mutex)
    {
      while((givenLocks == -1) ||
          (waitingWriters != 0))
      {
        mutex.wait();
      }

      givenLocks++;

    }
  }
```

This method is used to request the read lock. It locks our common object, mutex, to control access to the internal variables. If writers are waiting or if writers have a lock, they're allowed to clear before the lock is granted. givenLocks has a value of −1 when a writer has the lock:

```
public void getWriteLock()
{
  synchronized(mutex)
  {
    waitingWriters++;

    while(givenLocks != 0)
    {
      mutex.wait();
    }

    waitingWriters--;
    givenLocks = -1;
  }
}
```

When requesting a write lock, a thread signals that it is waiting by increment-ing the waitingWriters variable, waits until no more readers are holding the lock, and then takes a lock by setting givenLocks to −1 and decrements wait-ingWriters to signal that it is no longer waiting:

```
public void releaseLock();
{
  synchronized(mutex)
  {
    if(givenLocks == 0)
      return;

    if(givenLocks == -1)
      givenLocks = 0;
    else
      givenLocks--;

    mutex.notifyAll();
  }
}
}
```

To release a lock, the protocol is followed in reverse. To use this lock, an appli-cation must:

- Create a lock for each critical resource to be protected.
- Request the lock for read before reading from the resource.
- Release the lock for read after reading from the resource.
- Request the lock for write before writing to the resource.
- Release the lock for write after writing to the resource.

The application will allow shared reads but will require exclusive writes. In our case, the application would have significantly higher throughput for most caching applications. Relational databases have proven the utility of robust read/write locks for years. Caching is an example where throughput can be significantly improved through the implementation of a read/write lock.

As always, a much better solution than rolling your own is to use a prepackaged, respected utility. Many other resources exist for good concurrent programming in Java. Among the best is a book called *Concurrent Programming in Java: Design Principles and Practices*. In it, author Doug Lea describes locking considerations and other techniques for ensuring correctness. His website, http://g.oswego.edu/dl/, also includes `util.concurrent`, a well-respected collection of utilities for concurrent programming.

5.6   *Cooking the Cacheless Cow*

This chapter has shown that caching can add a substantial boost to performance when applications meet certain criteria. Real-world architectures have implemented caches on every level, from low-level hardware to operating systems, networks, and distributed applications. We also know that many applications neglect this important potential performance boost. The Command design pattern provides a convenient point to add a cache. This chapter has presented an unsophisticated cache solution, but many frameworks will build in command caches over time. Many of the applications that do cache unnecessarily limit throughput by falling into the trap laid by the Synchronized Read/Write Bottleneck antipattern or other mini-antipatterns defined in this chapter.

5.7   *Antipatterns in this chapter*

These are the templates for the antipatterns that appear in this chapter. They provide an excellent summary format and form the basis of the cross-references in appendix A.

The Cacheless Cow

> RELATED ANTIPATTERNS: Round-tripping. Poor caching strategies usually lead to round-tripping and poor performance.

> DESCRIPTION: Caches can be used to provide a significant performance boost with very little effort, but many developers neglect this basic enhancement. Most Internet applications take advantage of hardware and

web servers for caching of static content, but caching of dynamic content takes more time.

MOST FREQUENT SCALE: Application.

EXCEPTIONS: Some applications are not caching candidates. If there's no way to know when cache data is invalid, a cached solution won't work. If most data elements change too frequently, caches won't be effective. If a database is large and the cached data set is too diffuse, the cache won't be effective.

REFACTORED SOLUTION NAME: Dynamic Command Cache.

SOLUTION ALSO KNOWN AS: Model 2, Modified Model-View-Controller.

REFACTORED SOLUTION TYPE: Software or technology. Caches can be bought or built.

REFACTORED SOLUTION DESCRIPTION: Cache dynamic content where possible. The Command design pattern and its relatives provide a convenient interface point for a cache. Most major web application server vendors have developed or are working on dynamic caching solutions, and rolling your own is well worth the effort when the prepackaged solutions do not fit.

TYPICAL CAUSES: Ignorance of the power of caching is the biggest culprit. Designing a data model without caching solutions in mind is another.

ANECDOTAL EVIDENCE: "The individual pieces seem to be working, but the application still seems slow."

SYMPTOMS, CONSEQUENCES: Applications suffering from this antipattern do a job many more times than is necessary. They can range anywhere from slug-slow to slug-slime-slow, depending on the read/write ratio and other factors.

SOLUTION ALTERNATIVES: Commercial versions of command caches exist. Sometimes, data that would otherwise be cached can be stored in the session state, at the application, session, or at page level.

Synchronized Read/Write Bottleneck

DESCRIPTION: The Java programming language locks on the object level for synchronization, but does not distinguish between readers and writers. This locking mechanism is too restrictive for applications such as databases and caches.

MOST FREQUENT SCALE: Microarchitecture.

REFACTORED SOLUTION NAME: Read/Write Locks.

REFACTORED SOLUTION TYPE: Software.

REFACTORED SOLUTION DESCRIPTION: Instead of synchronizing on methods or objects, use a read/write lock. As of the publishing date, Java had not yet included a read/write lock, but many examples exist in literature and on the Internet.

ROOT CAUSES: Ignorance. Java does not yet include a read/write lock, and information about this solution is not widely distributed.

SYMPTOMS, CONSEQUENCES: This antipattern must usually be detected by inspection, but occasionally a web application server can bog down without fully using available CPU resources.

SOLUTION ALTERNATIVES: A second solution for this problem is called Copy-on-Write. This solution involves creating a copy of a cache item, locking the copy, writing to the copy, and then deleting the original. Readers in this scenario do not lock.

Bitter memories

Kayakers and canoeists are not quite mortal enemies, but there's a healthy rivalry between them. As a child I canoed, but I made the switch to kayaks attracted by their stability, speed, and grace. I am now on an extended trip with three other kayakers--and one canoeist. The canoeist, Randy Barnes, and I spar verbally at every opportunity. I comment on his strong swimming skills, regretting that a canoe is so difficult to roll. Randy wonders aloud why I need the security blanket of a two-blade paddle when a canoeist can make do with a short, single blade. Our first day is spent on the Little River, a tight, technical run in the Smokey Mountains. I secretly marvel as Randy takes his canoe down a violent Class V rapid called the Sinks. I decide to walk around it; for me, the margin of safety is too slim. With outstanding control and incredible skill, Randy maneuvers his 12-foot canoe into places I have trouble taking my 7-foot kayak.

We are now running a Class IV+ rapid known as the Elbow. It's an extremely tight flume of water—in places just four feet wide. Bent tightly at two points, the Elbow drops nearly 20 feet down a 40-degree fall. Three kayakers at the bottom watch, stunned, as Randy's canoe hits the side of the chute, then the riverbed. The canoe tumbles all the way to the end of the run. Coughing up river water, Randy emerges as the kayakers jeer. Looking over the rapid as I prepare for my run, I remain silent.

6.1   *Understanding memory leaks and antipatterns*

In this chapter, we'll begin to explore antipatterns related to memory leaks. Some of you might think that memory-management discussions should be left to JVM vendors. Technically, a Java memory leak occurs when an object cannot be reached and it's not freed through an automatic process known as garbage collection. In this sense, the virtual machine vendors, rather than application programmers, should be the ones to concern themselves with memory leaks. However, we'll use the term *memory leak* in a much broader sense. For our purposes, an object that's not garbage-collected after it's no longer of use to an application is a memory leak. Some of you might consider this usage inaccurate, because Java is working precisely as it is designed. I chose the term memory leak because it best describes the behavior of the applications that suffer from these antipatterns: memory that we no longer need is not returned to the memory heap and will continue to "leak" away until we explicitly trace the source and fix the problem.

First, we'll examine memory management for other languages, such as C++. We'll also examine several garbage-collection techniques and identify the ones most JVMs use. In some places, we need to help the garbage collector to do its job. To that end, we'll present a series of antipatterns involving memory leaks. Finally, we'll look at tools and techniques that will help us solve memory leaks.

6.1.1   *Managing memory*

In any object-oriented language, each variable, regardless of scope, must be allocated. In most cases, memory can come from three primary sources: registers, the stack, and the heap. The compiler (or interpreter) closely manages registers and the stack, so we'll focus on the heap. We can think of the heap as a mailbox with different-sized slots. A compiler or interpreter will have a memory manager, analogous to a postmaster, to manage these slots. Implementations of memory managers can vary widely, from single runtime entities to static libraries. It's the manager's job to configure the size of the slots, allocate them as needed, and reclaim them for later use. For some low-level languages, like C++, the manager is a very thin layer. The programmer is responsible for explicitly requesting a block of memory (with `new` or `malloc`) and explicitly freeing the block (with `free`) when it's no longer required. C++ also forces the programmer to track individual addresses of memory blocks through *pointers*. This implementation makes C++ very flexible, but also tedious and problematic. Table 6.1 shows some of the bugs that a C++ programmer might encounter. We'll focus on the dangling pointer and the memory leak, because both are realized differently in Java.

Table 6.1   Problems encountered while managing memory in C++. The third column shows the types of program failure that you can expect.

Name	Description	Failure Symptoms
Memory leaks	Memory is allocated. Memory is not freed.	This is the classic memory leak. The program grows indefinitely, slows as free memory runs out, and eventually fails with an allocation error.
Free errors	Memory is freed with no allocation.	The program fails with a free error.
Dangling pointers	Memory is freed, but the pointers not updated.	As lists, trees, or other structures are traversed, the program crashes with unpredictable results.
Invalid pointer; lost pointer	Pointers to valid memory addresses are overwritten.	The program crashes.

Recall that Java implements a different strategy. Java applications request objects, and the interpreter allocates the memory for the object. Because Java handles allocation for the programmer and all variables are represented as higher level objects, the Java programmer doesn't need to bother with pointer arithmetic. In fact, pointer arithmetic was explicitly avoided in the Java design to increase the stability and security of the language. Memory is not explicitly freed. Instead, Java handles deallocation of memory through a process called garbage collection.

6.1.2 *Understanding garbage collection*

Heaps are usually managed as a linked list or with a reference table pointing to blocks of memory. An allocated block is marked in the table or taken out of the chain. With allocation, a suitable block is found, subdivided, marked, and returned to the requesting application. To prevent fragmenting, some memory managers periodically coalesce memory or combine contiguous blocks into one big block. Automatic allocation of memory isn't difficult. The size of the memory block and the block usage are known in advance. The memory manager simply goes to the heap and walks through the free blocks until a block of sufficient size is found.

Garbage collection is the act of periodically finding unused memory and returning it to the heap. Doing it well is much more difficult than allocation. The garbage collector cannot reliably guess the programmer's intent, so it must use some other means to identify memory blocks to free. We'll discuss two important garbage-detection techniques: reference counting and unreachable nodes.

6.1.3 *Reference counting*

Early garbage collectors used a technique called *reference counting*. With this algorithm, each object has a counter. When an object is allocated or used, the associated counter is incremented. When the object is no longer referenced, it is freed. The garbage collector can periodically sweep through all allocated objects and free any objects with a reference counter of 0.

In figure 6.1, the circles represent allocated objects in the form of a *directed graph,* or a group of interconnected objects. Connections between objects are called *edges.* In our case, the edges are directed because an object that explicitly references another provides direction for our arrows. Our graph's objects are labeled with a name and reference count in parentheses. The objects above the line are in use, and the objects below the line are no longer in use.

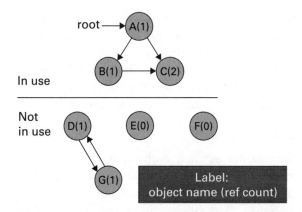

Figure 6.1 Some garbage collectors manage memory by counting references. Here, the objects with a reference count of 0 will be identified by the garbage collector and freed. Notice that objects D and G are not in use but will not be freed, due to a circular reference.

The problem with reference-counting garbage collection is that it cannot detect *cycles*, or objects that reference each other, though they might not be in use by any other object. In fact, we couldn't use the objects below the line if we wanted to, because we no longer have a reference. In our example, objects E and F would be freed, but D and G would not. D and G have positive reference counts, though we cannot possibly use them. This short program demonstrates an object that would be freed, and one that would not:

Listing 6.1 Demonstrating a circular reference

```
public class LinkedList                    ● Linked list class
  {
    public LinkedList next = null;

  }
.
.
.
public someMethod () {
  LinkedList a = new LinkedList();      ● Allocate A/B.
  LinkedList b = new LinkedList();        A/B reference counters = 1.
  a.link = b;                           ● A/B reference B/A.
  b.link = a;                             A/B reference counters = 2.
  a = null;
  b = null;                             ● Remove references to A/B.
}                                         A/B reference counters = 1.
.
.
.
```

This program does nothing, but it illustrates the anatomy of a memory leak for programs that use reference counting for garbage collection. Many programmers believe that circular references can lead to memory leaks in Java, but Java garbage collectors no longer use reference counting. (Some C++ frameworks do still use reference counting for garbage collection, which might account for some of the confusion on the subject.)

6.1.4 *Reachable objects*

Java garbage collectors use another technique, called *reachable objects*, to determine whether an object is in use. The garbage collector periodically travels the directed graph of allocated objects, attempting to visit every node by following valid references. If an object can be reached, it is marked, and the rest are freed. With this two-pass approach, sometimes called a *mark-and-sweep* algorithm, circular references are handled appropriately: They are freed only if they aren't reachable, effectively handling the problems shown in figure 6.2 and listing 6.1.

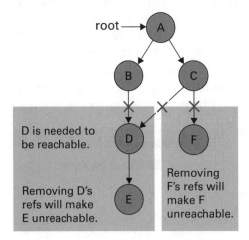

Figure 6.2   Java performs garbage collection by determining whether a node is reachable. An object cannot be garbage-collected if it is reachable. You can break reachability (D, F) by dereferencing an object or an object in the reference chain until it is no longer reachable (E).

6.2   *Trading C++ for Java*

Running through the Elbow after Randy, I'm glad to be in my tiny kayak. I am not expecting a problem making the S-turn, nor do I expect to hang up on the bottom. The two-blade paddle will help me brace on either side for stability. I need only make the initial critical turn, get into the flume, and brace. From that point on the turbulent water will steer me down the flume as it has the three kayakers before me. As I reach the initial turn, my front end hits turbulence—as I expected—but then skips over the water that I'd counted on to turn my boat. Out of control, I hit the same rocky outcropping as Randy. The mistakes are different, but the result is the same.

When I decided to eschew C++ and learn Java, I'd been frustrated with the amount of time required to handle tedious matters unrelated to my business problem. As a team leader, I'd spent hours tracking down dangling pointers, memory leaks, and off-by-one errors. C++ felt like a long, awkward canoe.

When I moved to Java, I felt *invulnerable* in my new "kayak." I marveled in condescending glee at the things that Java handled for free, while my C++ friends struggled with memory-management issues. Then, I encountered my first Java memory leak, and I discovered that my tools and skills were not adequate. I hadn't known that Java memory leaks could even exist, let alone how to find them. It took me a week to solve my first Java memory leak. My memory-management days weren't behind me, after all.

6.2.1   *Circumstances that cause Java memory leaks*

Though garbage collection in Java is sophisticated, certain patterns can still cause memory leaks. An object's transition through states from allocated to freed is known as its *life cycle*. From a garbage-collection standpoint, an object goes from being unallocated, to allocated, to live, to unused, to garbage-collected. A live object is one that is being actively used by a program. Java memory leaks tend to occur when a reachable object with a long life cycle has a reference to an object with a shorter life cycle. In short, memory leaks are objects that are reachable, but not live. Figure 6.2 shows two ways that garbage collection can occur:

- All references to an object by all reachable objects must be removed. In figure 6.2, F has references from object C, which must be removed for F to be collected.
- All references to another object, needed for an object to be reachable, must be removed. In figure 6.2, references from B and C to D will

make object E unreachable, and will be collected on the next garbage-collection pass.

Eventually, chains are garbage-collected as they fall out of use. However, if object B or C has a long life cycle, then objects D and E will remain reachable unless the references to D are explicitly broken. If the programmer no longer intends to use D and E, we have a classic Java memory leak. Most of the memory leaks in this chapter will deal with some type of anchor with a very long life cycle that references unused objects, such as collections, singletons, and listeners. If nothing is done to remove the reference, we'll have a memory leak.

6.2.2   *Finding Java leaks*

Java leaks can be especially difficult to find. For the most part, Java applications are at a higher level than C++ applications. We Java programmers are not well versed with the low-level tools and techniques that complex memory problems demand. Factors that contribute to the dilemma of finding and troubleshooting memory leaks in Java include:

- *Simply watching memory by using a monitor, like the Windows Task Manager, is not sufficient.* Garbage-collection scheduling varies, and memory is not freed until garbage collection is scheduled.

- *Under certain circumstances, the Java garbage collector is not executed at all.* Some garbage collectors are activated only when memory use reaches a certain threshold. In those instances, if tests do not model real-world usage scenarios closely, you could easily miss memory leaks or incorrectly assume leaks exist.

- *References are in clusters, so the impact of leaks is greater.* In Java, each block of memory is not explicitly freed. If you forget to remove a critical reference to a single object, it may reference many other objects. A Java interface developed with the Swing component library can have references to dozens or even hundreds of child classes. Further, since the classes also have back pointers, references to a child class can make an entire user interface tree reachable.

- *More than one reference might be causing the leak.* Because all references must be broken to make a class unreachable and eligible for garbage collection, breaking a single reference might not be enough. A correct fix may not have the desired impact if multiple bugs exist.

- *The symptoms are not as dramatic or immediate as those in C++*. In C++, a reference is not correctly updated, the result is often a crash due to a dangling pointer. In Java, the symptoms are not immediate, so generating failure test cases is not as easy.

This chapter will help you recognize some common types of memory leaks before they become problems. Coding conventions make it easier for you to account for key references that must be explicitly removed to achieve effective memory management. Now that we've reviewed memory management and seen some basic patterns that could lead to Java memory leaks, let's examine some specific antipatterns.

6.3   *Antipattern: Lapsed Listeners Leak*

The Lapsed Listener Leak is a common antipattern given its name by Ethan Henry and Ed Lycklama in an article titled "How Do You Plug Java Memory Leaks?" One design pattern with the potential for memory leaks is the Event Listener design pattern, which is used to establish interest in an event without forcing broadcast messaging. Objects request notification of an event by registering a listener or method that will be called if the event occurs. Java uses this design pattern in several places; three are interesting for the purposes of this antipattern. First, the Java user interface framework (called the AWT library) uses this design pattern for notification of actions. Second, generic JavaBeans can use an interface called `PropertyChangeListener` to establish notification for a changing property. Third, the Java Swing component library uses the Model-View-Controller design pattern. The model is registered with a user interface component, and the user interface is notified when the model changes.

Three factors make event-notification design patterns ripe for memory leaks:

- The event registry can be a collection with a long life cycle. A user interface component that is registered cannot be garbage collected until it is removed or the root registry object (or *anchor*) is garbage collected. If the anchor has a long life cycle, garbage collection may not occur at all.

- The symptoms for failing to remove the notification are initially benign. The benign symptoms make it easy for the leak to get through initial tests.

- Many visual programming frameworks, Swing programming samples, and wizards do not remove listeners. Whether these samples are created with a development environment or through cut and paste, memory leaks are not expected from these sources.

6.3.1 *Examining some dangerous practices*

The program shown in listing 6.2 was created with VisualAge for Java. It's a simple applet called TestView. Notice that the development environment registered a method to handle the button action without a corresponding remove method.

Listing 6.2 Dangerously registering an action without a corresponding remove

```
package memory;

public class TestView extends java.applet.Applet {

class IvjEventHandler implements java.awt.event.ActionListener {
    public void actionPerformed(java.awt.event.ActionEvent e) {
      if (e.getSource() == TestView.this.getTest())
        connEtoM1(e);
    };
  };
  IvjEventHandler ivjEventHandler = new IvjEventHandler();
  private java.awt.Button ivjTest = null;
  private java.awt.TextField ivjTextField = null;
  public TestView() {
    super();
  }

  private void connEtoM1(java.awt.event.ActionEvent arg1) {
    try {
      getTextField().setText("After");
    } catch (java.lang.Throwable ivjExc) {
      handleException(ivjExc);
    }
  }

  private java.awt.Button getTest() {
    if (ivjTest == null) {
      try {
        ivjTest = new java.awt.Button();
        ivjTest.setName("Test");
        ivjTest.setBounds(117, 166, 56, 23);
        ivjTest.setLabel("Test");
      } catch (java.lang.Throwable ivjExc) {
        handleException(ivjExc);
      }
    }
    return ivjTest;
  }

  private java.awt.TextField getTextField() {
    if (ivjTextField == null) {
      try {
```

● **Trigger for an event**

● **Event handler class**

● **Method is fired when the event handler gets called.**

```
      ivjTextField = new java.awt.TextField();
      ivjTextField.setName("TextField");
      ivjTextField.setText("Before");
      ivjTextField.setBounds(118, 100, 60, 29);
    } catch (java.lang.Throwable ivjExc) {
      handleException(ivjExc);
    }
  }
}
  return ivjTextField;
}

private void handleException(java.lang.Throwable exception) {
  exception.printStackTrace(System.out);
}

public void init() {
  try {
    super.init();
    setName("TestView");
    setLayout(null);
    setSize(426, 240);
    add(getTest(), getTest().getName());
    add(getTextField(), getTextField().getName());
    initConnections();
  } catch (java.lang.Throwable ivjExc) {
    handleException(ivjExc);
  }
}

private void initConnections() throws Exception {
  getTest().addActionListener(ivjEventHandler);
}
}
```

● Event is registered here. Danger!

In this case, VisualAge for Java has created event registrations with no corresponding remove methods. The application does not have a memory leak, because our registration class has a limited life cycle. However, we do have the foundation for one. If this code is reused with cut and paste, or if the life cycle of our registry changes, we'll have a leak.

How might the life cycle change? Suppose an application has a long-lived main window with many transient subwindows that are created and destroyed. Events registered to the class will prevent garbage collection of the child windows.

Another common implementation for object-oriented classes that can be shared is the singleton. With this design pattern, a single, shared object is created, typically with a long life cycle, and is used by many objects. Objects that need to use the singleton get an instance. Consider the program shown in listing 6.3, which was taken from "Plugging Memory Leaks," by Tony K.T. Leung. (Some cosmetic changes have been made for easier annotation.)

Listing 6.3   Leaking memory through registering to a singleton

```java
import java.beans.*;

public class Test
{
  public static void main(String[] args)
  {
    C c = new C();
    c = null;
    System.gc();
  }
}
```

References C, removes reference, and then runs `gc`, suggesting garbage collection.

```java
class C implements PropertyChangeListener
{
    private D d_ = null;

  public C ()
  {
    d_ = D.getInstance();
    d_.addPropertyChangeListener(this);
  }

  public void propertyChange(PropertyChangeEvent evt){}

}
```

A singleton, with a different life cycle from C.

This reference will prevent garbage collection.

```java
class D
{
  private static D singleton_  = null;
  private PropertyChangeSupport listeners_ =
    new PropertyChangeSupport(this);

  private D(){}

  public static D getInstance()
  {
    if (singleton_ == null)
      singleton_ = new D();
    return singleton_;
  }

  public void addPropertyChangeListener(
    PropertyChangeListener listener)
  {
    listeners_.addPropertyChangeListener(listener);
  }

  public void removePropertyChangeListener(
```

Static instance variable; `getInstance` method. Singleton!

Method registers the event (but there is no remove). Singleton!

```
    PropertyChangeListener listener)
  {
    listeners_.removePropertyChangeListener(listener);
  }
}
```

In this case, class C is registering a `propertyChanged` method with a static listener. Since D is a singleton (and has a long life cycle), it will remain reachable. Though the reference to C is removed in `main`, we have a memory leak. We can solve this solution in one of three ways.

6.3.2   *Solution 1: Explicitly remove the listeners*

You can solve this problem by explicitly removing listeners whenever you add them. With the graphical components, the places for removing listeners are well defined. The `Frame` and `Dialog` classes in the Java AWT library fire the `dispose()` method when the associated window is destroyed. Classes that add listeners and inherit from `Frame` or `Dialog` will also want to override the `dispose()` method and add a call to remove the event listener. For subclasses of components, cleanup can occur when the component is removed from the parent's container. This action fires the `removeNotify` method, which can be subclassed for the addition of the proper cleanup code. For property change listeners, the call is `removePropertyChangeListener`; for event listeners, the call is `removeActionListener`.

For other classes like the one in listing 6.3, there's no logical place. Since `finalize` is triggered by garbage collection and we're trying to remove references that will inhibit garbage collection, we have to invent a method and call it when we've finished using the class. It's better to place this code in close proximity to the code that registers the event listener. Both the `add` and the associated `remove` methods should be commented.

Finally, it's important to periodically verify that `addSomeKindOfListener` calls are paired with the associated `removeSomeKindOfListener` calls. If both lines are in close proximity, verification is simple. If not, the calls can be paired with a text search, like `grep`.

6.3.3   *Solution 2: Shorten the life cycle of the anchor*

One way to ensure that a listener will be garbage collected is to make sure that the listener registry can be garbage collected. Listing 6.2 does not have a memory leak because the registry is a short-lived component. This is usually not the best solution by itself, because it leaves `addActionListener` calls without the matching removeActionListener calls, which means the program is vulnerable to future memory leaks. It also takes a singleton class and changes it to a regular object, which must be instantiated for each use. The singleton may have been initially created to conserve system resources.

6.3.4 *Solution 3: Weaken the reference*

With the introduction of version 1.2, Java offers additional types of references that can be used to solve this problem. In addition to the standard object reference, Java has specialized *reference objects* that can work with the garbage collector in special circumstances. There are three types: weak, soft, and phantom references. For this solution, we need weak references. To the garbage collector, an object that can be reached only by using a weak reference is called *weakly reachable* and is a candidate for garbage collection. In figure 6.3, objects C and D are weakly reachable. Weak references can be placed in collections with longer life cycles, in situations that might normally inhibit garbage collection. Because objects can be garbage collected, the null condition should always be checked whenever you're accessing an object through a weak reference.

6.3.5 *Reference objects simplify memory management*

Each solution has its advantages and disadvantages. Weak references provide a generic solution that's suitable for frameworks and tools, like visual programming environments, but it isn't as clean a solution as explicitly removing each

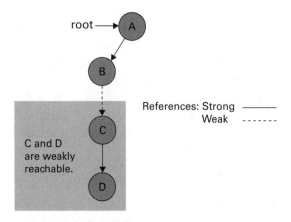

Figure 6.3 Weak references can be used to assist the garbage collector. An object is weakly reachable if it can be reached only through a weak reference. Weakly reachable objects are candidates for garbage collection.

listener that's added. On the other hand, weak references do add to our bag of tricks for memory management. Table 6.2 shows the strengths and weaknesses of each solution.

Table 6.2 These are the solutions to the Lapsed Listener antipattern. Each circumstance is unique, and each solution has pros and cons that must be considered.

Solution	Strengths	Weaknesses
Balancing removes and adds	The design is clean, readable, and intuitive. Implementing graphical components is straightforward.	The placement of the remove is not always intuitive, especially for objects that are not components.
Shorten the anchor's life cycle	The solution can be very easy to implement and is easy to tool.	The solution is vulnerable to bugs, resulting in memory leaks.
Weak references	This is the most generic solution, and is also very easy to tool.	The code for weak references is not as intuitive and readable as direct references.

6.4   *Antipattern: The Leak Collection*

The root of the Lapsed Listener antipattern is a collection with a long life cycle that has object references inserted but not removed. The references prohibit effective garbage collection because they make the referenced object reachable. The Leak Collection is a general case of the Lapsed Listener antipattern. Whenever we have a collection with a long life cycle that has the potential to contain objects that aren't removed, we have the possibility of a memory leak. Figure 6.4 shows the basic antipattern.

In essence, an application (A) allocates an object (B) with a short life cycle, registers the object in a collection (C) having a relatively long life cycle, and then removes the reference to object B. If the collection has a long life cycle— as many shared collections do—and if the object isn't removed from the collection before the reference is garbage collected, we'll have a memory leak.

Many different design patterns and problem domains call for singleton collections. Here are a few:

- Caches: A singleton hash table is the implementation of choice for a cache. When a cache doesn't have a policy to expire old entries, we have the potential for a leak.

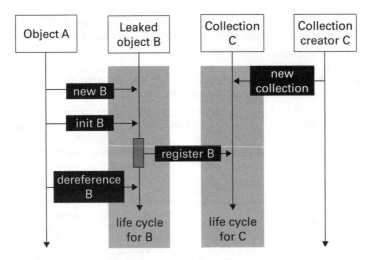

Figure 6.4 In the Leak Collection antipattern, an object with a short life cycle is registered in a collection with a long life cycle. Here we've shown a UML sequence diagram of such a memory leak. In this case, object B will be a memory leak, because the reference in collection C won't allow the garbage collector to free it.

- Session state: A well-publicized Tomcat bug turned out not to be a bug at all, but a session-management problem. By default, session management was turned on, and many didn't know it. In certain circumstances, the session dictionary grew until memory was gone. In general, session state is a good place to find a memory leak.

- User interfaces: Most modern user interfaces are collections of windows and components. Many times, these potentially massive collections have persistent anchors. Some common places to find singleton anchors might be print support, font management, and interapplication communication. Whenever a user interface is attached to an anchor with a long life cycle, leak conditions are present.

- EJB containers: An EJB container is essentially a smart singleton collection of EJBs.

6.4.1 *Causing trouble with caches and session state*

Two specialized uses of collection classes are especially troublesome. Session state captures the conversation context between the client and the server. Because HTTP is a *stateless protocol*, the infrastructure or the application must manage conversation details. The duration of Internet conversations varies wildly among consecutive communications from a given client, so the management of session state is particularly difficult. Currently, standard specifications for the various servlet protocols deal with expiration of session state through timeout. When a session is established, a timeout is specified. When the timeout expires, the conversation expires as well. Excessive timeout lengths can cause memory to be exhausted, while too short a timeout can cause frustrating user experiences.

A similar problem involves the cache. In many cases, a cache can exhaust memory if the data set is large and older data is not removed periodically. If the cache is allowed to grow unabated, memory will eventually be exhausted. With only minor changes, we can easily ensure that cache memory can be neatly managed.

6.4.2   *Solution 1: Search for common warning signs*

Collections can serve many different purposes and can be involved in many different types of leaks, but you can recognize common threads. Table 6.3 describes the common warning signs, along with the appropriate actions.

Table 6.3   Memory leaks are common in applications with certain characteristics.

Warning Sign	Description	Action
Mismatched life cycles	Whenever an object with a long life cycle references an object with a short life cycle, there is leak potential.	Examine objects with long life cycles. Try to make sure references to transient objects are removed.
Mismatched add/remove for shared collections	Whenever a shared collection exists, adds without deletes may provide references that prohibit garbage collections.	Make sure that any add has a corresponding delete or weak reference that allows garbage collection.
Singletons and static objects	Static objects and singletons have long life cycles, and have the potential for memory leaks.	Examine static objects and singletons to make sure that references to transient objects are removed and commented.
"May" conditions for registrations	Whenever a registration to a collection is voluntary ("may" versus "must"), absence of strict attention can lead to a memory leak.	Watch voluntary registrations especially closely, or weaken the references to allow garbage collection.
APIs that hide collections	Whenever an API hides an addition to a collection, it is possible that the associated remove will be missed.	Comment APIs that hide collections, and make sure that responsibilities are clear, or weaken the references to allow garbage collection.

The main indications that conditions are common for a leak are mismatched add/remove pairs, mismatched life cycles, and other kinds of anchors with longer life cycles. Singletons and static classes can often provide safe harbor for memory leaks.

6.4.3 Solution 2: Aggressively pair adds with removes

To effectively deal with collection-based memory leaks, you might have to change your programming hygiene. Consider collection management with all CRUD operators: Create, Read, Update, and Delete. Any time you add a row to a collection, you need to add the corresponding remove. In fact, you should do both at the *same time* so you don't forget. Further, if possible, ensure that the pairs are in close proximity in the code. In addition, you can tag the pairs with a comment or with the name of the collection so that you can easily use strategies to look for pairings when you have to refactor or deal with a memory leak. Then, you can use tools such as GREP to scan the program and look for pairs. In some cases, proximity may not be an option, like the use of a cache. For these collections, you can use a different utility to periodically prune the cache to remove elements that have timed out. In these cases, different strategies will be required.

6.4.4 Solution 3: Use soft references for caches

Though inconsistent implementation diminishes their value, caches (and session state managers, a special case of the cache) are collections that demand a different approach. We'd like the cache to use all available memory, and be freed only when the system needs the additional resources. Fortunately, Java soft references provide a mechanism that can do exactly that. An object is said to be *softly reachable* if it can be reached only through use of a soft reference. The Java 1.3 specification says that softly reachable objects can be freed at the garbage collector's discretion with two caveats:

- The garbage collector will attempt to free soft references before throwing an out-of-memory exception.
- The garbage collector should attempt to free soft references in least recently used order.

These properties make soft references ideal for the implementation of caches. In practice, some garbage collectors treat soft references like weak references, diminishing their value in caches. Clearly the intent of the soft reference is for use in such applications as memory-sensitive caches. While the JVMs should attempt to free soft references in the least recently used order, many do not.

6.4.5   *Solution 4: Use collections with weak references*

The Java 1.2+ specifications build in some collections that implement weaker references. WeakHashMap is a class that implements a hash table with weak references. Objects referenced solely from this hash table are weakly reachable. This type of collection is ideal for the optional registration of objects, and for applications where it's difficult to pair add/remove method calls managing the items in the hash table.

6.4.6   *Solution 5: Use finally*

Even when the calls are placed appropriately, exceptions can prevent the proper cleanup from ever occurring. Important cleanup should be placed in finally blocks. The Java finally block is executed after all code in a method, including exception management, is processed. finally will guarantee that a necessary block of code is executed, and is especially useful for cleanup.

6.5   *Shooting memory leaks*

These antipatterns can be used to identify existing leaks through inspection, but what techniques can help you troubleshoot applications with existing memory leaks? C++ programmers use spectacularly cumbersome tools and techniques to solve memory-related problems. For the most part, Java programmers prefer to stay above the fray. Sometimes, however, we aren't so fortunate. In this section, we'll look at the strategies that can help. The basic steps to finding memory leaks are determining whether a problem exists, isolating the problem, repairing the problem, and protecting against the problem in the future.

6.5.1   *Make sure there is a leak*

Much is left to the discretion of garbage collectors. In some cases, garbage collection can occur relatively frequently. In other cases, it may not run at all. Many of the faster JVMs try to limit the number of times that garbage collection is run. Some JVMs execute garbage collection only when memory resources are close to exhausted. In such cases, an application can appear to leak. Watching available memory on a simple memory monitor is not enough. A good strategy is to take memory snapshots before and after suggesting garbage collection with a call to System.gc. (This method call should seldom or never be used in production code.) Many tools can force garbage collection.

Tools are available to help you analyze memory leaks. A few are J-Insight (from alphaWorks), J-Probe (from Sitraka Software), and OptimizeIt (from

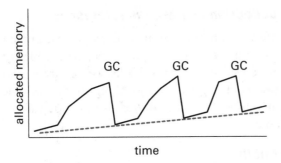

Figure 6.5   This is the classic resource chart of a memory leak. The solid black line shows actual memory use. The broken line projects reachable memory objects. The peaks and valleys are caused by garbage collection. The slowly rising valleys are characteristic of memory leaks.

Intuitive Systems). A well-behaved application should show a usage pattern that builds to peaks and then has distinct valleys. With similar types of activities, the valley floors should be consistent. The peaks represent normal object allocation over time. The valleys represent memory use just after garbage collection. If the valley floor continually creeps up between garbage-collection cycles, that's a sign of a possible memory leak. Figure 6.5 shows the graph of a classic memory leak. The GCs denote garbage collection at each of the peaks. The dotted line shows a slowly increasing amount of memory not garbage collected.

Sometimes, the symptoms of a production memory leak are clear. Of course, a `java.lang.OutOfMemoryError` is a clear sign of a leak, but the exception is not always generated before a more catastrophic system error occurs. Other symptoms may also point to a memory leak. In many cases, a leak will cause a relatively smooth decline with progressively worsening performance. As the system begins to swap or page more, the system performance will degenerate rapidly until the application fails or the system crashes. Low memory can cause many different types of failures, such as an inability to connect to a database or open a file, even though the root cause is lack of memory.

6.5.2   *Determine that the leak should be fixed*

Fixing memory leaks can be expensive. In some cases, we should push leak fixes lower on the priority chain, and maybe not even bother to do them. If an application's in-memory life span is relatively short, it may not make sense to patch all memory leaks, because garbage collection may never be run. If memory leaks and total memory usage is small, memory leaks may not be a concern. Table 6.4 offers some guidance as to whether memory leaks should be fixed at all.

Table 6.4 In some circumstances, fixing a memory leak may not be worth the effort. This table shows common memory leak characteristics, and provides a guideline for whether the fix will be worthwhile.

Application Characteristic	Fix Memory Leak?	Comments
Short application life cycle.	Seldom	Garbage collection may never be run.
Very small footprint.	Seldom	The leak should be fixed only if the application has a long enough life for the cumulative leaks to be a problem.
Fixing hurts code readability.	Sometimes	Readability is not the overriding concern, but may discourage fixing a leak in some circumstances.
Footprint is large.	Often	The leak should be fixed if the application life cycle is long or if resources are likely to become a problem.
Fix is very easy.	Yes	A memory leak is a bug. If the fix has been identified and has no other side effects, it should be fixed.
Code runs 24x7.	Yes	The leak will eventually become a problem.
Code is a target for reuse.	Yes	Regardless of other characteristics, if the code is a reuse target, it should be fixed

You should be especially vigilant about fixing leaks in two instances: when an application runs 24x7, and when code is a target for reuse. Leaks in either circumstance should nearly always be plugged. In any case, to prevent the spread of bugs through cut and paste, if a leak exists and you don't fix it, then you should at least document it.

6.5.3 *Isolate the problem*

Once you've determined there is a leak, and that the leak should be fixed, you need to isolate a test case that creates the problem. Effective testing can be much more productive than the use of low-level memory debuggers, so it's important to make the test case as narrow as possible. Unfortunately, that isn't always possible. The complexity of user scenarios and the degree of coupling between elements of the application will collectively determine how effectively a memory leak can be isolated through scenarios. After you've isolated a leak, add the test to the application's regression test suite.

6.5.4 Determine the source and fix the problem

Once you've generated the narrowest possible test case, the next step is to determine the source of the problem. Without a doubt, this is the most difficult part of the process. These strategies may help:

Use good tools

You must have effective tools to be able to track memory leaks in Java. You need tools that let you:

- Trigger garbage collection on demand.
- Examine the size of the heap collectively over time.
- Examine the contents of the heap, including objects on the heap.
- Determine the references to an object (that prevent garbage collection).

Inspect code by hand

Many times, you can locate memory leaks by looking in the likely places. With close attention to collections, listeners, singletons, and long life cycles in general, you can spot many possible leaks. Further, searching tools can aid manual inspection. Simply counting the number of adds and removes to a problematic collection using GREP or an editor can help you identify an imbalance that may lead to a leak.

Force garbage collection between repeated test cases

Most good profiling tools can force garbage collections. In this way, a code segment can be repeatedly exercised, garbage collection run, and the heap examined for growth. With the profiler's snapshot of the heap (graphs of allocated space versus free space over time work well), you can make the test case narrower.

Use object reference graphs when the search is sufficiently narrow

Most good profilers will show the references from an object on the heap. Since you're looking for reachable objects not garbage collected, profiling is a powerful tool when combined with garbage collection on demand. When you find a reachable object that should have been garbage collected, you can follow the reference chain to find the culprit.

Iterate

When you find a problem, fix it and start over. Patching one leak can solve others as well. Many leaks are interrelated—sometimes in surprising ways—and you'll find it much easier to fix links one at a time than to try to solve them all with a single pass.

Fixing leaks usually turns out to be relatively easy after you've identified a problem. You must make the object unreachable by using one of the techniques described in this chapter. These techniques can make an object unreachable, and thus a candidate for garbage collection:

▶ **Fixing Java application memory leaks**
When an object with a long life cycle maintains a reference to an object with a short life cycle, we have the potential for a memory leak. These possible fixes remove references to make an object unreachable and eligible for garbage collection.

- Remove the object reference directly by setting it to another value.
- Remove an object from a collection.
- Weaken the references using Java reference objects.
- Shorten the life cycle of the referent.
- Shorten the life cycle of the object.
- Remove the object from the code.
- Refactor the code.

6.5.5 *Protect against the problem for the future*

When coding problems occur, you should examine the cause. If the problem is an isolated case of programming error, no further action may be necessary. These steps will help keep the problem from occurring in the future:

- Add to the test suite to make sure that the new case is covered. This will ensure that if the problem crops up again through poor change control or cut and paste, it will be found.
- If the problem has occurred in the past, an antipattern should be documented and shared.
- If the antipattern or solution lends new significant insight, it should be published at some level. Publishing paths can be as focused as emails to peers or presentations in department meetings, and as broad as writing a book or speaking at a conference.

Antipatterns work best when we establish a pattern, solve a problem in a general way, and disseminate the wisdom.

6.6 *Mini-Antipatterns: Little Hogs*

One little hog cannot eat much, but many little ones can have devastating appetites. This chapter title may have led you to expect a whole chapter on dealing with strings and the little things that a programmer can do to save a few bytes here and there. This section is the last in the chapter because I do not think that little optimizations should be emphasized, especially in cases where they can affect performance. There are some places where memory can become an issue, such as in pervasive environments, very large object trees, and massive collections of objects. In these extreme cases, it makes sense to consider the microtechniques, which can collectively yield considerable savings. In other cases, I do not advocate reckless or careless memory use. I simply prefer readability to a few bytes of memory savings, and trust that I can make up the difference by optimizing the most important test cases first. With that in mind, let's consider some of the little memory hogs that can add up. In most cases, performance problems will be found in higher level designs, so low-level optimizations should be saved for later.

6.6.1 *String manipulation*

In memory-constrained situations, you should pay close attention to the proliferation of strings. A common offender is the + operator. If we string several + operators together to build a string, then each string argument will allocate an additional object and force more than one copy operation. This can get expensive, in terms of memory and performance. To clarify, consider the two following string treatments:

```
String s = "this code uses plus to break between "+
           "lines but doesn't result in any extra "+
           "objects as it still counts as a compile-time"+
           "constant";
```

This string works. The optimizer will allocate one `StringBuffer`, build the string up there, and then turn it into a single string. The following is much more dangerous:

```
String x = "Hello ";
   x += name;
   x += ", your birthday is ";
   x += birthday;
```

This fragment will take significantly longer to execute, because in this case, each individual string will be allocated and copied. It does have a memory impact, although it is negligible. The bigger impact is the cumulative time that it takes to reallocate and copy each individual string. In Java, this antipattern frequently occurs within loops that build queries, process parameters, or build XML documents. Instead, you should use a single `StringBuffer` and append each successive string into the buffer. Alternatively, you can keep the string together:

```
String x = "Hello " +
    name +
    ", your birthday is " +
    birthday;
```

In this way, you let the optimizer do the work for you. It will allocate a single string buffer to process the entire string, saving memory and plenty of CPU cycles.

6.6.2   Collections

We have seen that collections can have a dramatic impact on memory, because they tend to be used to manage objects in large numbers. Collections can affect memory in other ways as well. For example, large multidimensional arrays can consume staggering resources. Collection choice can also affect memory and performance.

Collections and allocation

Different Java types handle memory resources differently. Arrays allocate memory when they're created. Other collection types, such as sets, vectors, hash tables, and lists, allocate memory when items are added. Many times, preallocation is a good thing. If you know that you'll be allocating an explicit number of objects, that you'll be accessing the collection randomly or exclusively by a numerical index, and you know precisely when the resource will be used, then an array could be a good choice. Other times, preallocation can cause you to make incorrect assumptions or allocate much more memory than you are likely to use. Beginners frequently prefer arrays to more robust collections. If you know that you'll be adding a variable number of objects throughout the life cycle of the collection, or that access will be random by some other key, then a hash table may be a better choice.

Collections and access patterns

The type of access will also have an impact on the collection choice. If you must frequently access by a key other than an index, then a hash table, dictionary, or b-tree may be a better data structure than an array. If the order does not matter, a set may be a better choice. The key for success is to pick an abstraction that fits the collection type. If the size is fixed and you need to frequently enumerate the collection, an array could be the best choice.

Arrays

Because arrays can have a significant effect on memory, they warrant special consideration. These tips can help:

- If you have many collections with widely varied size, consider another collection that allocates dynamically.
- Delay initialization (and thus allocation) until the automatic variable is needed.
- If the array is sparse, it should be declared appropriately. You shouldn't create methods (such as accessors) that you don't plan to use.

6.6.3   *Inheritance chains*

We have all seen excruciatingly complex object hierarchies with inheritance chains that reach all the way to China. Similarly, just as databases can be normalized too far, object-oriented design can be taken to extremes beyond anything that can practically perform. If you aren't in a memory-constrained environment, let common sense be your guide. On the other hand, as inheritance chains get longer, the memory cost is higher. If memory is a serious concern and other avenues have been exhausted, reducing the length of inheritance chains can save some valuable memory. This practice should never compromise reuse, design principles, or readability, but when considering whether to add one more subclass, you'll find that memory can be a tiebreaker.

6.7   *Summary*

Let's clean up this chapter by reviewing what we have covered and presenting our antipattern templates. We began by discussing memory-management philosophies of C++ and Java. We presented the old and new strategies of garbage collection, and showed that Java garbage collection is based on a concept called reachable objects. We then showed that even Java is prone to memory leaks, and we described general symptoms and specific antipatterns called Lapsed Listeners, Leak Collections, and Little Hogs. Finally, we examined common strategies that you can use to shoot down memory leaks, and looked at some "little hogs" that can make a big cumulative impact.

6.8   *Antipatterns in this chapter*

These are the templates for the antipatterns that appear in this chapter. They provide an excellent summary format and form the basis of the cross-references in appendix A.

Lapsed Listeners

DESCRIPTION: The Publish/Subscribe design pattern requires applications or classes with an interest in an event to register. The Lapsed Listener is one form of memory leak where an event listener is registered without being removed. If the life cycle of the listener registry is long, then a memory leak will occur.

RELATED ANTIPATTERNS: The Leak Collection. The Lapsed Listener is a special case of the more general Leak Collection.

MOST FREQUENT SCALE: Application.

REFACTORED SOLUTION NAME: Weak References, or Pairing Register with Remove.

REFACTORED SOLUTION TYPE: Software.

REFACTORED SOLUTION DESCRIPTION: One solution to this problem is to explicitly remove the listener. For clarity, register and remove listeners in add/remove pairs. If this cannot be done in the same method, the two methods should be in close proximity. Another solution is to weaken the reference with Java weak reference objects.

TYPICAL CAUSES: Programming hygiene is a common cause. When registrations are not placed in close proximity to removes, it is easy to neglect the remove, because the symptoms are delayed.

ANECDOTAL EVIDENCE: "I didn't know you could have a memory leak in Java." "The system gets slower and slower, and then it hangs or traps."

SYMPTOMS, CONSEQUENCES: Some objects are not garbage collected, even though their primary user is. This leak will cause the system to slow over its life cycle, until it's terminated or eventually dies.

SOLUTION ALTERNATIVES: Remove the reference appropriately or shorten the life cycle of the registry. Adding a listener without a weak reference or a corresponding remove is possible if the life cycle of the registry is short, but this is vulnerable to changes in life cycle and cut and paste.

Leak Collections

DESCRIPTION: If a collection has a long life cycle, it can have long-lived references that are never removed. These will prevent large blocks of memory from being freed.

MOST FREQUENT SCALE: Application.

REFACTORED SOLUTION NAME: Weak References, or Pairing Add with Remove.

REFACTORED SOLUTION TYPE: Software.

REFACTORED SOLUTION DESCRIPTION: One solution to this problem is to explicitly remove the reference from the collection. For clarity, add and remove objects in pairs. If this cannot be done in the same method, the two methods should be in close proximity. Another solution is to weaken the reference with Java weak reference objects.

TYPICAL CAUSES: Programming hygiene is a common cause. When adds are not placed in close proximity to removes, it is easy to neglect to remove, because the symptoms are delayed.

ANECDOTAL EVIDENCE: "I didn't know you could have a memory leak in Java." "The system gets slower and slower, and then it hangs or traps."

SYMPTOMS, CONSEQUENCES: Some objects are not garbage collected, even though their primary user is. This leak will cause the system to slow over its life cycle, until it's terminated or eventually dies.

SOLUTION ALTERNATIVES: Remove the reference appropriately or shorten the life cycle of the registry. Adding a listener without a weak reference or a corresponding remove is possible if the life cycle of the registry is short, but this is vulnerable to changes in life cycle and cut and paste.

Bitter connections
and coupling

Bouncing beside the mountain guide in my SUV, my partner Mike and I notice that we are awfully close to the cliff next to the dirt road. The 72-year-old guide trusts neither of us to drive. As I watch him gently guide the vehicle down near-vertical drops and around turns a scant 3 feet from the cliffs, I am inclined to agree with him. Every now and then the SUV slides sideways, but he patiently coaxes it back onto the trail with a feather touch. Other times, he is close to asking us to get out of the vehicle and help guide it down a particularly slick or steep section, but each time he seems just confident enough to continue.

We are here to run the Gunnison River in Colorado—if we ever get there. After a full hour on the road, I have my doubts. When planning the trip we realized that we'd have to run many river miles, but didn't fear getting caught by darkness because the current was swift and the rapids easy. We won't need to scout much. On the map the shuttle road looked short and close to the river. Ah, patience. With luck, we'll easily finish by nightfall.

When we hired the guide, he noted my 8:00 a.m. start time but suggested 6:00 a.m. instead, "to be safe." Now I see why. After driving for an hour and a half he finally stops the SUV and begins to unload our gear—at the top of the canyon. I look in dismay at the tiny footpath leading to the winding river below.

7.1   Making connections

Most Internet architects see black lines on a white piece of paper and imagine their characteristics. They ask questions. What is the physical network? What protocols are established? Is there enough bandwidth? How fast is it? What are the peak loads? These questions assume that a software connection is already successfully established. Questions related to creating and terminating a connection are easily dismissed.

This philosophy is easy to understand; just a few short years ago, most connections were fairly static. Today, however, many solutions call for quick connections, and new frameworks make it easier for you to establish those connections. In this chapter, we'll look at some antipatterns related to how connections are established and terminated. We'll then examine some technologies you can use to decouple interfaces between systems.

7.2   Antipattern: Connection Thrashing

Over the years, database performance has been a weak spot among Java developers. I am not sure why. Perhaps we're accustomed to working with well-behaved subsystems that need little or no tuning—file systems, for example.

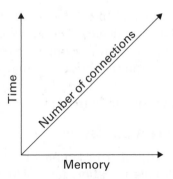

Figure 7.1 Consider the cost of connections. Each additional connection has fixed costs, in both units of time and system resources (such as memory). It isn't unusual for database connections in an application to take longer than all of the data access combined.

Maybe it's because the performance of so many of our systems is out of our control. Or perhaps we simply do not take the time to learn good practices.

One critical factor that never ceased to amaze my customers was the total expense of establishing a database connection. As you can see in figure 7.1, each connection has a fixed cost that must be paid in two different currencies. The first is time. Many Internet applications feature very quick database transactions, and it isn't unusual for a system to spend more time establishing communication than processing a given transaction. The second cost is the early exhaustion of system resources, including memory and file handles. Since each connection must set aside buffers for communication and database resources, as well as files for logging, the overhead can become significant in a hurry. For many architectures, if the number of users is not well defined, it is easy for a connection to strain the allocated resources on either the database machine or the web server. To solve this problem, many systems maintain a connection for a limited amount of time.

Two problems affect connection performance. First, the total number of concurrent connections is limited. When a system hits a resource wall due to a high number of connections, performance will crash or deteriorate rapidly, as a result of excessive swapping or paging. Second, determining the number of connections required at peak periods can be difficult, because Internet application loads are inherently hard to predict. Well before the creation of the Java development environment, many of my customers had problems managing individual connections for client/server architectures. Though their applications had a fixed number of connections and well-defined peak times and loads, the problems were significant. In the IBM database lab, we worked on early connection pools that were deployed at the application level, and we had some internally developed technical manuals called red books dedicated to solving the problem. The Internet brings a whole new level of uncertainty to this planning process. The total number of users is much harder to predict, and their browsing habits are uncertain.

7.2.1 Creating and terminating with every access

Listing 7.1 shows our ongoing bulletin board example. Though we'll be accessing the same database and running the same query with the existing connection, we create and terminate every connection as needed.

Listing 7.1   Creating and terminating the connection per invocation

```
Class.forName("COM.ibm.db2.jdbc.app.DB2Driver").newInstance();
  String url = "jdbc:db2:board";
  connection = DriverManager.getConnection(url);
  connection.close();       ● Close the connection.
```

Make the connection.

For client/server programs, many times a single program works around this problem by maintaining an active connection through the entire life cycle of the application. Internet applications can't do that, because the potential user population is much larger. Instead, the programmer often decides to create and close connections as needed. This is the approach that we've chosen for all of our program examples so far. To improve the process, we'll limit the number of connections and reuse them.

7.2.2 Solution: Reuse connections with a pool

Mike and I reluctantly gather our gear and start hauling it down the narrow, winding trail. Twice we see other parties; for the most part, pack mules effortlessly carry their loads. I glare at my partner accusingly, but Mike, who has made this run twice before, just smiles. As a partner-in-crime for more than five years, he knows how much I hate to shoulder my boat. We continue to wind between the cliffs, over the fallen trees, and beside the increasingly closer cliffs. When we reach the bottom of the canyon, I expect to be right at the river. Instead, the trail continues overland. I feel as if I've run a marathon when we finally arrive at the river. Four hours after leaving the campsite, we put our first paddle in the water.

After our trip to the Gunnison Gorge, I decided that I liked boating much more than I liked driving. Hiking and driving took time and energy away from the river. Once I reached the river, I vowed to try to find runs in the future with less driving and hiking and more river time. We should be so diligent as programmers and attempt to minimize the setup time in favor of providing service. Java has a connection framework that allows us to do exactly that by offering pooling and other services. Connection pooling can mean a dramatic difference in performance: Making any connection is an expensive process, and a pool of connections reduces the setup costs by allowing you to reuse a connection.

How much of the total transaction cost might the connection represent? I ran a test twice that summed up all the numbers in a database column. I did this calculation 1,000 consecutive times. With the first test, I reconnected each time I computed the sum. With the second test, I pooled connections. The second test took less than half the time that the first example did, as shown in figure 7.2.

Figure 7.3 offers another view of the savings. Here we see the database-related costs of a servlet. We have to process a connection before we can proceed with the real work, and then we close the connection. If we were to use connection pooling, after we prime the connection pool all of the work involved in connecting to a database and closing that connection becomes unnecessary. In figure 7.3, the black boxes represent redundant work. For the normal case, we have a penalty that consists of a fixed cost per open connection (c1) and a cost for the connection close (c2). This penalty will be paid for

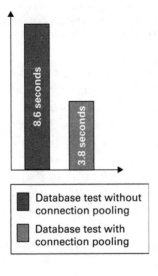

Database test without connection pooling

Database test with connection pooling

Figure 7.2
My program computed the total of a database column 1,000 times. The first column shows the results without connection pooling; the second column shows the impact of sharing the connection.

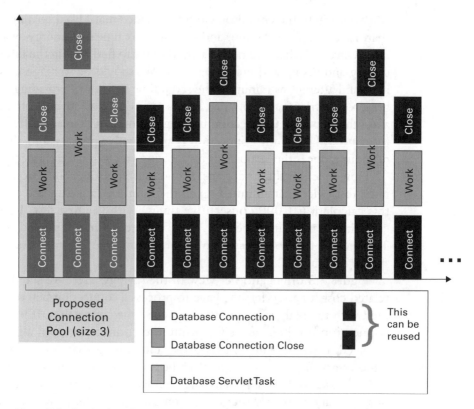

Figure 7.3 Servlet-based programs tend to connect and disconnect from a database repetitively, to control transactions and user context. The black boxes represent the unnecessary connections—work that can be saved through the use of a connection pool. Note that connection pooling will continue to pay dividends as long as the servlet runs, after the pool is primed.

every service. Theoretically, the cost is infinite. We can take a pool of n connections of cost c and limit our total cost to $n*(c1+c2)$. For a servlet with a theoretical infinite lifespan, the connection cost will approach zero over time. In reality, once our connection pool is primed, we'll pay only for the management of the connection pool.

We can claim additional benefits. For example, we can restrict the number of connections in our pool to a reasonable number. Then, we can formulate a definitive statement about the total connection cost of our system, which makes it easier to effectively plan the capacity of our system. When we use approaches like this one, our system performance as measured by throughput becomes much more predictable, because it won't degenerate rapidly due to the exhaustion of memory.

Let's look at the steps involved in using connection pooling.

Once at initialization

1   *Import the appropriate packages.* We need the packages for JDBC access and Java Naming and Directory Interface (JNDI), because data sources are named objects.

2   *Create the naming context.* This is a JNDI call to establish a naming context for the data source.

3   *Get a data source.* This is a factory object that will be used to create connections or get them from the connection pool as needed. It is a JNDI named resource.

Once per connection

1   *Get a connection from the data source.* This method will actually get a connection from a pool if an active connection exists; otherwise, it will create one.

2   *Close the connection.* This method maintains the connection, but frees it to the connection pool.

7.2.3   *Refactoring our BBS to add pooled connections*

The program in listing 7.2 demonstrates how to use connection pooling with Java 1.2. Most programming environments allow you to use a wizard to create a database application that pools connections. Our program was taken from a WebSphere application. The JDBC access can be vendor neutral; the JNDI access, however, will probably have some vendor-specific libraries, but you should use the common JNDI interface.

Here, we see connection pooling in practice. At a high level, we're creating a naming context (for the JNDI), a data source, and a factory. The factory is bound to the data source (a named resource that we can find through the JNDI). We then use that pair to create a connection.

Listing 7.2   A method that provides a pooled connection

```
protected Connection getPooledConnection(String driver, String URL, String
   userID, String password)
   {
     Connection conn = null;

     try
     {
       Hashtable parms = new Hashtable();
       parms.put(Context.INITIAL_CONTEXT_FACTORY,
                 CNInitialContextFactory.class.getName());
       Context context = new InitialContext(parms);
       ds = (DataSource)context.lookup(getDataSourceName());
       conn = ds.getConnection(userID, password);
     }
     catch (Throwable t)
     {
       try
       {
         DataSourceFactory factory =
           new DataSourceFactory();
         Attributes attrs = new Attributes();
         attrs.name = getDataSourceName();
         attrs.driver = getDriver();
         attrs.url = getURL();
         attrs.max = 30;
         ds = factory.createJDBCDataSource(attrs);
         try {
           factory.bindDataSource(ds);
         } catch (NamingException namingExc){
           namingExc.printStackTrace();
         }
         conn = ds.getConnection(userID, password);
       }
       catch (Throwable t1)
       {
         t1.printStackTrace();
       }
     }
     return conn;
   }
}
```

① Create parameter list to access naming system.

② Access naming context

③ Get data source factory object.

④ Get connection from data source object.

⑤ Data source not found; try to build one.

⑥ Create data source factory.

⑦ Create a JDBC specific data source.

⑧ Bind the factory to the data source.

① Our data source will be a named resource, so we need to get a context. The parameters to the context constructor are stored in a hash table, which is then passed to the constructor. We'll use the context to find the data source that we create in steps 7 and 8.

② This is the call to the context constructor. The context is part of the JNDI specification and represents a group of named-resource pairs. Our named resource will be the data source.

③ Here we use the context, created in steps 1 and 2, to obtain a data source. The data source is the construct that manages our connection pool. If there is no data source in the context, the context lookup will fail, and we'll create a factory object and data source within the `catch` statement block beginning at step 5.

④ In this step, we use the data source that was obtained from the context to get a connection. We'll get an active connection from a pool if one exists; otherwise, we'll create one. This connection is then returned to the invoker of this method.

⑤ We are inside the `catch` loop, which probably means that we've failed to get the data source. We assume that we don't yet have an instance of the data source factory.

⑥ We create a data source factory.

⑦ The `Attributes` type is a WebSphere type that encapsulates the attributes to `DataSourceFactory.createJDBCDataSource ()` per the Java specification. Here, we create the JDBC data source that will be used to pool our connections.

⑧ We bind the resource. We now have a named resource that we can find through the context that we created in steps 1 and 2.

This seems like a significant amount of overhead, but notice that we have no remote communications and no loops. This is a small fraction of the overhead we'd normally experience for each database connection. Using the connection is similar, but not identical, to our previous example.

7.2.4 *Using getPooledConnection*

We now have a method to obtain a pooled connection. This method will be called from our command beans, within the `initialize()` methods. We'll assume that we've broken out the driver, URL, user ID, and password as separate attributes with getters and setters. This is how the method is used:

```
connection = getPooledConnection(getDriver(),
        getURL(),
        getUserID(),
        getPassword());

connBean = new DatabaseConnection(connection);
```

We can then use connBean as we would any JDBC connection. Many tools can create command beans automatically, which makes this command architecture so attractive. A lot of these tools already use connection pooling.

It is critical, then, that:

- Existing applications already use connection pooling.
- Development wizards, classes, and templates can fully enable database connection reuse through pooling.

7.2.5 *Using the J2EE connector architecture*

A database is but one form of an enterprise information system (EIS). Likewise, connection pooling through data sources is only one part of the total package. J2EE defines a transparent architecture for connecting to a generic EIS. This framework allows a vendor to achieve robust connection support, with connection pooling, security, and other complex considerations, through the support of a single specification. Web application server vendors can support a single interface and gain access to an increasing number of systems.

Figure 7.4 shows how the connection architecture works. EISs access web application functions through special adapters, provided by the individual EIS vendor. This adapter collaborates with the web application server to provide

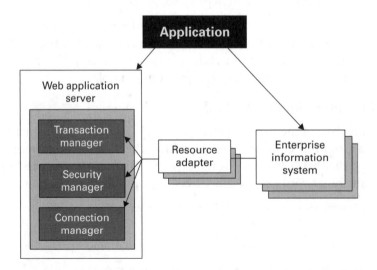

Figure 7.4   The J2EE common connector architecture uses vendor-provided adapters, operating through a common interface, to collaborate with the web application servers to provide transaction integrity, security, and efficient connection management. Connection pooling is included in the specification.

specialized services, such as transaction support, security, and connection management. Applications can then use the EIS interfaces directly or through common web application server interfaces. With this common connection framework, the context of a connection can be maintained to achieve unprecedented compatibility, transaction support, and interoperation between application components.

7.3 *Antipattern: Split Cleaners*

In chapter 6, several antipatterns involve the conservation of resources. While the following antipatterns are not specifically memory related, we can see similar themes. One such antipattern is the Split Cleaner, presented by Eric E. Allen in an article titled "Diagnosing Java Code: The Split Cleaner Bug Pattern." Figure 7.5 shows the scenario. We have an application that has a multistage process. Each stage of the process is managed by a different object, or at least in a different method. Each stage of the process will need access to some connection. We must create and free the connection somewhere in the application. One way to solve the problem is to manage the connection inside one or more of the process stages, passing the connection as a parameter. Consider this little application. The application needs to compute first the total cost and then the tax for the items in a shopping cart. To do this, it takes a two-phase process: adding the total costs in one process, and adding the total tax in another.

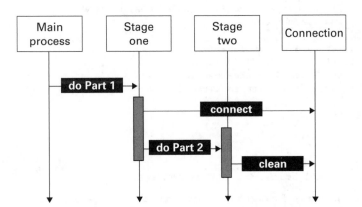

Figure 7.5 This is a UML sequence diagram showing the Split Cleaner antipattern. The resource is allocated and freed in a different place. Future enhancements can easily lose the cleanup for the connection, creating a bug.

Listing 7.3 Splitting the initialization and cleanup

```
package splitcleaner;
import java.sql.*;

public class CostProcessor {                    ● The master process controller

  public static void main(java.lang.String[] args) {
    String url = "jdbc:db2:shop";

    try {
      Class.forName ("COM.ibm.db2.jdbc.app.DB2Driver").newInstance();
      Connection con = DriverManager.getConnection (url);     ● Making the
      Adder adder = new Adder();                                 connection
      float total = adder.addCosts(con);   ● Calling phase 1
      System.out.println("Total cost: " + total);

    } catch (Exception e) {
      throw new RuntimeException(e.toString());
    }
  }
}
                                                      ● Implementation
public class Adder {                                     for phase 1
  public static final int COST_COLUMN = 1;
  public float addCosts(Connection con) {
    float sum = 0;
    float total = 0;
    try {
      Statement stmt = con.createStatement();
      ResultSet rs = stmt.executeQuery("SELECT cost from cart");
      while (rs.next()) {
        float cost = rs.getFloat(Adder.COST_COLUMN);
        sum = sum + cost;
      }
      Taxer taxer = new Taxer();
      total = taxer.addTaxes(con, sum);
    } catch (Throwable theException) {
      theException.printStackTrace();
    }
    return total;
  }
}

public class Taxer {                              ● Implementation
  public final static int COST_COLUMN = 1;          for phase 2

  public float addTaxes(Connection con, float total) {
    float sum = total;
    try {
      Statement stmt = con.createStatement();
      ResultSet rs = stmt.executeQuery("SELECT cost from cart");
      while (rs.next()) {
```

```
        float cost = rs.getFloat(Taxer.COST_COLUMN);
        sum = sum + cost * 8 / 100;
    }
    con.close();
    } catch (Throwable theException) {
        theException.printStackTrace();
    }
    return sum;
    }

}
```

● **Closing the connection
(the split cleaner!)**

A good clue that this application is poorly designed is that the objects are named after processes instead of entities. Other forms of the Split Cleaner are subtler, spreading connection management across different well-formed methods. When connection management is distributed, it's easier to lose the connection cleanup and create another kind of leak. For this example, if it was determined that tax may or may not be charged, then a condition could be added to the Adder class to add tax only if the condition is met. In this case, we'd leave an open connection. In fact, as our application grows in complexity, we'll have to add cleanup to every branch that uses the resource.

7.3.1 *Exceptions can lead to Split Cleaners*

Another variation of the Split Cleaner is exception processing. In our programs so far, cleanup has occurred at the end of a command's execute method, like this:

```
public void execute()
    throws
        IOException,
        DataException {

    try {
        // retrieve data from the database
        Statement statement = connection.createStatement();
        result =
            statement.executeQuery("SELECT subject, author, board from posts");
        while (result.next()) {
            subject.addElement(result.getString(SUBJECT_COLUMN));
            author.addElement(result.getString(AUTHOR_COLUMN));
            board.addElement(result.getString(BOARD_COLUMN));
        }
        result.close();
        statement.close();
        connection.close();
    } catch (Throwable theException) {
```

```
    theException.printStackTrace();
  }
}
```

If we have an exception situation, the close will fail to be executed. If we're forced to process closes in every exception condition, we have a Split Cleaner pattern, with the same potential for failure.

7.3.2 *Solution: Pair connection with cleanup, in finally*

This antipattern again calls for refactoring. To solve the problem, we perform three discrete steps:

1 Refactor the program to have a single entry point and a single exit point, to make logical slots for cleanup code.

2 Make a `finally` block for the connection cleanup, in the method where it is allocated.

3 Release the resources in the `finally` block.

For listing 7.4, the refactored solution is clear. We simply add a `finally` block to `main` with the appropriate cleanup.

Listing 7.4   A refactored Split Cleaner, pairing the connection and close

```
try {
  Class.forName ("COM.ibm.db2.jdbc.app.DB2Driver").newInstance();
  Connection con = DriverManager.getConnection(url);
  Adder adder = new Adder();
  float total = adder.addCosts(con);
  System.out.println("Total cost: " + total);
} catch (Exception e) {
  throw new RuntimeException(e.toString());
}
finally {
  try {
    con.close();
  } catch (Exception e) {
    throw new RuntimeException(e.toString());
  }

}
```

Of course, for this program, the repair is a bit like simply repainting a Gremlin after a head-on collision with a semi. For our BBS example, we've broken our service method into two pieces to allow us to separate initialization and validation from the main line processing. This is a Split Cleaner, but because the intent of the command architecture is clear and the `execute` and `init` methods can be in close proximity, the design is relatively safe. Nevertheless, we should continue our refactoring to ensure that our connections are cleaned in the event of an exception. We do this by moving the cleanup to a `finally` block:

```
public void execute ()
  throws
    IOException,
    DataException {
    .
    .
    .

  } catch (Throwable theException) {
    theException.printStackTrace();
  } finally {
    result.close();
    statement.close();
    connection.close();
  }
```

In truth, we could be even more defensive. If `result.close()` or `statement.close()` throw runtime exceptions, `connection.close()` doesn't get called. Also, if there's a failure before the result set is built, `result` will be null. You should test for a null result before closure.

7.4   *Antipattern: Hardwired Connections*

The previous examples dealt with tightly coupled connections that are likely to be found entirely within our own walls. When we're sharing a business-to-business connection, we should pay careful attention to the coupling between systems. Different types of interfaces should have couplings of different strengths. Object-oriented languages let us keep the coupling between objects fairly loose. Direct access through an object's interface may be sufficient for many purposes. For the boundary between the model and view, we should loosen the coupling. In chapters 3 and 4, we did so through a command layer. The layer between client and server should employ still looser coupling, which we accomplish through the servlet API over HTTP over TCP/IP.

When you're dealing with two disparate systems that cut across organizational boundaries, you need to be especially careful when designing the interfaces. Experience has shown that loosely coupled systems are easier to maintain, and many decisions that you make can affect the strength of the coupling between your systems. The Hardwired Connections antipattern deals with several traditional technologies and decisions that may force a tighter coupling than you'd like. Most connections fall in one of three families:

- *The transactional approach.* For this one, transactional middleware—like CICS, Encina, or Tuxedo—is used to execute a process on the target system. A communications buffer is passed to serve as input or output parameters. Sometimes, this approach is used to maintain additional transactional integrity. Other times, the approach is used solely as a distributed RPC.

- *The message-based approach.* For this approach, a sender ships a block of data to a listener, who processes the message and decides how to react. Messaging-oriented middleware and Internet architectures are examples of this approach.

- *The RPC approach.* With this approach, a distributed procedure call is made, passing parameters through a predefined signature.

7.4.1 *The communications buffer*

In the past, the centerpiece for all three approaches has been the *communications buffer*, a block of data passed between two systems. We'd then map out specific fields related to our interface. Figure 7.6 shows this strategy for a credit card transaction. For a transactional system, we have a sender and a dedicated listener method that is synchronously fired with the communications block. For a messaging equivalent, a sender routes the message to a waiting listening process or thread, much like the HTTP server routes our PUT or GET to a servlet on a web server. Setting the mechanism aside, we have a very similar solution. The listener must now parse the communications area, and the format must be exact. Most interface changes have to occur simultaneously at the client and server. While this approach has been very common, it is very tightly coupled.

A good analogy is management style. Poor managers tend to delegate poorly. They assign a task, and describe in excruciating detail how that task must be done. This approach limits flexibility and hinders efficiency by locking us out of more efficient solutions to the problem. The communications buffer has many of the same problems. The request is bound to the delivery vehicle, and the communications area is usually described in details beyond those required to do the task.

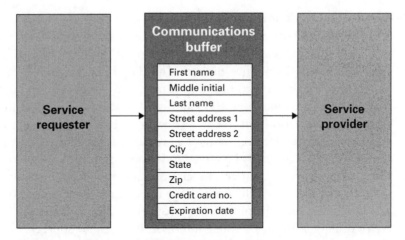

Figure 7.6 When we use a fixed communication area to connect two systems, we tightly couple the requester and provider. Changes to the interface—for example, an added country or a nine-digit ZIP code—can render the interface obsolete.

For example, consider the communications buffer in figure 7.6. If we were to switch from five-digit to nine-digit ZIP codes, then both the service requester and the service provider would have to change their interfaces at the same time. Added or deleted fields can also lead to problems. If changes occur without the notification of one side or the other, we'll have a bug. Using a fixed parameter set through communication-area mapping algorithms or some form of RPC (including CORBA) can improve the situation somewhat. In this case, the software can enforce our rigid interface. We'll catch some of the error conditions, but we'll still have to deal with the difficulties of coordinating interface changes.

When this changing interface is between two organizations or even companies, the consequences can be dramatic. The problems are compounded as new clients are added to the interface. Here are some possible ways we can deal with the change, all with significant disadvantages:

Synchronizing schedules

We can try to synchronize schedules. That means that the service provider must wait until all the clients of the interface can change. This is one of the many reasons that software development for large organizations is so tedious and takes so long. Managing interfaces like this can occupy entire departments for years.

Creating multiple interfaces

The service provider can support a new interface. This approach works pretty well for the first change, but it breaks down with multiple changes. Let's consider first going from a five-digit to a nine-digit ZIP code. We can solve this problem by adding a second full interface, with a new communications area that supports the nine-digit ZIP code. We'll continue to support the old interface. Now, if we also want to add a country code before all of our clients have adopted the new interface, we have a problem. Depending on the priorities of our clients, we'll probably be forced to support multiple versions of each interface. At the worst, we'll need to support four interfaces instead of one: versions for the old ZIP with and without the country code, and versions for the new ZIP with and without the new country code, as in figure 7.7. Because we're dealing with only a single interface, it is easy to appreciate how quickly these combinations can explode.

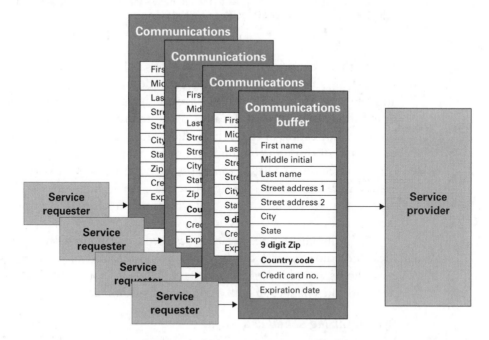

Figure 7.7 Dealing with tightly coupled interface changes through maintaining old versions can lead to a proliferation of interfaces. Here, we are going from five- to nine-digit ZIP codes and adding a country code in independent changes. To satisfy all of our clients, we keep back-level interfaces.

The hybrid approach

Under these circumstances, we might choose a combination of both techniques: synchronization of schedules and multiple interfaces. We block together a number of changes, and then deal with the complexities of supporting a small number of back-level interfaces. This approach gives us some of the best, and lots of the worst, of both techniques. The pace of improvement is limited by the need to aggregate and coordinate changes, and the approach requires supporting back-level interfaces or even custom combinations of old and new interfaces. Many companies that have used these technologies to carry out e-commerce deal with the same issues after decades of struggle. Making such a cumbersome process work is not easy, and many an IT department has collapsed under the weight of managing interfaces across organizations. Fortunately, help is on the horizon.

7.4.2   Premature binding

Another problem with the communication area is early binding. Clients must decide at an early stage who will be providing the service, and service providers must find their clients in traditional ways. We make these producer-consumer business decisions and hardwire our information systems to the proposed solution. We are then bound to those decisions, whether or not business conditions change or we face significant consequences.

7.4.3   Solution 1: Decouple with XML messages

Returning to our management analogy, good managers delegate by describing a *task*, and not the *way* the task should be completed. This is the XML approach: We describe the task in an XML schema and give the description to both the client and the server. That way, both ends of the transaction have a degree of freedom. Specification in a neutral, flexible language like XML does not dictate the actual byte structure of the data block that serves as our new communication area. Instead, it lends structure and meaning to the data so that we can make more intelligent processing decisions. XML can help us in many ways:

- XML lets us deal with tangible business objects with deeply nested relationships, instead of a disorganized collection of parameters. This increased organization helps servers understand how to process data, and gives additional clues to which data sets are valid and which are not.
- Clients and servers both have a better description of the interface, along with a wider array of deployment choices.

- XML is rich enough to handle changes in the interface. For example, adding optional fields has no impact on a client, and the client can take advantage of the added functionality at its discretion. In addition, some required fields could be satisfied with default values, which allows the client to use those fields only when needed.

- XML has a number of technologies that can quickly and efficiently translate one XML schema (or type) to another. This ability makes XML extremely flexible and efficient.

Not every interface has to be so loosely coupled. Within our applications, we'll doubtlessly have many object-to-object method calls, and we may even have distributed communications through EJBs or other interfaces. For those major interfaces between major systems that demand a looser coupling, XML is a good alternative to hardwiring an interface to a static communication area.

Listing 7.5 features an XML message that we might use instead of the communications area described in figure 7.6. Notice that we are sending a communications block but that the format is an XML document, instead of a tightly managed collection of fields.

Listing 7.5   XML message for credit card transactions

```
<creditCardTransaction>
  <customer>
    <firstName>Bruce</lastName>
    <middleInitial>A</middleInitial>
    <lastName>Tate</lastName>
    <address1>1234 McMerican Trail</address1>
    <city>Austin</city>
    <state>Tx</state>
    <zip>78732</zip>
    <country>USA</country>
  </customer>
  <creditCard>
    <creditCardNumber>0u812</creditCardNumber>
    <expirationDate>03/03</expirationDate>
    <amount>3.35</amount>
  </creditCard>
</creditCardTransaction>
```

The service requester can generate the XML message using a variety of techniques, including custom applications, exports from existing applications, or translations from existing XML documents. Then, the service provider can use one of several approaches to process the XML message; for example, the provider could use one of the XML programmatic APIs. Elements of this message can be processed sequentially, so we could probably get by with the Simple API for XML (SAX). If instead the provider needed to construct the entire tree to process the elements of the message out of sequence, the provider would probably need a more robust API, such as the DOM API.

We also have some flexibility in managing changes in the interface. We can add processing steps at the client or server to translate between different XML formats, or even convert to a format that is not XML at all by using Extensible Stylesheet Language Transformations (XSLT). We could even use XSLT to translate this message format to a valid communication block for an older interface. XML, combined with the incredible flexibility and tools at the client and server sides, lets us decouple important interfaces.

7.4.4 Solution 2: Delay binding with web services

XML allows us to decouple interfaces by adding an abstraction layer and structural clues to the message. We also have a technology that addresses the problem of premature binding: web services let us describe our interface as a service that clients can register and bind. The interesting part of this process for us is *delayed binding*.

Figure 7.8 shows how this works. The provider describes a service in an XML-based markup language called Web Services Description Language (WSDL), and publishes the interface in a distributed registry. The requester can search the registry for a service and then bind to the service. The standard for the open registration of resources is called Universal Discovery Description and Integration (UDDI), which specifies a common XML description of an

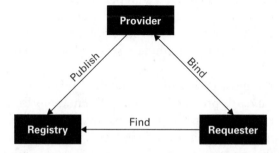

Figure 7.8 Web services loosen coupling between the provider and the requester by delaying the binding process. Providers publish their service in a distributed registry. Requesters can then search the registry for an appropriate service. When one is found, the service is bound between the requester and provider.

interface, as well as a method for organizing the full directory of web services. Web services use XML in many ways. Though the messaging protocol is not mandated, the common implementations today use Simple Object Access Protocol (SOAP), an XML-based standard messaging protocol. The message content is, of course, in XML, and the definition language for services is an XML derivative.

The web services architecture, and the open standards that form its foundation, is based on standards that are simple, adequate for the task, and flexible. Table 7.1 describes the benefits of web services.

Table 7.1 By allowing us to describe our interface as a service that clients can register and bind, web services provide significant benefits.

Feature	Benefit
Loose coupling	Reduced maintenance and integration cost.
Late binding	Improved flexibility in business process and implementation.
A comprehensive, open standard	One widely available and deployed standard addresses service encapsulation, binding, invocation, distribution, and description.
Dynamic and robust technologies	Improved flexibility of implementation.
Platform and language neutrality	Improved flexibility of deployment, wider vendor support, and wider market penetration.

7.5   *Mini-antipatterns for XML misuse*

We have seen that XML can loosen the coupling between two systems, providing better insulation to change and more independence between the client and service provider. The key to effective XML interfaces is a good, flexible schema. Clean XML documents describing a service lead to smoother, more flexible connections.

XML is perhaps the most powerful new standard related to the Internet. Although previous standards provided open implementations for communication, messaging, presentation, and applications, the missing link was a standard language that provided structure and meaning to *data*. However, keep in mind that XML is subject to misuse. Next up, we'll look at some antipatterns related to XML.

7.5.1 *XML's Golden Hammers*

The book *AntiPatterns* described Golden Hammers, a series of good technologies employed for ill-suited tasks. In a perceptive paper called "XML for Data: Four Tips for Smart Architecture," Kevin Williams points out two ways that we can miscast XML. Let's take a look. (For more information, you can see this paper at www-106.ibm.com/developerworks/xml/library/x-xdtips.html.)

XML is not a search engine

XML provides native searching tools, such as XPath. Even so, XML may not be the best format for data that is subject to extensive searches. XML parsing can be expensive, especially when we're frequently searching for relatively small fragments or complex relationships in data. We must parse an entire XML document to perform a reliable search in the proper context. If we intend to search an XML document regularly, it is best to load the document into a tool built for that purpose—a database, for example. In his article, Williams points out that the nature of the document should help you make the right decision. If the document is text oriented, such as a manuscript, XML provides a good native format. If the document is data oriented, like an insurance policy, then a database would probably be the better option.

XML is a poor choice for large-scale summarizing

For complex data reporting and summarizing purposes, relational database reporting functions are more powerful than those of XML. XML also does not combine documents into intermediate formats as efficiently. However, some technologies allow indexed XML, which *can* provide an effective intermediate format for communication to a relational database engine. In this way, the two technologies can be used effectively together.

7.5.2 *XML's bitter transitions*

When XML bridges two subsystems controlled by a single organization, keeping the schema current and each part relevant is easy. Using XML documents across major interfaces presents additional challenges. Table 7.2 shows some of the areas you must watch. In particular, you should throw away anything that you are not likely to use, and you should look for data in a structure and format that it is likely to be used.

Table 7.2 XML translation technology is simple and effective. Often, translation is eschewed in favor of expensive application development or manual effort, without regard to performance considerations.

XML warning signs	Potential problems
XML documents are used as shipped.	The document may not be in the optimal format for use as shipped.
Elements, types, and attributes contain formats and data proprietary to other organizations.	Additional data is expensive to parse and store. These can all be translated in a single step and save the application developers significant time.
Applications parse XML data into a model and immediately restructure it.	XSLT translations are usually easier to code and maintain than application translations.
Different documents that contain the same data are created independently.	New applications or manual effort to create a new format for existing data is much more expensive than the alternative. Instead, XSLT translations should be used to repurpose data.
Applications use proprietary parsing technology to render XML.	When manual parsers are written for XML data, it may be a sign that someone is reinventing the wheel. Instead, XML programming extensions like DOM or SAX should be used, or even the XSLT scripting alternative.

Fortunately, with XML you can quickly translate documents between different formats. You can combine XSLT with cascading style sheets (CSS) to create a simple and effective presentation. You can also make adjustments to a document over a major interface. It doesn't matter if the target format is XML or not; XSLT can easily translate to non-XML targets as well.

7.6   *Mini-antipatterns: Rigid XML*

XML gives you a degree of freedom, compatibility, and flexibility that isn't possible with other languages. You can extend languages and vocabularies that describe proprietary data. XML lets you forge e-businesses by describing a transaction rather than dictating the implementation. However, if you box yourself in by designing rigid, inflexible XML, many of the advantages are lost.

An excellent resource is a collection of best practices moderated by Roger L. Costello at http://www.xfront.com/BestPracticesHomepage.html. The mini-antipatterns in this section are based on the content on that site.

When you build an interface across a major organizational boundary, you'll probably make a significant investment negotiating the XML schema of the transaction messages. The key to taking advantage of this investment is to build schemas that can be extended so that future negotiations are easier. Let's examine some of the practices that can get in the way of extensible schemas.

7.6.1 Name collisions

XML shares a primary goal with object technologies: reuse. When we're building a large schema, we'll often combine parts of existing schemas. Suppose we own a company that sells mountain bikes. Like many such companies, ours doesn't make its own frames. Instead, it buys parts from disparate sources and assembles the bikes. Let's say we want to build an XML specification describing a bike, and we plan to use this specification to communicate with our distributors and suppliers. We want to use one vendor's frames and another vendor's components. To build the specification, we combine the component set definitions from an existing standard specification with the frame portion of a competing specification for an XML bike definition. We round it out with some custom XML describing our proprietary wheel sets and forks. Figure 7.9 shows our plan for the combined XML document schema. We've reused portions of specifications for the frame and component (`frame.xsd` and `comp.xsd`) and combined those with new schemas for the wheel set and front suspension. We've called those new schemas `wheel.xsd` and `fork.xsd`. We combine all the schemas to form a bike specification that meets our needs. The problem is that XML allows only a single definition for entities, attributes, and type definitions.

Shortsighted designers might decide to ignore name collisions altogether. Some organizations, through either ignorance or the belief that namespaces are cumbersome, decide to control naming collisions with prefixes and longer

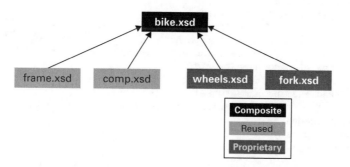

Figure 7.9 With XML, we can build a new schema out of existing specifications. In this example, we combine reused schemas for the bike frame and components with proprietary schemas for wheels and the fork, and come up with an entirely new specification with a fraction of the total effort.

variable names. If we accept the premise that control of an XML schema has some value, we should strive for designs that don't force us to prepend variable names with proprietary extensions. A namespace is the XML schema extension designed to handle this problem.

In listing 7.6, we first create a namespace. Next, we declare namespaces for both of our reused schemas (**1**). Within our composite document (`bike.xsd`), we can then import the namespaces (**2**), and use the types within to create a type called `bike`. Let's assume that both our frame and component companies use the identifier `classification`. Usually, these types within the `comp.xsd` and `frame.xsd` would collide, but the namespace will protect us (**3**).

Listing 7.6   XML namespaces help resolve naming collisions.

```
<xsd:schema xmlns:xsd="our-URL"
            targetNamespace="http://www.bikespace.org"
            xmlns:frame="url-for-frame-namespace"
            xmlns:component="url-for-component-namespace"
            xmlns:wheel="url-for-wheel-namespace"
            xmlns:fork="url-for-fork-namespace" />
```
1 Defining the namespace

```
<xsd:import namespace="url-for-frame-namespace"
            schemalocation="frame.xsd" />
<xsd:import namespace="url-for-component-namespace"
            schemalocation="comp.xsd" />
<xsd:import namespace="url-for-fork-namespace"
            schemalocation="fork.xsd" />
<xsd:import namespace="url-for-wheel-namespace"
            schemalocation="wheel.xsd" />
```
2 Importing the namespace

```
<xsd:element name="bike">
  <xsd:complexType>
    <xsd:sequence>
      <xsd:element name="frame"
                   type="frame:frameType"/>
      <xsd:element name="component"
                   type="component:componentType"/>
      <xsd:element name="fork"
                   type="fork:forkType"/>
      <xsd:element name="wheel"
                   type="wheel:wheelType"/>
    </xsd:sequence>
  </xsd:complexType>
</xsd:element>

</xsd:schema>
```
3 The types can share names without colliding

As you can see, the namespace can resolve conflicting names. Many intricacies make mastering namespaces seem like black magic, but if you can learn to do so, you can unleash significant power. At design time, you must decide whether to use exposed versus hidden namespaces, how to set the default namespace, and how to determine the number of namespaces. Such intricate issues are beyond the scope of this book. For additional information, consult the "XML Schema: Best Practices" page at http://www.xfront.com/ BestPracticesHomepage.html.

Our example hardwires the schema location to the type. In the next section, we'll learn how to make the association between type and the implementation for a type more dynamic.

7.6.2 Rigid constructs

Some of the time, we want tight control over an XML definition and how it can be extended. The rest of the time, we should strive for flexibility. Now, we'll look at practices that can limit the flexibility in an XML document. None of these practices are always inherently bad, but they do have the negative consequence of limiting flexibility.

Hardwiring components to a namespace

Choosing a namespace for a schema unnecessarily binds the schema to that namespace early in the process. When we do so, we're also adopting the *semantics* of the namespace to our schema. We can delay the binding process by creating compact nameless schemas and letting the application that uses the schema map a better namespace onto the schema. Through this delayed binding, we can choose the best namespace at the application level, thus controlling the target application semantics and ensuring flexibility.

Hardwiring a type reference to a type implementation

When we define a type in one document and rigidly fix the type within an import, we're constraining the type implementation to the imported specification. This implementation is probably one of the most common. The following line binds a type to a type implementation:

```
<xsd:import namespace="http://www.frame.abccorp.com"
            schemalocation="frame.xsd" />
<xsd:element name="frame" type="frame:frameType"/>
```

We can delay the binding between type and schema location (and thus the type implementation). We don't have to specify the schema location; it's an optional parameter. Instead, when we create an *instance* of this document, we can specify a type specification for frame_type. We'll then have a flexible and powerful schema.

Using static content models

A limited-content model will not allow instance models to extend the types beyond what is in the schema definition. Consider the definition of a photograph:

```
<xsd:element name= "Photograph">
  <xsd:complexType>
    <xsd:sequence>
      <xsd:element name="photographer" type="string" />
      <xsd:element name="subject" type="string" />
    </xsd:sequence>
  </xsd:complexType>
</xsd:element>
```

In this example, we'll always be limited to a sequence containing the photographer and the photograph subject. If we stay with the same schema, we'll never be able to extend the photograph element by adding, say, a color or black-and-white field, a resolution field, or a size field.

Instead, we can add placeholders to the schema in spots that we are likely to extend:

```
<xsd:element name= "Photograph">
 <xsd:complexType>
    <xsd:sequence>
      <xsd:element name="photographer" type="string" />
      <xsd:element name="subject" type="string" />
      <xsd:any namespace="##any" minOccurs="0" />
    </xsd:sequence>
  </xsd:complexType>
</xsd:element>
```

With the revised schema, we can add any number of new elements or types to our photograph schema, and the added components can be contained in their own namespace to avoid collisions.

Element over type

Preferring interfaces over abstract classes is one of the Java programming hygiene rules we'll introduce in chapter 9. Abstract classes limit us to a single inheritance chain and restrict how our code can be extended, while an interface gives us much more flexibility. In XML, we're often faced with making a similar decision between types and elements. In a schema, many times elements are specified, which of course limits flexibility.

Instead, we should prefer type definitions to elements. If necessary, we can always replace the type with an element in another schema document. This way, we have the ability to choose compatible subtypes or different elements at a later time. In essence, we're delaying the binding of a specific element to a schema. As with Java interfaces, minor exceptions exist, but the general rule is that in schemas, we should use XML types rather than elements.

7.6.3 *Restrictive variable-content containers*

Many XML designs call for containers of variable content. A *variable-content container* is a collection of components; these components may be of similar or unrelated types, either simple or complex. Examples include inventory lists, sales catalogs, and recipes. The XML Schema: Best Practices website describes four approaches, with varying flexibility

Use an abstract element and substitute an element

With this approach, we declare an abstract element and a substitution group. In this example, we're inventorying office furniture, and our inventory list contains desks and chairs. This is the code:

```
<xsd:element name= "InventoryList">
  <xsd:complexType>
    <xsd:sequence>
      <xsd:element ref="FurnitureItem"
                   maxOccurs="unbounded" />
    </xsd:sequence>
  </xsd:complexType>
</xsd:element>

<xsd:element name= "Desk"
             substitutionGroup="FurnitureItem"
             type="DeskType" />

<xsd:element name= "Chair"
             substitutionGroup="FurnitureItem"
             type="ChairType" />
```

This approach is fairly flexible, but it does force us to derive elements of the inventory from the FurnitureItem's type. In essence, we're limiting ourselves to custom types. We're also limiting the *structure* of the derived types to the base types.

Use choice elements

We can instead implement our schema with an unbounded list of choices. This is the code for the <choice> approach:

```
<xsd:element name= "InventoryList">
  <xsd:complexType>
    <xsd:choice maxOccurs="unbounded" >
      <xsd:element name= "Desk"
                   type="DeskType" />
      <xsd:element name= "Chair"
                   type="ChairType" />
    </xsd:choice>
  </xsd:complexType>
</xsd:element>
```

We don't limit the structure of the choice types because the types are no longer derived from a common type. Unfortunately, we can no longer extend our list by adding new elements to our substitution group. With this approach, we have taken one step forward and one step back.

Use an abstract type and type substitution

A third approach is to define an abstract type within our schema, and then substitute a type in our instance document. Here is our schema:

```
<xsd:element name= "InventoryList">
  <xsd:complexType>
    <xsd:sequence>
      <xsd:element ref="FurnitureItem"
                   type="FurnitureItemType"
                   maxOccurs="unbounded" />
    </xsd:sequence>
  </xsd:complexType>
</xsd:element>
```

FurnitureItemType is our abstract type. We can substitute a compatible type—meaning any type derived from the abstract type—in the instance document. We have the same extensibility advantages as with the first example, and less coupling. We can also process the list items over a common interface. However, we're still limited to elements that are derived from the same type.

Use a dangling type (not supported yet) or the any construct

With this approach, we're going to define a type that's defined in another namespace. We'll then import the type, but in the schema, we won't specify the schema location. This will allow us to delay the binding of our type until runtime, since the schema location can be provided in our runtime document.

Listing 7.7   Variable-content containers can delay type bindings

```
.
.
.
<xsd:element name= "InventoryItem"
            type="i:InventoryItemType" />               Defining the
.                                                        namespace
.
.
<xsd:import namespace="http://www.inventoryItem.org" />  No schema
.                                                         location in the
.                                                         import!
<xsd:element name= "InventoryList">
  <xsd:complexType>
    <xsd:sequence>
      <xsd:element name="InventoryItem"                 Use the imported
                   type="i:InventoryItemType"           type in another
                   maxOccurs="unbounded" />             namespace.
    </xsd:sequence>
  </xsd:complexType>
</xsd:element>

</schema>
```

Listing 7.7 shows this approach is appropriately called the dangling type. We'll bind to the schema location in the instance document. Using this approach, we delay binding of the types until runtime. We can then let individual instances define types appropriate to their application. We gain all of the benefits of the first three approaches, and we enjoy the additional benefit of complete type freedom. Unfortunately, as I am finishing *Bitter Java*, the dangling type is not yet implemented in the major schema validators. The way around this is to use anyType:

```
<xsd:element name= "InventoryItem"
            type="anyType " />
```

7.6.4   *XML versioning*

In the section "Creating multiple interfaces," we mentioned that we might want to collect different versions of the same interface to preserve compatibility. With XML, we can avoid some of the problems that lead to interface versioning, but sometimes we're faced with incompatible versions of the same schema. Here's how we can provide better versioning support:

▶ **Reducing the impact of new XML versions**

Creating new versions of XML schema definitions can trigger painful, rippling change. These steps can reduce or eliminate problems caused by inflexible version control.

- *We should capture the XML version in our schema.* Many mechanisms can be used to do this, and each approach has strengths and weaknesses. The important thing to do is to pick an approach for capturing a version number and stick with it.

- *We should capture compatible versions in the instance.* By explicitly listing compatible versions of the interface, we avoid guesswork. We explicitly list compatible versions.

- *Where possible, we should make compatible changes.* We can make added elements optional, or we can make newly changed types less restrictive than the original.

- *Older versions should be available.* We can support multiple versions of the same schema within the same processing application. Within the same XML application, we can query the version number and process accordingly.

- *We should use translation technologies to bridge incompatible XML specifications.* A powerful use of XSLT technology is quick translations between incompatible types.

These techniques won't necessarily eliminate the changes associated with churning a major interface. However, they will reduce the impact of any changes.

7.7   *Summary: Sweetening bitter connections*

Many Java programmers and architects understand the importance of a well-performing connection but fail to consider the costs associated with establishing and terminating connections. In this chapter, we examined antipatterns related to connection creation and cleanup.

Connection Thrashing is an antipattern that creates and terminates a connection at significant expense, though the connections might easily be reused with a connection pool. Database administrators have used the connection-pooling concept for years, and the benefits are well documented. Because the total cost of making and closing a connection can easily approach fully half of the total cost of a database transaction, this approach should be near the top of the list of performance enhancements that promise significant bang for the buck.

The Split Cleaner is an antipattern related to connection cleanup. When a resource is requested and released in different methods, the potential exists for cleanup-related problems. Connections not properly cleansed can lead to leaks. Connections cleansed too soon will lead to exceptions. Both are bugs that we can avoid by placing allocations and frees in close proximity.

Finally, the Hardwired Connection antipattern can make business-to-business connections very difficult to maintain. We can use technologies (such as XML) and APIs (such as Web Services) to decouple systems, and make both the service and the client much easier to maintain.

7.8 Antipatterns in this chapter

These are the templates for the antipatterns that appear in this chapter. They provide an excellent summary format and form the basis of the cross-references in appendix A.

Connection Thrashing

DESCRIPTION: When database connections are created from scratch with each new user connection, the performance can be poor, because database connection costs are prohibitive. This antipattern can happen for other connection types as well.

MOST FREQUENT SCALE: Application.

REFACTORED SOLUTION NAME: Connection Pooling.

REFACTORED SOLUTION TYPE: Software.

REFACTORED SOLUTION DESCRIPTION: Design patterns and software with built-in connection pools are widely available, and Java has a new connection framework.

ROOT CAUSES: Haste, sloth, ignorance.

ANECDOTAL EVIDENCE: "We'll just add connection pooling later."

SYMPTOMS, CONSEQUENCES: Since database connections are expensive, the primary symptom is strain of system resources such as memory or file handles, causing errors or poor performance. In extreme cases, it is not unusual for over half of an application's total work effort to go toward managing connections. Along with Round-tripping and the Cacheless Cow, this antipattern is the biggest performance drainer in the book.

Split Cleaners

DESCRIPTION: When a resource is allocated separately from where it is freed, cleanup can be lost.

MOST FREQUENT SCALE: Application.

REFACTORED SOLUTION NAME: Pairing Connections with Cleanup.

REFACTORED SOLUTION TYPE: Software.

REFACTORED SOLUTION DESCRIPTION: Connections should be allocated and cleared in close proximity, and `finally` blocks should be used for connection cleanup. In this way, inspection will quickly show whether a connection has been cleansed appropriately.

ROOT CAUSES: Haste, sloth.

ANECDOTAL EVIDENCE: "That connection probably gets cleaned up somewhere else."

SYMPTOMS, CONSEQUENCES: Resources, like database or file connections, run out prematurely.

Hardwired Connections

DESCRIPTION: For business-to-business connections, a common implementation is to enumerate all of the fields in an entire interface, complete with parameter and return types. The connection is then made through some form of a remote procedure call. This approach makes the connection difficult to maintain and support as the interfaces change.

MOST FREQUENT SCALE: Enterprise.

REFACTORED SOLUTION NAME: Web services or XML messages.

REFACTORED SOLUTION TYPE: Software.

REFACTORED SOLUTION DESCRIPTION: Connections should be made with common standards that allow a dynamic description of the transaction, including the parameter set and the message construction. Web services provide such a wrapping, through open standards, including SOAP for messaging and XML for the description of the parameter and message format.

TYPICAL CAUSES: The solution described by this antipattern is actually one of the most common implementations of business-to-business connections. Many have not yet migrated to XML-based solutions for a variety of reasons.

ANECDOTAL EVIDENCE: "We should connect via interface version 12.23.345." "You can't change that field length without six levels of management approval, because you will break everyone." "We can have the nine-digit ZIP code ready for testing in two years."

SYMPTOMS, CONSEQUENCES: Multiple versions of the same interface is a tell-tale characteristic. Interface support that significantly lags the capabilities of both the client and server systems is another symptom of this problem.

XML Misuse

RELATED ANTIPATTERNS: This antipattern is a subset of the Golden Hammer antipattern in *AntiPatterns*, since we are applying an ill-suited technology to a purpose.

DESCRIPTION: XML, like many powerful technologies, can be misused. In this case, we're using XML to do large-scale search or summary missions.

REFACTORED SOLUTION NAME: Databases, Indexed XML, or other appropriate technologies.

REFACTORED SOLUTION TYPE: Software or technology.

REFACTORED SOLUTION DESCRIPTION: XML indexing solutions or relational databases are better technology fits for these problems.

TYPICAL CAUSES: This antipattern is caused by the assumptions that some convenience facilities in XML are scalable and robust, which is not necessarily their intent.

SYMPTOMS, CONSEQUENCES: Applications using XML to do significant sorting or summarizing perform poorly.

Rigid XML

DESCRIPTION: Some design choices can restrict the extensibility of XML. Namespaces can collide and some constructs are more restrictive than others.

REFACTORED SOLUTION NAME: Extensible, Flexible XML.

REFACTORED SOLUTION TYPE: Software.

REFACTORED SOLUTION DESCRIPTION: Design choices can affect the flexibility of XML. In general, we should use namespaces to control collisions, prefer types to elements in a schema, use dangling types or `anyType` for implementations of variable content containers, and limit the impact of XML versioning by observing best practices.

ROOT CAUSES: Ignorance or apathy.

SYMPTOMS, CONSEQUENCES: The problems with rigid XML are similar to those for hardwired, inflexible code: difficult maintenance and changes that ripple into other parts of the system. The primary symptom of Rigid XML is a schema that requires significant maintenance. It does not contain changes to isolated areas and so must be heavily revised for every minor change or new use. Other symptoms include having to redesign schemas from scratch even when solving similar problems, and the lack of effective reuse.

ANECDOTAL EVIDENCE: "We always need a new version when we change the XML." "I don't know what the X stands for, but it is not eXtensible."

Bitter beans 8

I watch Eric line up his run on the easy Class II rapid in North Alabama. At the bend, the river is about 45 feet wide, and there is only one danger spot: a notorious feature called a pour-over. This one is easily visible. Merely five feet wide, it's difficult to hit. The bulk of the current swings around the bend, away from the pour-over, but it appears Eric will hit it anyway. Although he's a beginner, we've practiced for months for this run. Texas has been dry, so our practice has been on slow water. Eric can steer, power, and roll his kayak. He can even roll without a paddle, a skill that belies his beginner status. When it's dry, it's easy to look for challenges in unlikely places. As we watch with amusement (and some apprehension), Eric's brain appears to lock as he approaches the pour-over. He just stares, and it pulls him in like a tractor beam. He goes over the powerful 2-foot wave behind the rock and stares at the 4-foot drop and the powerful hydraulic beyond. He knows that he's going to flip and maybe get hammered by the hole ... so what does he do? He drops his paddle.

8.1   A brief Enterprise JavaBeans review

EJBs—the "bitter beans" of this chapter's title—build in extensive functionality that dramatically simplifies database, message-oriented, and transactional programming. This chapter will not cover message-oriented EJBs because they're relatively new, and we programmers don't have enough experience to develop antipatterns based on their use. A technology as complex and ambitious as this must provide fertile grounds for antipatterns. We will not be disappointed.

In this chapter, we'll review the basic characteristics of EJBs and discuss how they are built and deployed. Next, we'll return to our BBS application and consider an EJB implementation. This time, since we have so much code, we'll break away from the practice of providing a complete example, but we'll include enough detail to give you the full flavor of the application. Next, we'll revisit some existing antipatterns, such as Round-tripping, in greater detail. We'll discuss what happens when we run into the antipattern Everything Is an EJB, and then we'll see what happens when we make bad choices for our EJB deployments.

8.1.1   The component-based distributed architecture

The EJB architecture is a component-based, distributed architecture. On the server, a set of services support a container, which in turn supports the components, called EJBs, within the container. The components can communicate with clients via a *stub* approach. This is essentially the approach that CORBA, the distributed objects standard, uses to communicate between client and

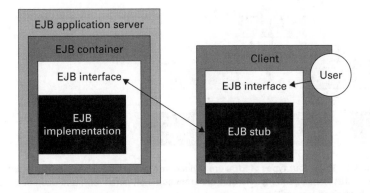

Figure 8.1 EJBs use client-side stubs to communicate with server-side objects. Users of the client-side EJBs use the remote interface, which in turn uses the proxy, which then uses the distributed interface and the local implementation. The server supports a container, which provides critical features to EJB components.

server. An object's interface is separated from the implementation. The interface is deployed on both the client and the server. On the client side, a simple stub is used, which communicates with the server-side distributed interface, as shown in figure 8.1. Users can then use the client-side interface, which communicates with the stub and, by proxy, the remote interface, and eventually the remote implementation.

8.1.2 *Types of EJBs*

There are two major types of EJBs in common use (with more on the way): Session beans provide distributed transactional support, and entity beans provide a mechanism for building *shared, transactional, persistent* models:

- *Shared* means that many different implementations can use the same model, conserving resources and improving complex distributed communications.
- *Transactional* means that the database can support complex, multipart transactions. We've heard the same idea with the database term *unit of work*.
- *Persistent* means the data is stored in a database. Though the structure of the model is object-oriented, rich relational database support is provided.

Figure 8.2 shows the different subtypes of EJBs. Only the dark gray ones may be used; the other nodes simply help us organize and categorize the types of support. The two types of session beans are *stateless* and *stateful*. Stateless

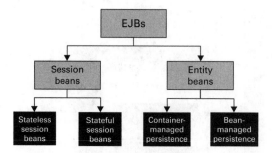

Figure 8.2   These four types of EJBs are divided into two major classes: entity beans and session beans. Entity beans build models that are transactional, persistent, and secure. Session beans wrap distributed transactions.

session beans have no persistent state. They're used as small, fast wrappers around distributed transactions, and they ensure transactional integrity. Stateful session beans provide transactional support, with a primitive ability to support state. This state doesn't assure persistence after a crash. Entity beans with container-managed persistence are entity beans that can save their state, usually in a database, through the services of the container. They'll persist through a crash of the EJB application server. Entity beans with bean-managed persistence are the same, but they must provide the persistence mechanism. Each of these types of beans has a specific purpose and can be efficient within that role. When we step out of that role, we can have problems with performance, maintenance, manageability, or scalability.

8.2   Bitter BBS with EJBs

In this example, we'll first introduce a full object model for our BBS. As with all of the "before" examples in this book, we'll make some mistakes. Our solution will suffer from round-tripping and will map every class onto a container-managed entity bean. Many sources warn against the perils of this type of architecture, including *Core J2EE Patterns*, various sources on java.sun.com, and conferences such as Java One. Still, programming tools and a lack of education lead to solutions like this one with alarming regularity. Braden Flowers, a well-published architect at IBM, has seen numerous poor EJB examples through his many years of working with IBM's largest customers. He has agreed to play the role of a novice and provide the examples in this chapter.

The nature of wrapping legacy architectures is such that we won't always have a clean, object-oriented design throughout the application, but we

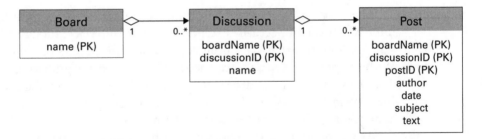

Figure 8.3 This entity-relationship diagram shows the organization of our BBS. We have a board that represents a collection of discussions around a central topic, containing discussions. We also have discussions, representing a single discussion, containing posts. Our posts are an atomic statement by a single author at a given time, on a given subject.

should have a good, consistent model for representing the user interface, even when the rest of the design is lacking. This example will introduce a fully object-oriented model on the server side. Figure 8.3 shows an entity-relationship diagram describing our application.

A *board* is a logical discussion topic, and it will hold a list of *discussions*. (Earlier examples used *thread*, the more common name for BBS discussions. Unfortunately, thread is a reserved keyword in Java.) A discussion contains one or more *posts*. A post is a composition by an author and is the leaf node of our BBS. The entity-relationship (ER) diagram in figure 8.3 shows the relationships between the entities and is ideal for this type of modeling.

In the next step, we'll generate the interfaces for our BBS. We'll show an initial attempt at refactoring. As usual, our design will fall short of our expectations.

8.2.1 *Elements of an EJB application*

EJB applications have five different parts: the remote and home interfaces, the bean and primary key classes, and the deployment descriptor.

The *remote interface* is the primary interface of an EJB, and is the interface that we'd define in a modeling tool. This is where we specify the business attributes and methods of a given EJB. Because the container manages most of the details, such as security, persistence, and context, we are free to focus on the interface. The remote interface is a formal Java interface, meaning we won't specify an implementation here. The *home interface* describes the object known as the EJB Home and is similar to a description of a factory object. We define methods to manage the bean's life cycle, such as creating and adding it to a container, removing and destroying it, and finding it.

The *bean class* is responsible for implementing the methods in the remote interface. It doesn't actually extend the remote interface, though the method signatures must match. This bean concentrates on specifics of the model logic. With the *primary key class*, we specify an entity bean's primary database key. This is a simple class that defines the set of fields that in turn will uniquely define the rows in our database. We also have the usual responsibilities of supporting a generic object, including comparison, hash codes, and equality for the class.

As we mentioned, the container supports many of the management services of an EJB, so we probably won't see methods to handle such services as security, transactions, context, naming, or even distribution. While we don't have to develop those services, we do need to configure them through a *deployment descriptor.* These files use XML to describe how an EJB is to be deployed. They allow us to delay binding of the container's services until runtime. A deployment descriptor's format is specific to each classification of enterprise bean, since each major category will need subtly different information. Each bean class has its own deployment descriptor, which can be generated manually or automatically through the development environment or proprietary framework. I've used both approaches, and either will work reasonably well.

We have seen all of the basic pieces of an EJB application. Table 8.1 shows each piece, with the corresponding Java interfaces that are implemented and the role that each plays. Next, we'll implement our bulletin board example with EJBs. At that point, we'll be free to dive into the antipatterns that plague EJB applications.

Table 8.1   Here are the parts of an EJB program: the common name of the artifact; the formal construct used to build the program; the Java interface that is extended; and the role that the construct plays in EJB development.

Program artifact	Construct	Extends	Role
Remote interface	Java interface	`javax.ejb.EJBObject`	Defines the business methods and attributes.
Home interface	Java interface	`javax.ejb.EJBHome`	Defines life cycle methods.
Bean class	Java class	`javax.ejb.EntityBean`	Implements remote interface methods.
Primary key	Java class	Serializeable	Identifies the database key.
Deployment descriptor	XML file	N/A	Defines properties of services used by the bean.

8.2.2 Building the remote interface

As we explained earlier, the board is a collection point for discussions around a single topic, denoted by the board name. Listing 8.1 shows the remote interface to our `Board` bean.

Listing 8.1 The remote interface to our Board bean

```
package com.bitterjava.bbs.ejb;                        Remote interfaces
                                                       always extend
public interface Board extends javax.ejb.EJBObject {●  EJBObject

  int addDiscussion(java.lang.String threadName)
    throws javax.ejb.CreateException, java.rmi.RemoteException;
                                                              A method
  String getName() throws java.rmi.RemoteException;           wrapper

                      Accessor for the name attribute ●

  com.bitterjava.bbs.ejb.Discussion getDiscussion(int discussionID)
    throws java.rmi.RemoteException;

  java.util.Collection getDiscussions()
    throws java.rmi.RemoteException;

  void removeDiscussion(com.bitterjava.bbs.ejb.Discussion discussion)
    throws java.rmi.RemoteException, javax.ejb.RemoveException;
}
```

For a distributed persistent object, the interface is remarkably simple. We aren't forced to deal with the complexities—the container in our application server masks all of those complexities from us. Here we can see the power of the EJB architecture.

Next, we'll look at two additional remote interfaces, for discussions and posts.

The remote interface for Discussion

The `Discussion` interface is used to provide a collection point for a discussion, or a collection of posts. We have the methods that you'd expect: add, remove, and get a post. We also have attributes for the name and a collection of posts, wrapped with accessor methods:

```
package com.bitterjava.bbs.ejb;

public interface Discussion extends javax.ejb.EJBObject {

  int addPost(String author,
              Date date,
              String subject,
              String text)
    throws javax.ejb.CreateException,
```

```
                         java.rmi.RemoteException;

      String getBoardName()throws java.rmi.RemoteException;

      String getName() throws java.rmi.RemoteException;

      Post getPost(int postID) throws java.rmi.RemoteException;

      Collection getPosts() throws java.rmi.RemoteException;
      int getDiscussionID() throws java.rmi.RemoteException;

      void removePost(Post post)
         throws java.rmi.RemoteException, javax.ejb.RemoveException;

      void setName(java.lang.String newValue)
         throws java.rmi.RemoteException;
   }
```

The remote interface for Post

The Post interface is a little simpler. Because its members are all primitive objects and not collections, they consist of only getter and setter methods. Later, this will make the implementation class much simpler. If we view our object model as a tree, then a post is a leaf node:

```
package com.bitterjava.bbs.ejb;

public interface Post extends javax.ejb.EJBObject {

   java.lang.String getAuthor() throws java.rmi.RemoteException;

   java.sql.Date getDate() throws java.rmi.RemoteException;

   int getPostID() throws java.rmi.RemoteException;

   String getSubject() throws java.rmi.RemoteException;

   String getText() throws java.rmi.RemoteException;

   void setAuthor(java.lang.String newValue) throws
      java.rmi.RemoteException;

   void setDate(java.sql.Date newValue) throws java.rmi.RemoteException;

   void setSubject(String newValue)
      throws java.rmi.RemoteException;

   void setText(java.lang.String newValue)
      throws java.rmi.RemoteException;
   }
```

Together, these three interfaces make up the business types in our domain. We'll also need an interface to add and remove these items from a container, and finder methods to locate groups of these objects, because these methods do not logically belong on a single object.

8.2.3 *Creating the home interface*

The home interface, shown in listing 8.2, supports methods related to a class that aren't contained in the bean class. Creating (❶), finding (❷), and removing are all handled by the home interface. These life cycle methods help the container manage the bean. In our case, we have no reason to remove a board once it is created, so there's no remove interface.

Listing 8.2   The home interface to our Board bean

```
package com.bitterjava.bbs.ejb;

public interface BoardHome extends javax.ejb.EJBHome {

    com.bitterjava.bbs.ejb.Board create(java.lang.String argName)
        throws javax.ejb.CreateException, java.rmi.RemoteException;
```
❶ **Creator method for Board**
```
    com.bitterjava.bbs.ejb.Board findByPrimaryKey(BoardKey key)
        throws java.rmi.RemoteException, javax.ejb.FinderException;
```
❷ **Finder (by primary key)**
```
}
```

We will have two more home interfaces, for `discussions` and `posts`. First, the `Discussion` home:

```
package com.bitterjava.bbs.ejb;

public interface DiscussionHome extends javax.ejb.EJBHome {

    com.bitterjava.bbs.ejb.Discussion create(
                                java.lang.String argBoardName,
                                int argDiscussionID)
        throws javax.ejb.CreateException, java.rmi.RemoteException;

    Enumeration findAllForBoard(String boardName)
        throws java.rmi.RemoteException, javax.ejb.FinderException;

    com.bitterjava.bbs.ejb.Discussion findByPrimaryKey(DiscussionKey key)
        throws java.rmi.RemoteException, javax.ejb.FinderException;
}
```

This interface also has another finder. We'll need to find all of the `discussions` on a given board. We've chosen to put this function in the home interface for `discussions`, since it returns an enumeration of `discussions`. We have one more home interface, for `posts`. It is straightforward:

```
package com.bitterjava.bbs.ejb;
```

```
public interface PostHome extends javax.ejb.EJBHome {

  Post create(java.lang.String argBoardName,
              int argPostId,
              int argDiscussionID)
    throws javax.ejb.CreateException, java.rmi.RemoteException;

  public Enumeration findAllForDiscussion(String boardName,
                                          int discussionID)
    throws java.rmi.RemoteException, javax.ejb.FinderException;

  Post findByPrimaryKey(PostKey key)
    throws java.rmi.RemoteException, javax.ejb.FinderException;
}
```

Once again, we have two finders: one to find by primary key, and one to find all posts on a discussion. Now that we've defined the interfaces, we should examine the bean classes that will handle our implementation.

8.2.4 *Implementing the bean class*

In the bean classes, we'll implement the methods that make up our BBS. Since the container handles most management details for us, we'll work primarily with methods that make up the primary functions of a BBS.

The bean class for Board

Listing 8.3 shows the implementation for Board. The bean class implements the methods defined in the remote interface.

> **Listing 8.3   The implementation for Board**

```
package com.bitterjava.bbs.ejb;

import java.rmi.RemoteException;
import java.security.Identity;
import java.util.Properties;
import javax.ejb.*;

public class BoardBean implements EntityBeean {
  private javax.ejb.EntityContext entityContext = null;
  private String name;
  private java.util.Vector discussions;
  private DiscussionHome discussionHome = null;
  final static long serialVersionUID = 3206093459760846163L;

  public int addDiscussion(String discussionName)
    throws RemoteException, CreateException {
    int nextID = 0;
    for (int i = 0; i < discussions.size(); i++) {
      Discussion discussion = (Discussion)discussions.elementAt(i);
      int discussionID = discussion.getDiscussionID();
```

① Extends
EntityBean,
one of four
possible types

② Adds a discussion
to a board

```
      nextID = Math.max(nextID, discussionID+1);
    }
    Discussion newDiscussion = getDiscussionHome().create(name, nextID);
    newDiscussion.setName(discussionName);
    discussions.addElement(newDiscussion);
    return nextID;
  }
```
Must appear to satisfy an interface, even if empty.

```
  public void ejbActivate() throws java.rmi.RemoteException {}
```
❸

```
  public void ejbCreate(java.lang.String argName)
    throws javax.ejb.CreateException, java.rmi.RemoteException {
    name = argName;
  }
```
Fired when bean is added to container.

```
  public void ejbLoad() throws java.rmi.RemoteException {
    try {
      java.util.Enumeration e = getDiscussionHome().findAllForBoard(name);
      discussions = new java.util.Vector();
      while (e.hasMoreElements()) {
        discussions.addElement(e.nextElement());
      }
    } catch (FinderException e) {
    }
  }
```
❹

```
  public void ejbPassivate() throws java.rmi.RemoteException {}

  public void ejbPostCreate(java.lang.String argName) throws
  java.rmi.RemoteException {}

  public void ejbRemove() throws java.rmi.RemoteException,
  javax.ejb.RemoveException {}

  public void ejbStore() throws java.rmi.RemoteException {}

  public javax.ejb.EntityContext getEntityContext() {
    return entityContext;
  }

  public String getName() {
    return name;
  }
```
❺ **An attribute wrapped in an accessor**

```
  public Discussion getDiscussion(int discussionID)
    throws java.rmi.RemoteException {
    Discussion rcDiscussion = null;
    for (int i = 0; i < discussions.size(); i++) {
      Discussion thisDiscussion = (Discussion)discussions.elementAt(i);
      if (thisDiscussion.getDiscussionID() == discussionID) {
        rcDiscussion = thisDiscussion;
        break;
      }
    }
    return rcDiscussion;
```
❻ **Get a single BBS discussion from the board.**

```
    }
    private DiscussionHome getDiscussionHome() {
      if (discussionHome == null) {
        try {
          Properties env = entityContext.getEnvironment();
          String providerURL = env.getProperty("providerURL");
          String discussionHomeName = env.getProperty("discussionHomeName");

          Properties p = new Properties();

          p.put("java.naming.provider.url", providerURL);
          p.put("java.naming.factory.initial",
  "com.ibm.ejs.ns.jndi.CNInitialContextFactory");
          javax.naming.InitialContext ic  = new javax.naming.InitialContext(p);

          java.lang.Object homeObject = ic.lookup(discussionHomeName);
          discussionHome =
  (DiscussionHome)javax.rmi.PortableRemoteObject.narrow((
                  org.omg.CORBA.Object)homeObject,
                  DiscussionHome.class);
        } catch (Exception e) {
        }
      }
      return discussionHome;
    }

    public java.util.Collection getDiscussions() {
      return discussions;
    }

    public void removeDiscussion(Discussion discussion)
      throws RemoteException, RemoveException {
      for (int i = 0; i < discussions.size(); i++) {
        Discussion thisDiscussion = (Discussion)discussions.elementAt(i);
        if (thisDiscussion.isIdentical(discussion)) {
          discussions.remove(i);
          thisDiscussion.remove();
          break;
        }
      }
    }

    public void setEntityContext(javax.ejb.EntityContext ctx)
      throws java.rmi.RemoteException {
      entityContext = ctx;
    }

    public void unsetEntityContext()
      throws java.rmi.RemoteException {
      entityContext = null;
    }

}
```

❼ **We need the discussionHome's interfaces.**

❽ **Removes a discussion from the board.**

❶ This is the class for the implementation of our EJB. We have two major requirements:

- *Satisfy the* EntityBean *interface.* The compiler will enforce this rule.
- *Satisfy the interface of the remote interface.* This will be enforced by the EJB extensions.

❷ This adds a discussion to a board. This method satisfies the namesake in the remote interface. Note that the method signatures match exactly. This is a requirement, and is enforced by the EJB environment.

❸ Because we're satisfying an interface, all of the methods must be present, even if we don't use them.

❹ When our bean is added to the container, we'd like to be able to read all of the discussions in a board. We use discussionHome's interface to find all of the discussions in the board, and then we use the returned enumeration to populate our board. Likewise, we'll remove them when we remove the board EJB from the container.

❺ All of our attributes are wrapped with accessor methods. This practice makes it easier for us to provide remote interfaces and to consistently wrap services around the elements of our interface.

❻ This method finds a given discussion. Here, we simply scan the collection for the discussion that we want. No database access is required, because the container is managing that complexity for us.

❼ We need the discussionHome's interfaces to get the discussions related to a board. Since a home object is a named resource, we'll get a naming context and use it to find our discussionHome object. This type of method is called a *finder*.

❽ This method removes a discussion from the board.

Bean class for Discussion

Most of the code for the Discussion class is the same. Here are the interesting methods:

```
public int addPost(String author, java.util.Date date, String subject,
  String text) throws RemoteException, CreateException {
  int nextID = 0;
  for (int i = 0; i < posts.size(); i++) {
    Post post = (Post)posts.elementAt(i);
    int postID = post.getPostID();
    nextID = Math.max(nextID, postID+1);
  }
```

```
Post newPost = getPostHome().create(boardName, nextID, discussionID);
newPost.setAuthor(author);
newPost.setDate(new java.sql.Date(date.getTime()));
newPost.setSubject(subject);
newPost.setText(text);
posts.addElement(newPost);
return nextID;
}
```

First, in `addPost`, we need to play the same trick as earlier to find the maximum value. We don't have direct access to SQL aggregate functions, so we iterate through the board, looking for the largest element. Here, our IDs are relative to a post, so we pay only a modest penalty. A better implementation might be to include a unique ID generator. Many possible implementations exist. Next, let's look at how we load the EJB:

```
public void ejbLoad() throws java.rmi.RemoteException {
  try {
    java.util.Enumeration e =
      getPostHome().findAllForDiscussion(boardName, discussionID);
    posts = new java.util.Vector();
    while (e.hasMoreElements()) {
      posts.addElement(e.nextElement());
    }
  } catch (Exception e) {
    System.out.println(e.toString());
  }
}
```

We simply request to load all of the posts in a discussion. Then, we put them all into a vector called `posts`. This method is fired when the EJB is loaded into the container. Next, we have a finder for a post within the discussion:

```
public Post getPost(int postID) throws java.rmi.RemoteException {
  Post rcPost = null;
  for (int i = 0; i < posts.size(); i++) {
    Post thisPost = (Post)posts.elementAt(i);
    int thisID = thisPost.getPostID();
    if (thisID == postID) {
      rcPost = thisPost;
      break;
    }
  }
  return rcPost;
}
```

In this method, we iterate through the `posts` vector (populated in `EJBLoad`), and then return the one that has the specified ID. Finally, let's look at `remove`:

```
public void removePost(Post post) throws RemoteException, RemoveException
  {
  for (int i = 0; i < posts.size(); i++) {
    Post thisPost = (Post)posts.elementAt(i);
    if (thisPost.isIdentical(post)) {
      posts.remove(i);
      thisPost.remove();
      break;
    }
  }
}
```

Here, we remove a post from the discussion. We find the post by iterating through the vector. We then remove it, break, and return. You can find a complete version of the class at http://www.bitterjava.com.

The bean class for Post

The `PostBean` class is full of primarily getters and setters, so it's not as interesting as the earlier ones. To illustrate the concept, we'll show an attribute and the associated accessors:

```
  public String author;

public java.lang.String getAuthor() {
  return author;
}

public void setAuthor(java.lang.String newValue) {
  this.author = newValue;
}
```

This entity bean is a leaf node in our database. It doesn't have any additional collections; thus, the implementation is fairly bland. The container does almost everything for us, after some simple housekeeping. Again, you can find a complete version of the class at http://www.bitterjava.com.

8.2.5   *Defining the primary key*

Let's look at the primary key class for `boardBean`. The primary key class helps to identify the database fields that represent a true database primary key, which is a set of fields used to uniquely identify a row in a table. We'll see the definitions of equality, and as good citizens, whenever we override equality, we also should override hash code:

```
package com.bitterjava.bbs.ejb;

public class BoardKey implements java.io.Serializable {
  public java.lang.String name;
  final static long serialVersionUID = 3206093459760846163L;
```

```
public BoardKey() {
  super();
}

public BoardKey(java.lang.String argName) {
  name = argName;
}

public boolean equals(Object o) {
  if (o instanceof BoardKey) {
    BoardKey otherKey = (BoardKey) o;
    return ((this.name.equals(otherKey.name)));
  } else {
    return false;
  }
}

public int hashCode() {
  return (name.hashCode());
}
}
```

Of course, session beans do not need a primary key class.

We've looked at all of the Java interface and implementations for our model. We now need a deployment descriptor, which will be used to define the runtime behaviors and properties that the application server will need to deploy our object model.

8.2.6 *Creating a deployment descriptor*

Most environments create deployment descriptors automatically. Though VisualAge for Java can also create XML deployment descriptors, it's much easier to use the user interface to handle deployment details. Even so, we'll provide a portion of an example of a deployment descriptor for the refactored project shown in the upcoming section "Antipattern: Round-tripping." We chose this deployment descriptor because it also has a session bean, with a slightly different syntax:

```
<?xml version="1.0">
  <ejb-jar id="ejb-jar_ID">
    <description>Generated by Export Tool for
                 Enterprise Java Beans 1.1 version 1.0
                 from IBM VisualAge for Java version 4.0.
    </description>
    <display-name>BitterJavaEJBs</display-name>
```

This header information contains the XML version, a description of the bean, and the pretty name, suitable for display, for the EJBs in the archive file. The meat of the Java Archive (JAR) will follow.

```
<enterprise-beans>
   <entity id="Board">
      <ejb-name>Board</ejb-name>
      <home>com.bitterjava.bbs.ejb.BoardHome</home>
      <remote>com.bitterjava.bbs.ejb.Board</remote>
      <ejb-class>com.bitterjava.bbs.ejb.BoardBean</ejb-class>
      <persistence-type>Container</persistence-type>
      <prim-key-class>com.bitterjava.bbs.ejb.BoardKey
      </prim-key-class>
```

Here, we see the class names for the home, remote, bean class (ejb-class), EJB entity bean persistence type, and the primary key defined for Board.

```
      <reentrant>False</reentrant>
      <cmp-field id="Board_name">
         <field-name>name</field-name>
      </cmp-field>
      .
      .

      <env-entry id="EnvEntry_1">
         <env-entry-name>ejb10-properties/providerURL
         </env-entry-name>
         <env-entry-type>java.lang.String</env-entry-type>
         <env-entry-value>iiop://localhost:900
         </env-entry-value>
      </env-entry>
      .
      .

   </entity>
```

The Board description is one of the fields that we specified in our interface, followed by information that the detailed environment might need to manage the bean, such as properties and types. We have several similar fields and environment entries, which we've removed here for brevity. The full version is available at http://www.bitterjava.com:

```
      <session id="BoardManager">
         <ejb-name>BoardManager</ejb-name>
         <home>com.bitterjava.bbs.ejb.BoardFacadeHome</home>
         <remote>com.bitterjava.bbs.ejb.BoardManager</remote>
         <ejb-class>com.bitterjava.bbs.ejb.BoardFacadeBean
         </ejb-class>
         <session-type>Stateless</session-type>
         <transaction-type>Container</transaction-type>
```

Here, we have an entry for a session bean, which is the facade that we'll use in the refactoring exercise. A facade is a new interface layer that we'll place between the EJB client and server. Because it isn't an entity bean, there will be no fields or primary keys. We do have tags for the home, remote, and bean-class interfaces and implementations. We also have a tag showing that this bean is a session bean, and it implements the stateless session bean protocol from an EJB container.

```
<env-entry id="EnvEntry_5">
    <env-entry-name>ejb10-properties/postHomeName
    </env-entry-name>
    <env-entry-type>java.lang.String</env-entry-type>
    <env-entry-value>com/bitterjava/bbs/ejb/Post
    </env-entry-value>
</env-entry>
    .
    .

</enterprise-beans>
```

We then have environment entries for the bean, describing the parameter names in detail and providing descriptive information that we'll need to manage the bean. We omit similar descriptions for other session facade session beans, as well as our discussion and post entity beans.

```
<assembly-descriptor id="AssemblyDescriptor_ID">
    <container-transaction id="MethodTransaction_1">
        <method id="MethodElement_1">
            <ejb-name>Board</ejb-name>
            <method-name>*</method-name>
        </method>
        <trans-attribute>Required</trans-attribute>
    </container-transaction>
    .
    .

</assembly-descriptor>
</ejb-jar>
```

The assembly descriptor describes security roles (we don't have any here). The descriptor also includes transactional details. Since many different EJBs might have the same transactional and security details, they are broken out into a separate section so that they might be handled in a single pass.

8.2.7   *Using the model*

Conceptually, this model can be used in the place of our command model in the triangle architecture specified in chapter 3. We'd use the controller to provide entry points for various actions required by our user interface. In a high-performance environment, we'd typically deploy the EJB server on different hardware from the web application server. Such a deployment would force us to pay careful attention to the interface between the hardware containing our JSP and controller and the hardware containing our model. We'd have to populate the fields on our user interface through remote calls to our model. Such a design can hurt our performance, and it is our first bitter bean.

8.3 Antipattern: Round-tripping

As we populate our bulletin board remotely, we can quickly build up a staggering number of communications. To build a board, we also have to fetch the discussions in a board; to build a discussion, we have to build all of the posts in the discussion. This quickly leads to many remote communications that spin out of control. Indeed, one of the most common EJB antipatterns is called Round-tripping. Many EJB consultants have made a living going from customer to customer solving this problem, and preparing the same report that details causes and solutions. Though there may be many subtle differences, the causes for the most part are the same. EJB frameworks and environments make it easy to take an existing model, press a button, and spit out an EJB-centric object model. This model is then deployed on different hardware from the base web architecture. As the model is instantiated, the communication costs explode. Let's take a look at figure 8.4.

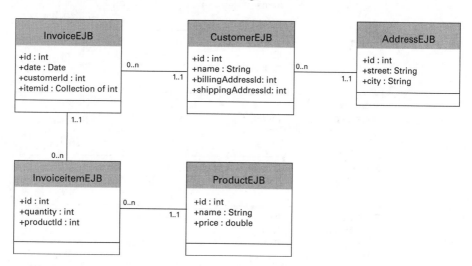

Figure 8.4 This ER diagram shows an object model for an invoice solution. We create an object model in a design tool or programming environment, press a button, and generate an EJB model. This model looks good, but if we deploy it as a distributed solution, it will not perform well.

8.3.1 *Computing the cost of a distributed deployment*

Figure 8.4 shows an ER diagram for a classic EJB implementation of an invoice solution. If we decide to deploy this solution with distributed entity beans, and if our controller and JSP are on the client, we'll need to populate the fields on our user interface based on the fields in the model. While single communication round-trips are not expensive, we have containment relationships that can get out of hand in a hurry. Table 8.2 shows the fields, multipliers, and costs associated with displaying a view of this model.

Table 8.2   Without a façade layer, individual fields must be accessed one at a time. If a field points to an object (such as Customer) or collection (such as Items), then those individual pieces must also be retrieved. These nested costs can multiply quickly. The costs for these composite fields are shown in bold.

Object	Contents	Number of round-trips	Total number of round-trips
Invoice	Id Date Customers Items	1 + 1 + **8** + **4N** =	 10+4N
Customer	Name ID Addresses	1 + 1 + **6** =	 8
Addresses (for 2 addresses)	Id Street City	2 + 2 + 2 =	 6
Items (for N items)	Quantity Products	1N + **3N** =	 4N
Products (for N items)	ID Name Price	1N + 1N + 1N =	 3N

To compute the total cost, it is best to go out to the leaf nodes and work back to the root object. Table 8.2 shows the leaf nodes at the bottom and works up to the root `Invoice` class. For the variable costs, we have three fields per product and one field in the item, for a total of four units per item. For the fixed costs, we have a customer with two addresses (eight fields), and two fixed fields on the invoice. The total cost is $10*4N$. That does not seem too bad, but let's look at some real-world numbers.

If we assume 50 milliseconds per network transaction, this is the cost of fetching a single invoice:

- For 1 invoice with 2 items
  - 18×50 mSec = 900 mSec—almost an entire second
- For 1 invoice with 20 items
  - 90×50 mSec = 4500 mSec—4.5 seconds

These times are relatively slow, but reasonable. However, it's probably unrealistic to expect our users to fetch a single invoice. In reality, they'll probably usually fetch several and drill down to the one they're seeking. The math for multiple invoices is grim:

- For 10 invoices with 2 items
  - 9000 mSec—9 seconds
- For 10 invoices with 20 items
  - 45 seconds!
- For 100 invoices with 20 items
  - 450 seconds, or 7.5 minutes

We aren't fetching too many bytes in any single instance; we're simply taking too many round-trips. Some might quibble with our assumptions, but if we allow users to fetch more than a single invoice at a time, this architecture won't hold up to even the most basic performance requirements. We have the same problem with our bulletin board example. Boards contain discussions that contain posts. We simply have to refactor.

8.3.2 Chatty interfaces

The UML sequence diagram is the perfect tool for identifying round-tripping. Figure 8.5 shows the sequence diagram for the Invoice example. We've combined the local EJB and its home for simplicity. In this case, we're looking at the interface between the EJBs and the view, since each of those method calls will be expensive distributed invocations. First, the controller issues a find to the invoice home, which triggers cascading finds on other EJBs. Next, we include get methods to populate our user interface. Let's assume that we're building a data bean in our controller that we'll pass to our JSP. Because we have accessor methods for all of the attributes that will fill the interface, we

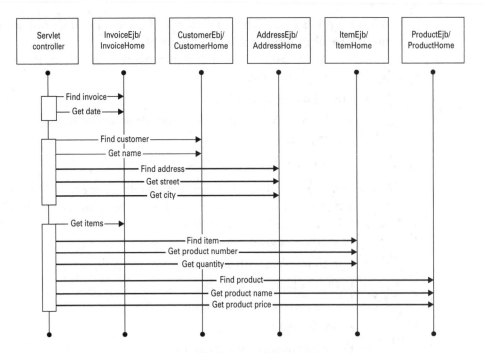

Figure 8.5   This sequence diagram graphically illustrates the round-tripping problem. We have a distributed interface between the controller and the EJB objects. The bold lines indicate places where we have significant looping. The UML sequence diagram is ideal for detecting round-tripping.

have a problem. Bold lines in the sequence diagram indicate looping, and we have a significant number of them. Ideally, we'd like to group all finds and gets together in a single distributed call. That way, all of the calls to the accessors will be local, giving us a significant performance boost. That is precisely the solution that we'll implement with the session facade.

8.3.3   Solution: Group together round-trips with a facade

To batch all of the round-trip calls in a chatty interface into a single collection and handle all of the work with a single conversation, we'll implement a facade. With this technique, we're creating a new layer with a formal interface in our architecture. We can use distributed commands for this purpose, but we can just as easily use stateless session beans. Figure 8.6 shows the impact of a facade.

What a difference a simple refactoring step can make! We've taken a design with several round-trips and boiled them down to one. The communication mechanism doesn't matter too much. We can wrap a variety of different

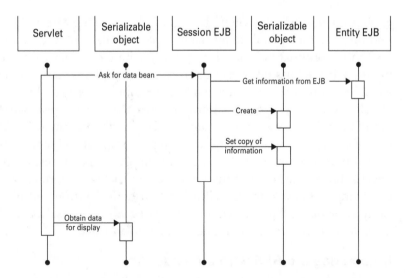

Figure 8.6   This sequence diagram is characteristic of the facade design pattern. The distributed interface appears just before the session EJB. Note that the communication is reduced to a single call. (Actually, one additional call at lower levels is required to initialize the communication with the stateless session bean.)

mechanisms with our command architecture, or we can use session EJBs. The key is to reduce chatty interfaces by collecting multiple communications around a single point.

8.3.4   *Roots of round-tripping*

As all beginners on the riverbanks watch, the pour-over cartwheels Eric's kayak several terrifying times before finally releasing him. Frantically, we fumble for ropes and throw one end uselessly behind him. Suddenly Eric rolls up, effortlessly, without his paddle. The beginners now see Eric's mishap in a different light: he didn't blunder over the pour-over--he aggressively fought the current to get his boat right in that monstrous maw in the river. He then bravely disdained his sole means of control and propulsion, as if to say, "I don't need a stinking paddle." He executed some carefully planned linked moves in the hydraulic, disengaged, and did an Eskimo roll, sans paddle. On this day, Eric is everyone's paddling idol.

When Eric went into his first rapid, he was equipped with a new tool: a hands Eskimo roll. It was an advanced technique that few had mastered, and one that gave him a false sense of security. He went into the rapid underequipped and overconfident. Though his roll worked in this instance, he knew it wouldn't be enough to guarantee his safety throughout his paddling career. Should he ever find the need for a paddle in his hands *after* his roll, he'd need to learn to apply his tools appropriately. Likewise, using distributed frameworks and development environments does save us from many implementation details, but it should not absolve us of understanding the tools that we employ.

The Round-tripping antipattern made database-stored procedures popular, even in the face of significant maintenance and design trade-offs. The performance costs for round-tripping were simply too great to ignore. This antipattern also doomed many CORBA and Smalltalk architectures, though we can refactor them with some of the same techniques that we present in this chapter. Many EJB environments allow us to use distribution and persistence as easily as we might flip a switch, but we *must also understand the implications of using that switch*. One such implication is performance.

8.3.5 Refactoring the BBS with a facade

We can think of our distributed interface as low-tech communication across a turbulent river. Each request for information must be written down on a piece of paper and carefully ferried across the dangerous river. We could tediously paddle every page across the river individually. Eventually, we might decide that we'd like to collect several papers together and take them all at once. We could simply wait for all of the papers related to a single request, box them, and take them on a single trip. We could box the entire response in the same way.

This is the approach that we'll take with the facade on our BBS example, allowing us to dramatically reduce our round-trip communications. We'll use a stateless session bean as a local client of our object model, instead of using the EJB objects directly from a JSP or controller object. We'll wrap the important public interfaces in the facade, called `BoardFacade`. Since this will be a stateless session bean, we won't have a primary key class, but we will have home and remote interfaces, a bean class, and a deployment descriptor.

The remote interface for BoardFacade

First, listing 8.4 contains the remote interface. We're collecting the methods for accessing the BBS application here. Because we don't want to expose the EJB entity bean implementation to our controller, our methods that return boards, discussions, or posts return primitive object types, and our collections return vectors. Otherwise, there are no surprises.

This facade provides three different ways to aggregate information in a single round-trip: We can specify a longer parameter list, use a compound object with many smaller atomic parts, or use a collection.

Listing 8.4   Buffering with a facade

```
package com.bitterjava.bbs.ejb;

public interface BoardFacade extends javax.ejb.EJBObject {

    Vector addPostToDiscussion(String boardName,
                         int discussionID,
                         com.bitterjava.bbs.ejb.Post post)
        throws javax.ejb.CreateException,
               java.rmi.RemoteException,
               javax.ejb.FinderException;

    Vector addDiscussionToBoard(String boardName, String discussionName)
        throws javax.ejb.CreateException,
               java.rmi.RemoteException,
               javax.ejb.FinderException;

    com.bitterjava.bbs.Board createBoard(String boardName)
        throws javax.ejb.CreateException,
               java.rmi.RemoteException,
               javax.ejb.FinderException;

    com.bitterjava.bbs.Board getBoard(String name)
        throws java.rmi.RemoteException, javax.ejb.FinderException;

    java.util.Vector getPostsInDiscussion(String boardName, int
    discussionID)
        throws java.rmi.RemoteException, javax.ejb.FinderException;

    java.util.Vector getDiscussionsInBoard(String boardName)
        throws java.rmi.RemoteException, javax.ejb.FinderException;

    void removeBoard(String boardName)
        throws java.rmi.RemoteException,
               javax.ejb.RemoveException,
               javax.ejb.FinderException;

    Vector removePostFromDiscussion(String boardName,
                         int discussionID,
                         com.bitterjava.bbs.ejb.Post post)
        throws java.rmi.RemoteException,
               javax.ejb.FinderException,
               javax.ejb.RemoveException;

    Vector removeDiscussionFromBoard(String boardName, Discussion
    discussion)
        throws java.rmi.RemoteException,
               javax.ejb.FinderException,
               javax.ejb.RemoveException;

}
```

❶ Buffering in the parameter list

❷ Buffering with a collection

❸ Buffering with a composite object collection

❶ This interface uses all three techniques to aggregate information, but we are most interested in the parameter list. In this list, we have a `boardName` and `discussionID`. We also have a collection of attributes that we bind together with a `post` object that is nothing more than a collection of fields. In the original interface, we needed to make several method calls, whereas this interface uses just one. We can use this technique to collect several sets into a composite interface with a single method call. The command interface uses this approach by having many local set calls, a distributed `execute` call, followed again by local `gets`.

❷ This interface illustrates the use of a collection to aggregate many round-trips into one. We'd normally have to make a round-trip for every object in the vector. Instead, with this interface, we retrieve a single buffer that has many objects. We also collect many different `get` calls into a single interface, because we'd normally have to use the remote accessors for each of the attributes. Instead, we call once.

❸ This interface demonstrates the collection of several round-trips with a single composite object. In this example, we have three composite objects.

This is the object for the board:

```
package com.bitterjava.bbs;

public class Board implements java.io.Serializable {
  private java.lang.String name;
  private java.util.Collection discussions;

  public java.lang.String getName() {
    return name;
  }

  public java.util.Collection getDiscussions() {
    return discussions;
  }

  public void setName(String name) {
    this.name = name;
  }

  public void setDiscussions(java.util.Vector discussions) {
    this.discussions = discussions;
  }
}
```

We aren't interested in encapsulating any behaviors here, since our behaviors are captured in our model. We simply need a helper class so that we can organize all of the different parameters in our interface.

The home interface for BoardFacade

Since we have a session bean, the home interface is extremely simple, having only the `create` method:

```
package com.bitterjava.bbs.ejb;

public interface BoardFacadeHome extends javax.ejb.EJBHome {

  com.bitterjava.bbs.ejb.BoardFacade create()
    throws javax.ejb.CreateException, java.rmi.RemoteException;
}
```

The bean class for BoardFacade

This class has the implementation of the two previous interfaces. We'll see this facade interact with all three of the EJBs. We simply have to pass requests straight through the facade to the EJB interface.

Let's look at some of the method implementations in our facade solution. I've chosen a representative set of the implementation but left off some of the similar implementations and much of the exception management for brevity. For the full implementation, go to http://www.bitterjava.com.

```
package com.bitterjava.bbs.ejb;

import java.rmi.RemoteException;
import java.security.Identity;
import java.util.Properties;
import javax.ejb.*;

public class BoardFacadeBean implements SessionBean {
  private javax.ejb.SessionContext mySessionCtx = null;
  final static long serialVersionUID = 3206093459760846163L;

  private static BoardHome boardHome = null;
  private static DiscussionHome discussionHome = null;
  private static PostHome postHome = null;
```

We use these three instance variables as convenient placeholders for our home interfaces, where we have our finders and the life cycle methods. We expose several of them within our interface.

```
  public java.util.Vector addPostToDiscussion(String boardName,
                                              int discussionID,
                                              Post post)
    throws RemoteException, FinderException, CreateException {

  Discussion discussion = getDiscussionHome().findByPrimaryKey(
                   new DiscussionKey(boardName, discussionID));
    discussion.addPost(post.getAuthor(),
               post.getDate(),
               post.getSubject(),
```

```
                    post.getText());
     return getPostsInDiscussion(boardName, discussionID);
  }
```

In this method, we add a post to a discussion. We first find the home interface for the discussion and execute a finder by primary key. We then add a post with this interface. Note that we have conveniently collected all of the elements of the post within a small helper object called post, to help simplify the interface.

```
public com.bitterjava.bbs.Board getBoard(String name)
  throws java.rmi.RemoteException, FinderException {

    com.bitterjava.bbs.ejb.Board boardEjb =
      getBoardHome().findByPrimaryKey(new BoardKey(name));
    return marshallDataObject(boardEjb);
  }
```

Here, we use a technique to convert an EJB to one of our helper objects. We use one of three marshallDataObject methods. An example is shown further here.

```
private BoardHome getBoardHome() {
  if (boardHome == null) {
    try {
      Properties env = mySessionCtx.getEnvironment();
      String providerURL = env.getProperty("providerURL");
      String boardHomeName = env.getProperty("boardHomeName");
      Properties p = new Properties();
      p.put("java.naming.provider.url", providerURL);
      p.put("java.naming.factory.initial",
            "com.ibm.ejs.ns.jndi.CNInitialContextFactory");
      javax.naming.InitialContext ic  =
        new javax.naming.InitialContext(p);

      java.lang.Object homeObject = ic.lookup(boardHomeName);
      boardHome = (BoardHome) javax.rmi.PortableRemoteObject.narrow(
        (org.omg.CORBA.Object)homeObject, BoardHome.class);
    } catch (Exception e) {}
  }
  return boardHome;
}
```

The Java home objects are named resources, so we can find them through the naming context and the JNDI interface. Many of these property values are established in our deployment descriptors.

```
Vector getPostsInDiscussion(String boardName, int discussionID)
  throws java.rmi.RemoteException, javax.ejb.FinderException {

  java.util.Vector posts = new java.util.Vector();
  try {
```

```
    java.util.Enumeration e = getPostHome().findAllForDiscussion(
                              boardName, discussionID);
    while (e.hasMoreElements()) {
      java.lang.Object o = e.nextElement();
      com.bitterjava.bbs.ejb.Post postEjb = resolvePost(o);
      com.bitterjava.bbs.Post post = marshallDataObject(postEjb);
      posts.addElement(post);
    }
  } catch (NullPointerException e) {}

  return posts;
}
```

In this method, we're collecting all of the posts in a single discussion. The while loop in bold would have been executed right on an interface boundary in our original design. The original methods that performed the tasks of the methods in italics were all distributed in our original design.

```
private com.bitterjava.bbs.Board marshallDataObject(Board boardEjb)
  throws RemoteException {

  com.bitterjava.bbs.Board board = new com.bitterjava.bbs.Board();
  board.setName(boardEjb.getName());

  java.util.Vector discussions = new java.util.Vector();
  java.util.Collection discussionEjbs = boardEjb.getDiscussions();
  java.util.Iterator iter = discussionEjbs.iterator();
  while (iter.hasNext()) {
    java.lang.Object o = iter.next();
    com.bitterjava.bbs.ejb.Discussion discussionEjb =
resolveDiscussion(o);
    com.bitterjava.bbs.Discussion discussion =
marshallDataObject(discussionEjb);
    discussions.addElement(discussion);
  }
  board.setDiscussions(discussions);
  return board;
}
```

Here, we're taking an EJB object and creating generic data objects from a collection of EJBs. This approach provides a helper for generic data objects, so that we can easily hide the implementation of our model.

```
private Post resolvePost(Object o) {
  return (Post)javax.rmi.PortableRemoteObject.narrow(
    (org.omg.CORBA.Object)o, Post.class);
  }
}
```

This method helps us resolve the remote address of the object passed to our method.

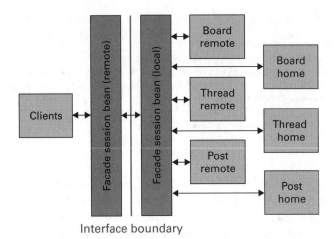

Figure 8.7   This facade will dramatically reduce our round-tripping. We've consolidated the interfaces of six different classes down to a single facade interface. Further, the individual methods are much more coarse, so one method will perform many smaller operations. For example, one method gets all of the discussions in a board with one single call, returning a vector.

This completes our facade implementation of our BBS. Figure 8.7 shows the result. We have our base EJB model with home and remote interfaces. We use a facade object to hide those interfaces and to present a local interface to our EJB. The application will do less round-tripping for the EJB layer and provide much better performance.

A good facade

Like any other interface, a good facade is an art form. We'd like to build a logical grouping of methods into a single facade; it's foolish to build an interface across too many separate facades. Instead, we should design a logical packaging that will make sense to our users. Where transactional issues exist, the facade should use the capabilities of the session beans to manage the transactional logic. A good facade is not a haphazard implementation.

8.4   *Antipattern: Square Bean in a Round Hole*

In *AntiPatterns*, the authors presented an antipattern called the Golden Hammer. This is what they had to say about the anecdotal evidence:

"I have a hammer and everything else is a nail." "Our database is our architecture." "Maybe we shouldn't have used Excel macros for this job after all."

For EJBs, the Golden Hammer is usually the entity bean with container-managed persistence. This is also the EJB classification with the most overhead. If every object in our model is a container-managed entity bean, we might want to hunker down behind the desk to prepare for the deluge of customer complaints about performance. We should instead limit the use of entity beans to problems that need them. The characteristics of this EJB classification are:

- *Transactional.* The application should have transactional characteristics. Entity beans will maintain their value after a crash, and they will also maintain transactional integrity. Such functionality is valuable, but it comes at a cost.

- *Persistent.* This is the most obvious of the characteristics. None of the examples in this chapter require you to write a single line of database code. The container will do all of that for you.

- *Shared.* We can share the same model across many different users, which is one of the founding concepts of EJBs.

These characteristics are incredibly valuable. Distributed, transactional, shared, and persistent architectures that used to take years can be developed in mere months. The danger is that entity beans become our Golden Hammer.

In the coming section, we'll break form slightly. We'll show a series of mini-antipatterns followed by solutions. In the first, we will show that we can also go overboard with our entity beans.

8.4.1   *Mini-antipattern: Bean-Managed Joins*

My first question when I saw that I could create entity beans with bean-managed persistence was, "Why would I?" Isn't that like ordering a hamburger without the meat? "Yes, I'm ready to order. I'll have a persistence framework, hold the persistence." Like any framework, Java's bean-managed persistence handles some problems better than others. For example, join algorithms are handled more quickly in the database engine.

The first mini-antipattern involves processing a join, but outside the database engine. A *database join* is the process of combining two sets of database rows by merging all database rows where selected fields in two different tables match. Database engines are highly optimized and process joins many times faster than we can. One common place that entity bean solutions can encounter application joins is with reporting. Because reports often present renormalized (joined) data, container-managed entity beans can lead to implementations that perform poorly.

One-to-many joins occur frequently with object models. For example, when we build the invoice in figure 8.4, container-managed persistence would be forced to process several joins in our application.

Reporting can often be best handled outside the realm of EJBs, perhaps with a view. Too many entity beans can lead to application joins and to the next problem. One particularly common problem is the creation of relationship EJBs. DBAs create relationship tables in a database environment, but in the EJB domain, relationship objects can lead to too many joins and poor performance.

8.4.2 Solution: Views, mappers, bean-managed joins

One painful solution to entity bean joins is to measure performance and make improvements where significant problems surface. We can use bean-managed joins in those problem areas and then code the database joins manually. This solution tends to break the portability of a solution between databases, but good attention to open SQL programming can alleviate this concern.

A more elegant alternative is to provide a view and use a facade instead of an entity bean. Or you can use object relational mapping software, such as WebGain's TopLink. These solutions allow objects with complex relationships to be saved and restored efficiently.

8.4.3 Mini-antipattern: Entity Beans for Lightweight Functions

If a method simply returns a list, there may be times we should go right to the database rather than use a full-blown EJB model. For our BBS, the list of boards is a perfect example. Extending our model to load full boards when all we need is a list of board names is extremely heavy-handed.

Instead, we can simply add a JDBC interface to our facade. It's an easy extension to make. This method signature is added to the remote interface, which is added to `BoardFacade.java`:

```
java.util.List getBoardNames() throws java.rmi.RemoteException;
```

Listing 8.5 contains the implementation, which is added to `BoardFacade-Bean.java`.

Listing 8.5 Use JDBC instead of a full entity bean for lightweight problems

```
public java.util.List getBoardNames() throws java.rmi.RemoteException {

  java.util.Vector names = new java.util.Vector();
  java.sql.Connection conn = null;
  java.sql.PreparedStatement stmt = null;
  java.sql.ResultSet rs = null;
  try {
    conn = getPooledConnection();
    String sqlString = "SELECT DB2ADMIN.BOARD.NAME AS NAME" +
                       " FROM DB2ADMIN.BOARD";
    stmt = conn.prepareStatement(sqlString);
    rs = stmt.executeQuery();
    marshalBoardNames(rs, names);
  } catch (Exception e) {
    throw new RemoteException("Database exception: " + e);
  } finally {
    if (rs != null) {
      try { rs.close();
      } catch (java.sql.SQLException e) {
      }
    }
    if (stmt != null) {
      try {
        stmt.close();
      } catch (java.sql.SQLException e) {
      }
    }
    if (conn != null) {
      try {
        conn.close();
      } catch (java.sql.SQLException e) {
      }
    }
  }
  return names;

}
```

● **We use a pooled connection (chapter 7).**

● **Cleanup is in finally (chapter 7).**

This approach lets us return a simple list of board names without having to load all the board EJBs, which would do much more work than we need. We may choose instead to extend our model to keep things consistent, but this option is available as a performance optimization. A scary number of entity beans do nothing but provide a simple reference table. In this case, the EJB implementation will be more difficult and will provide much more capability than we need. For reference tables, we don't have to map a full object model on a relational database. We have no need for the robust transactional support, either. It's much better to build a light implementation with a more basic technology.

8.4.4 Mini-antipattern: Entities for Read Only

A more specialized case of the Entity Beans for Lightweight Functions antipattern is the large list that is read but not written. In some cases, we have stable data that will seldom (or never) change. In these cases, a full entity bean is overkill. Some examples of objects that are read but not written are lists of states in a nation, cities in states, tax tables, and ZIP codes. In these cases, we can use a session bean like the one in the previous section as a lightweight wrapper around a database table. Or we may decide to load such data into a shared hash table once in a client-side cache.

8.4.5 Mini-antipattern: Entity Beans for Write but Not Read

Believe it or not, occasionally we might need to record data that will probably never be read. That concept seems strange to me, but there are examples of data that should be recorded, where the *expected case* is that the data will never be accessed. Transaction logs, audit files, and system logs are good examples of this type of data.

Clearly, the use of entity beans is overkill for these situations; a more primitive construct than a database is called for. We should optimize the expected case: writing the data. We may opt for file services, since the data organization doesn't need to be optimized for frequent random access.

8.4.6 Troublesome scrollable lists

Scrollable lists present interesting challenges to EJB developers. Instead of returning an entire list, many web pages display some subset of the result and allow users to navigate the entire list with links. The problem is that the list can change while the user navigates the list. If we do a full database query every time to populate the list, performance can suffer. For this reason, management of such a request can be difficult.

The stateful session bean is ideal for this type of problem. When model-related conversation state (the list contents) is required only for the duration of a session, a stateful session is a better candidate. This bean can serve as a facade, and the list data and user's current location in the list can be stored in the bean. Implementations vary, and some implementations may prove problematic in solutions deploying application server clusters. Capabilities in this area are changing rapidly, so check with your vendor to be sure.

8.4.7   *Overall solution: Pick the right bean for the job*

Table 8.3 shows the different EJB classifications, the general characteristics of appropriate solutions, and a list of problems that it can solve. Doubtlessly, EJBs will continue to evolve, and the imbedded services such as container-managed persistence and session states will become more robust. Table 8.3 describes the state of the art, as we understand it today.

Table 8.3 This table shows each EJB classification, with a generic description of the types of problems that it can solve. The last classification is not an EJB, but is used to categorize solutions that are not well suited for EJBs.

EJB classification	Description	Solution examples
Entity beans (container managed)	Transactional, shared, persistent. Simple object relationships.	Server-side persistent object models.
Entity beans (bean managed)	Transactional, shared, persistent. Complex object relationships.	Optimizations for the above, with relational joins, or persistence to other data stores.
Stateless session beans	Transactional distributed access without state requirements.	Adding transactional integrity to a method or procedure. Adding a facade to consolidate interfaces across major interface boundaries.
Stateful session beans	Transactional, distributed access with limited conversational state requirements, within the bounds of a single session.	Saving session state. Scrolling through large, multi-part lists.
None	Not necessarily transactional, persistent, shared, or secure. All aspects of an application that *do not* have compelling reasons to be EJBs should not be EJBs. This is the default implementation.	Log and property files. Quick hitters that do not belong in the model. Nontransactional data. User interface–related aspects of the application.

8.5   *Mini-antipattern: Everything Is an EJB*

After interviewing five consultants and programmers for this book, I discovered that the one common antipattern was the application of EJBs to trivial problems. This antipattern is a more direct example of the Golden Hammer antipattern. Each consultant had an example of bright programmers using this advanced technology to build simple applications. One gave an example of a three-tier EJB application built to display a few time sheets. Another had a team who used EJBs to build read-only reports that used a single database table. Many saw customers replace working, robust applications built on solid, well-suited technologies simply to stay current (a nebulous benefit under the best of circumstances). EJBs can help save us from complex details of persistence, transaction integrity, security, and distribution—at a price. If our application doesn't need the capability, our costs will quickly outpace our benefits. An application should have many of these characteristics to be considered an EJB candidate:

- *Complexity.* If the problem is not complex, the effort and overhead should steer us toward a simpler architecture.
- *Persistence.* Sometimes, a persistence framework can simplify an application significantly. Still, other persistence solutions, such as databases or even files, may be more appropriate for simpler solutions.
- *Stringent transactional integrity requirements.* Building robust transactional applications takes effort, especially for persistent distributed applications.
- *Distributed or multitiered deployment requirements.* Stand-alone applications usually won't have the complexity or sophistication to mandate EJBs.
- *A complex, shared object model.* At a cost, EJBs provide the ability of layering an understandable object model over legacy systems and sharing that model across many users.

When few of these conditions are present, it is unlikely that EJBs will provide enough benefit to outweigh the performance and development costs. I am confident that many programmers will continue to use them anyway.

8.6 EJBs and caching

Programmers often use a design pattern called the ValueObject, which works like a small spot-cache to reduce round-tripping. Programming ValueObjects can be tedious and they must be coded for every instance, so a programmer may neglect them when working under a tight schedule. I prefer to spend more time on a general-purpose or a prepackaged cache.

When EJB application servers are deployed on major system boundaries, they too are targets for caching. This problem is unique to the EJB client machine. Because the model can keep data resident between calls, the cache between the EJB model and database is usually not necessary at the EJB server. Further, since many EISs have aggressive caching built in, a cache upstream of the EJB is generally not necessary. Nevertheless, we could benefit from a cache in certain circumstances:

- Models that don't use entity beans or stateful session beans are possible targets for a client-side and server-side cache, depending on the factors outlined in chapter 5, in the section "Solution 2: Cache commands."

- If the controller and JSP are deployed on separate hardware, the interface between the controller and the facade is an appropriate place for a cache. See the next section, "Implementing a cache with a facade," for details.

- For some EISs, such as transaction monitors, a cache can provide performance boosts *upstream* of the EJB server.

8.6.1 Implementing a cache with a facade

In this chapter, we have not yet considered a cache between the EJB server and the web application server. If we decide to deploy both the EJB server and the web application server on the same box, we won't need a cache. With other deployments, a cache will almost certainly provide some performance benefits by reducing the communication between the EJB client and server boxes. Let's look at three caching alternatives.

Command pattern within a session bean

One solution is to implement the Command design pattern with a session bean. This interface would be easy to cache for the same reasons as our original command: a series of set methods for input parameters, an initialize method to establish connections and do validations, an execute method to access the model, and a series of get methods to obtain the results of the command. We'd have a built-in key in a concatenation of the set parameters of the command interface, and a consistent place for the cache implementation in the `execute` method. With this approach, we can automate cached command generation with some careful thought and planning.

A cache between the facade and the controller

A second possibility is to design the facade to return atomic objects and collections that are easily cacheable, and then add appropriate hash and key fields to the returned objects. This approach is manual, but it can result in clear, elegant interfaces.

A distributed command

The Command pattern is very well suited to a distributed architecture. IBM has some of the best practical guides and papers on this topic. One book that has outstanding ideas for general architecture, although presented in a Web-Sphere context, is called *Design and Implement Servlets, JSPs, and EJBs for Web-Sphere*. Distributed commands give us a smaller, tighter footprint than a session bean, less overhead per communication, and integrated keys and attachment points for a cache. The downside is that this approach will probably mandate a proprietary implementation, though some promising work—such as the action objects of the Jakarta Struts framework—is moving the ball forward.

The key to success with EJBs is not to get lazy and expect the frameworks to guess our intentions and optimize for us. We can choose a number of successful approaches, and should not lose sight of the impact of a cache as a first line of defense for a distributed interface.

8.7   Smoothing out the bitter beans

In this chapter, we've reviewed the basics of EJBs. They are implemented as components that go into a container, which provides such important services as support for transactions, persistence, and security. The EJB architecture is distributed and uses the stub-based approach, similar to CORBA. You learned that there are two major classifications: session beans and entity beans. Session beans come in stateless and stateful varieties, and entity beans have persistence that is managed either by the container or the bean itself.

Of the antipatterns that we examined, the worst was Round-tripping. We looked at an example that showed how complex object relationships can have a multiplier effect that can bring system performance to its knees. We did reveal a silver bullet that can kill this beast: the facade. We can wrap a chatty interface with a facade that combines many different round-trips into one, saving network traffic and boosting performance significantly.

The rest of the antipatterns in the chapter relate to the type of EJB used to solve a particular problem. EJB entity beans in particular are like golden hammers, and the whole world looks like a nail. Also, there may be situations where we use bean-managed persistence or a relational mapping tool to optimize performance, session beans to reduce overhead, or stateful session beans for a lighter approach to keeping session-duration conversations. The key to the successful use of EJBs is not to be lulled to complacency by the ease of implementation and pay attention to performance concerns.

8.8   *Antipatterns in this chapter*

These are the templates for the antipatterns that appear in this chapter. They provide an excellent summary format and form the basis of the cross-references in appendix A.

Round-tripping

- RELATED ANTIPATTERNS: The Cacheless Cow. Some specializations of this antipattern exist. Lack of a cache can also cause round-tripping.

- DESCRIPTION: Round-tripping occurs when a chatty interface falls on a distributed boundary. For EJBs, a client (usually a controller or JSP) accesses the remote interface of a distributed entity bean. Since an entity bean usually exposes many fields and sometimes collections, this results in many round-trip communications, absolutely murdering performance.

- MOST FREQUENT SCALE: Application.

- REFACTORED SOLUTION NAME: The Facade.

- REFACTORED SOLUTION TYPE: Software.

- REFACTORED SOLUTION DESCRIPTION: The most common solution to this problem is the facade. This interface is implemented with a distributed call, like a session bean. The interface combines many chatty communications into a single, consolidated call.

- TYPICAL CAUSES: A common cause is the use of major frameworks like EJBs near interface boundaries without modification.

- SYMPTOMS, CONSEQUENCES: Applications are slow.

- **ALTERNATIVE SOLUTIONS:** The distributed command can also be used to control round-tripping. Also, refactoring can frequently shift an interface so that logical tasks are grouped together into a single physical round-trip. Other alternatives can help performance. A cache can help after the first load. (Often, both a cache and facade are desired.) The EJB can also be deployed on the same box, though many times, strong reasons motivate separation.

Round Bean in a Square Hole

RELATED ANTIPATTERNS: The Golden Hammer, in *AntiPatterns*.

DESCRIPTION: Many times, a classification of EJB is used inappropriately. Several different variations of this problem exist. A complex object relationship may fit bean-managed persistence better than container-managed persistence. In other cases, a problem may not require the full support of an entity bean. Similarly, entity beans may be overkill for applications that exclusively read or write.

MOST FREQUENT SCALE: Microarchitecture.

REFACTORED SOLUTION NAME: Use the Correct EJB for the Job.

REFACTORED SOLUTION TYPE: Software.

REFACTORED SOLUTION DESCRIPTION: The correct bean should be employed for the application:

- For applications having a relationship corresponding to a relational join (one to many or n-ary relationships), frequently an entity bean with bean-managed persistence should be employed.

- For lightweight functions, session beans have much less overhead than entity beans.

- For write-only applications like system logs or audit trails, files or JDBC may be the best choice.

- For read-only applications, session beans with JDBC or SQLJ could be better choices.

ROOT CAUSES: Inexperience or apathy.

ANECDOTAL EVIDENCE: "This development environment builds the whole model for me automatically. I don't even have to think."

SYMPTOMS, CONSEQUENCES: Applying the wrong bean to a problem leads to ugly designs or poor performance.

ALTERNATIVE SOLUTIONS: Other layers, like relational mappers, can automatically manage entity beans with complex relationships.

Everything Is an EJB

RELATED ANTIPATTERNS: The Golden Hammer, in *AntiPatterns*.

DESCRIPTION: This is the generic form of the Round Bean in a Square Hole antipattern. If a problem is not well suited, an EJB solution is likely to be too difficult or poorly performing.

MOST FREQUENT SCALE: Micro-architecture.

REFACTORED SOLUTION NAME: Apply EJBs Appropriately.

REFACTORED SOLUTION TYPE: Software.

REFACTORED SOLUTION DESCRIPTION: EJBs should be used only where they provide significant value, and the problem domain has complexity that warrants a distributed, transactional architecture. See the section "Everything Is an EJB" for more details.

ROOT CAUSES: Inexperience or apathy.

SYMPTOMS, CONSEQUENCES: Using entity beans for everything is too heavy-handed, and has common performance consequences.

ALTERNATIVE SOLUTIONS: Simpler, lower-level technologies such as JDBC and servlets can work.

Part 3

The big picture

As the years went by, we found ourselves running more serious rivers. We also learned to appreciate the bigger picture. Class IV+ Wilson's Creek is a short, very steep run. Driving a road high above the creek along its full length, we weren't able to see any fine detail, but we could identify geology changes that marked the most serious rapids. We could observe features from the car that we couldn't see from the cockpit of the boat. We later used that knowledge because steep canyon walls on either side prevented us from scouting the hardest rapid from river level.

In chapters 9 through 11, we'll look at Java antipatterns at a higher level, in a broader context. In chapter 9, we'll explore programming hygiene and its surprising impact on antipatterns. In chapter 10, we'll take a look at some antipatterns affecting scalability and performance. Some are related to process, and others to programming or architecture. In chapter 11, I'll offer some parting thoughts about antipatterns in the Java community.

Some programmers will wonder why higher level topics such as hygiene and performance belong in this book at all, while I've left out issues such as security, usability, and other deployment concerns. Early on, I was struck by the tight connection between low-level server-side antipatterns and these topics. To this end, I included the hygiene chapter and placed it late in the book so that you could view the rules with related antipatterns fresh in your mind. I also included the performance chapter so you could learn to deal with performance issues at a higher level. I didn't consider usability because of its loose relationship with server-side programming and relative independence from

Java. Similarly, many security concerns are determined beneath the level of the programming standards (at the HTTPS level). Others are either too specific or addressed as deployment issues. I left deployment details for another book to allow me to focus on Java application development details. The compromises weren't easy, but I hope you can appreciate the result.

Bitter hygiene

_9_

I am in Colorado, looking at a quarter-mile-long, class V+ rapid called Pine Creek. I prefer the steeper, tighter runs of the East to these powerful western rapids, but here I am. Neither my friends nor I have run anything so dangerous, technical, and demanding. We all decide to portage the first and most difficult part of the rapid and maybe the rest as well. The crucial move is an S-turn around some massive turbulence called the Pine Creek Hole. The Hole regularly traps kayaks and even larger craft with dire consequences for some. The 30-foot hydraulic can be fatal. We ultimately decide to put in just below the Hole.

After staring at the hydraulic from 50 feet up, we decide that the rest of the rapid's features look relatively placid. As we shoulder the boats down to river level, we find that the mind-numbing size of Pine Creek Hole has biased our perception of the rest of the rapid. Before our eyes, the Class IV rapid that we expect slowly morphs into an expert-level Class V-. The 5-foot wave trains we expected are twice as high. The numerous little 3-foot drops have grown to 8 feet.

Feeling confident in my ability and the ample space to avoid dangerous obstacles, I get into my boat and start my run. As I approach the fourth massive wave in the initial train, I flip. I've never had to execute a roll in such violent conditions before, but with the power and speed of the river this time, swimming could be disastrous. Submerged under a large wave I hold my breath for what seems to be forever, waiting for my chance to roll.

9.1   Why study programming hygiene?

Why should we even consider something as banal as coding standards in *Bitter Java*? Shouldn't we leave this tedious subject to be covered in coding guidelines buried on a server or team leader's desk? In the past, I'd have been the last person to write a chapter about coding style guidelines, but my recent programming experiences have convinced me of their value. In many cases, bad Java can be traced directly to bad form. Good programming hygiene keeps intentions clear, makes it easier to share a code base, and enables efficient refactoring.

In this chapter, we'll review some of the coding conventions we've discussed so far in *Bitter Java*. We'll also examine common hygiene-related missteps, and we'll provide a helpful set of conventions. Finally, we'll present a real-world style guide and a summary of coding standards.

9.1.1   Extreme programming requires good hygiene

My experience at allmystuff with extreme programming (XP) convinced me of the value of good coding standards. XP has a small number of rules that make possible powerful improvements in programming cycle time, deliverable quality, and project success. Many of these rules, outlined in table 9.1, demand that you pay close attention to programming hygiene. For example, in XP the entire code base is shared, and programmers have to follow strict conventions so that anyone on the team can quickly read any line of code. Another rule is that programming is done in pairs, which means teammates must agree on such mundane issues as brace, tab, and comment treatments. Frequent refactoring mandates consistent style so that code fragments can move throughout the code base freely. Readability is shattered if programmers ignore these common conventions.

Table 9.1 Extreme programming (XP) requires good programming hygiene to work effectively.

XP Rule	XP Rule Value	XP Hygiene Requirements
Program to common standards.	Standards are required for refactoring as a team. See the next row.	Enough said.
Refactor mercilessly.	The cost of maintaining and fixing poorly designed code dwarfs the cost of refactoring.	Refactoring often involves moving code fragments throughout the code base. For the style to be uniform, all must observe common standards.
Share the entire code base.	The correct solutions can be developed without regard to ownership or "turf wars."	If many different teams can touch a class, only common standards can keep the style uniform.
Move people around.	Programmers have better focus and motivation. Losing one person will not doom a project.	Changing responsibilities also changes the set of classes that a team will affect.
Program in pairs.	Tunnel vision is avoided, and bugs are caught early.	Both programmers must agree on standards.
Value simplicity.	Simple is usually sufficient, and is much easier. Cycle times are much shorter.	Many coding conventions promote simplicity.

9.1.2   *Coding standards protect against antipatterns*

While coding standards protect against antipatterns, some antipatterns cannot survive good hygiene. Take the Lapsed Listener and Leak Collection antipatterns from chapter 6 and the Split Cleaner antipattern from chapter 7. Adhering to two simple coding standards helps diffuse each of these antipatterns:

- Ensure that every added resource or registration has a corresponding remove.

- Place resource requests and releases in close proximity, and in the same method if possible. Also place collection adds and removes in close proximity. Many of the antipatterns are refactored much more easily when we also apply common coding standards.

We can often take things a step further by using coding standards as a weapon against antipatterns. Figure 9.1 shows a process we can apply when fighting antipatterns. We start with isolated problems. In isolation, a bug or poor design does not rise to the level of an antipattern. When we have enough occurrences to cause concern, we document an antipattern. We refactor the generic antipattern, and then publish a guide that demonstrates how to refactor existing occurrences. Programmers use the antipattern and refactoring guide to identify and fix existing occurrences. We then put protective measures in place to prevent the problems from occurring. This is where coding standards can help. Coding standards range from formatting and style to usage guidelines or even light structural guidelines. In many cases, these guidelines can gently steer us away from antipatterns. They are also a convenient collection point for these types of remedies.

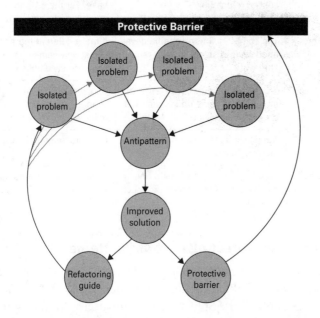

Figure 9.1 Effective use of antipatterns requires a process. In this one, when isolated incidents occur with sufficient frequency, they are used to document a generic antipattern. The refactored antipattern is used to build a guide for repairing existing problems, and to stimulate protective measures.

Now that we've reviewed the roles that coding hygiene can play in process and antipatterns, we'll dive into some specific examples. The next portion of this chapter will discuss antipatterns related to hygiene. These are actually groupings of many smaller mini-antipatterns, followed by a set of standards that can defeat them.

9.2   *Mini-antipatterns: Unreadable code*

In this section, we'll make a case for a class of standards that improve the readability of code. The benefit seems nebulous, but most experienced programmers understand the need. Mismatched quotes, comments, or braces have bitten almost all programmers at one time or another. Almost anyone who has done significant maintenance has been forced to deal with inconsistent style, poor commenting, or comments that do not match the code. True, readability is subjective, but the need for common, consistent standards is not.

9.2.1   *Names matter*

Good style communicates. If an application is designed with good object and method names, a story emerges that tells us exactly what is happening. Consider the fragments shown in listing 9.1.

Listing 9.1   Good and bad naming

This program illustrates the impact of good naming and bad naming. The first example, without comments, reads like a story. The second ... doesn't.

```
// good             ❶ Code with good naming communicates.

PurchaseOrder.setCustomer(shoppingCart.getCustomer());
purchaseOrder.setItems(shoppingCart.getItems());
purchaseOrder.totalCost = purchaseOrder.addLineItems()+
                          purchaseOrder.getTax()+
                          purchaseOrder.getShippingCost();
purchaseOrder.finalizePurchase();

// bad              ❷ Code with bad naming is hard to read.

po.setOther(sc.getOther());
po.setVector(sc.getVector(contents));
po.tc = po.addAll()+po.tax()+po.ship();

po.doIt();
```

---

❶ We can see exactly what's going on. It reads like a story. We first initialize the purchase order with the customer and items from the shopping cart. We then compute the total cost, including a sum of the line items plus shipping and tax, and we execute the transaction.

❷ If we don't have any other clues, we have no idea what this code fragment does. Abbreviations may save typing, but they don't clearly communicate the intentions of the programmer.

We have three ways to communicate with names: meaning, capitalization, and structure.

9.2.2   Standards for names

In all cases, choosing names requires common sense. Syntactically similar names can lead to bugs. For example, `theCustomer` looks too much like `the-Consumer`. `pass` can be a noun or a verb. Either of these conditions can lead to bugs, or at least reduce readability. We can be defensive and specific.

The meaning of names

The coding standard that will have the greatest impact is a naming guideline for variable names. Sometimes, teams of strong programmers leave off naming guidelines because the need is simply understood. Apart from code structure, naming provides the best clues for the purpose of any code fragment. Table 9.2 offers some common suggestions for naming.

Capitalization

Capitalization is a tool that can communicate clarity and structure. We use capitalization for two reasons:

- *Capitalization for word structure.* Java uses a convention called camel case (a variable would look like CamelCase) to communicate word structure. With camel case, the first letter of every new word, after the first, is capitalized. The rest are lowercase. For acronyms or abbreviations, we can capitalize the first letter or the whole thing as long as we are consistent:

```
processSqlStatement()
firstName
HttpServletRequest
```

- *Capitalization for program structure.* Certain identifiers will use different capitalization to denote program structure. Class names are capitalized, while attributes, automatic variables, parameter names, and

Table 9.2 Here are some coding conventions for naming. We've included an example of the intended usage, with the entities observing the rule in bold.

Naming rule	Usage
For fields and attributes, use descriptive nouns with restrictive adjectives where appropriate.	`StateTax` `shippingAddress`

Use a descriptive test prefix for Boolean *attributes*, like `is`, `contains` or `has`.	`if(anItem.`**`isTaxable`**`) {`
	`   // do something`
	`}`
	
	`if (collection.`**`hasTaxableItems`**`) {`
	`   // do something`
	`}`

Name Boolean *accessors* with a descriptive test, like `is`, `has`, or `contains`. `get` and `set` are not required.	`person.isPersistent()`
	`while(table.`**`hasMoreRows`**`()) {`
	`   // do something`
	`}`

Make collection names plural for clarification.	`shoppingCart.items`
For methods, use descriptive verbs with restrictive nouns indicating targets where appropriate.	`command.execute()` `computeInterest()`
Name accessors with `get` and `set`, followed by the field names.	`getCustomer()` `setCustomerName()`

Exception: Single letters are acceptable for loop counters, for the economy of space, as long as readability remains clear.	`for (i=0; i<10, i++) {`
	`   // do something`
	`}`

method names are not. Constants are capitalized, with words separated by underscores. Packages are all lowercase:

```
Customer              // class
customerFirstName     // attribute
java.lang             // package
CUSTOMER_COLUMN       // constant
```

Programmers don't always apply capitalization rules consistently. Acronyms and abbreviations are a particular source of confusion. For capitalization of abbreviations, which aren't the same as acronyms, the standard libraries are slightly inconsistent but generally go with full capitalization. Here are some examples:

```
URL
IOException
SQLException
SAXParser
HTMLEditorKit
```

Even this rule is not consistently applied. For example, HttpURLConnection combines the two styles. Either style is probably acceptable, as long as you pick a style and stick with it.

Hungarian notation and scope

In the Java community, the debate over the use of Hungarian notation has been waged for many years. This convention is commonly employed in such languages as C++ to provide additional information about a variable. For example, sCity denotes a variable of a type string named city. For the most part, Java programmers have avoided Hungarian notation, preferring a simpler style that tends to improve the English readability.

Using Hungarian notation might make sense when you need to clearly mark the differences between full class attributes and common automatic variables. Consider listing 9.2 (from Tapash Majumder on the http://www.bitter-java.com message boards).

Listing 9.2   A common Java bug pattern

The use of an attribute name and an automatic variable name within the same method is a common Java bug pattern. In this case, if users intend to have the value variable updated, they will be surprised.

```
public class SomeClass
   {
   //
   protected int value;                  ❶ This "value" is
                                            an attribute.
public int getValue(){
  return value;
}

public void setValue(int value) {
  this.value = value;
}

// lots of distracting methods here

public void readValueFromDatabase() {
    int value = 0;                       ❷ This "value" is a
                                            local variable.
// lots of distracting code here

  value = getFromTable(tableName);       ❸ Which "value"
                                            gets used?
}
```

We have an automatic variable and an attribute with the same name. We can easily confuse the two, leading to errors. Four common conventions can come into play here, and all have been used with good success.

1   Use a leading or trailing underscore (_) when dealing with attributes. In this case, at the value in ❶ in the previous example, we'd have int _value. We would also place the underscore at ❸. Doing so avoids all collisions at the cost of readability.

2   Precede all attributes with this. For that solution, at ❸, we'd have this.value = getFromTable(tableName), yielding the desired result. This approach has the advantage of reducing the number of collisions with little effect on readability.

3   Limit the access of all member attributes to the accessors. In this case, at ❸ we'd have setValue(getFromTable(tableName)) with no conflict. This has the advantage of hiding the implementation of all attributes, at the cost of real estate.

4   Finally, we could prohibit conflicting names. This method results in code with better readability, but it is error prone.

In order of preference, I like options 2, 1, 3, and 4, though I have seen each employed successfully. Table 9.3 lists the coding conventions for preventing collisions.

The best policy for any standard is flexibility. For attribute scope, we might decide to choose option 4 and revise the policy if bugs created by the collision

Table 9.3   Here are coding conventions for preventing collisions between attribute names and local variables. These types of errors are usually obscure and can be difficult to trace. They are preventable, at a cost.

Scope Rule	Example (Declare, Use)	Pros	Cons
Leading or trailing _ for all attributes.	`Public int _value;` `_value = 0;`	Prevents collisions.	Hinders readability with clutter.
Precede all attribute references with this.	`// no change in declaration` `this.value = 0`	Prevents collisions.	Hinders readability by taking up space.
Access attributes solely through accessors.	`// no change in declaration` `setValue(0)`	Prevents collisions. Isolates attributes.	Hinders readability by taking up space.
Disallow attribute names in the method body.	`// no change in declaration` `// no change in use`	Most readable alternative.	Allows collisions and human error.

of attributes with local variables plague us. Or we might decide to take a more extreme stance and revise it based on program readability.

Reserved names

Java does allow us to reuse package and class names from the standard Java packages and objects, although Sun strongly discourages this practice. It's easy to forget about reserved names. For instance, when we were building the EJB examples for this book, we originally chose the names of common bulletin board objects using the language common to that domain: posts, boards, and threads. Of course, a thread is also a Java construct. If we were to import both `bbs.thread` and `java.lang.*`, it wouldn't be clear which thread we would instantiate with this:

```
Thread = new Thread();
```

9.2.3   Braces and indentation

Few coding standards prompt as much controversy as the treatment of braces and indentation. This is probably another area where it is best to pick a standard and stick with it, but some rules should be established more strongly than others. Consider the following code fragment. Assume some of our premium customers are not charged for shipping.

```
if (purchaseOrder.isChargedForShipping())
  totalCost = totalCost+purchaseOrder.addShipping();
```

Now, let's assume that we want to add shipping surcharges for items under $10. We simply add the condition like this:

```
if (purchaseOrder.isChargedForShipping())
  totalCost = totalCost+purchaseOrder.addShipping();
  if (totalCost < 10)
    totalCost = totalCost+SMALL_ORDER_SUR_CHARGE;
```

We have just accidentally charged our premium customers. For this reason, it's best to bracket all `if`, `while`, and `for` statements with `{}` whether or not more than one line of code is used:

```
if (purchaseOrder.isChargedForShipping()) {
  totalCost = totalCost+purchaseOrder.addShipping();
}
```

You can avoid this error, and others like it, by using a good editor that auto-indents. We cannot know which editor or environment future owners of this code are likely to prefer, so it's best to be safe.

Which brace style is best?

Two major brace styles are commonly used. This one

```
if (condition) {
  // do something
}
```

values screen real estate more than clarity. This one

```
if (condition)
{
  // do something
}
```

values clarity over real estate. If we choose to adopt a standard that mandates the use of braces after conditionals, then the first style is usually sufficient, because it lets us have more lines of code on the screen at any given time. The most important thing is to pick a standard and stick with it.

Another consideration is indentation clues. It's important to be able to tell at a glance which braces belong together. Almost all coding standards use indentation as one clue. Commenting can be an additional clue, and may or may not be supported by a standard:

```
if(i>10){
  while(j==4) {
      // do something
  } // end while
} // end if
```

Because a good code editor will find matching parentheses, some programmers might think commenting is unnecessary or even distracting. In any case, code that has too many consecutive closes to be clear may benefit from refactoring.

9.2.4   Comments

Comments are meant to improve the readability of code for humans. The examples in this book are far from sterling examples for commenting, because the goals of documenting code for a book are far different from the goals of documenting for a production application. In a book, page space is at a premium, and we have other means of describing and annotating. A good rule of thumb is that comments should describe *why* something is being done, rather than *what* is being done. For production applications, we can use comments to document bugs and obscurities. Comments can clarify and mark.

Java supports three different types of commenting. Block, or C-style comments, are bracketed with /* and */ characters. Documentation comments, usually used at the top of type definitions and member functions, are bracketed with /** and */. End-of-line comments are preceded with // and extend to the end of the line. Table 9.4, and the program that follows, describes the comment classes with examples.

Table 9.4 Java has three comment styles.

Comment Style Name	Example of Comment Style	Usage of Comment Style

Documentation comments	`/**`
	`* ClassName`
	`* @author: Bruce Tate`
	`*/`
		Use for comments that are useful in code, and in automatically generated documentation (JavaDoc).

Block, or C-style comments	`/* step 1`
	`* step 2`
	`* step 3`
	`*/`
		Use to block a piece of code from executing, or to document a long description or algorithm.

End-of-line, or single-line comments	`i = 1;   // a comment`	Use to drop in annotations at the end of a line, or to drop in short comments between lines.

```
/**
 * CommentClass: This class shows the three types of comments.
 * @Author: Bruce A. Tate
 *
 */
public class CommentClass {
  int someVariable;            // This variable serves no purpose.
/*
  imp anotherVariable;         // Why won't this work?
*/
}
```

Documentation comments are processed by the JavaDoc utility, which produces documentation from tags in the comments. We use end-of-line comments to document variables and individual lines of programs. We use block style comments to block out segments of code from execution for testing purposes, or to provide algorithm type comments in the middle of a member function.

Block style comments can also be bug prone, and they can interfere with the placement of block comments for debugging purposes. They should not be used mid-line or for smaller sections. In my opinion, the unclosed comment is a particularly insidious bug that can be very difficult to track, especially in distributed code. This is another case where a good editor is worth its weight in gold. Bugs like this one, and the related bug of matching closing quotes, are easy to spot with an editor that distinguishes comments, strings, identifiers, and keywords with visual clues such as color, font, and style.

After you choose a comment style, you have to decide how much to comment. This topic is also debated in the Java community, and no clear answers have emerged. Some purists argue that comments provide additional bug-prone lines of code that are hard to keep in sync through maintenance. Others argue for documenting everything profusely. Some in the middle ground opt for commenting only type definitions and methods. I tend to fall between the most extreme camps. As I stated earlier, we should describe *why* something is done, not *what* is being done. Commenting should always add something, and never take anything away. If a line of code is obvious, it needs no comment. If intentions are not clear, the best course is to make them clear. The next best alternative is to document the decision. For various reasons, including conflicting priorities and unit testing, bugs may be discovered but not fixed. These should *always* be documented.

In a self-published coding standard document, Scott Ambler offers the following example. This line of code has an unclear initialization:

```
int index = -1;
```

A comment makes it clear:

```
int index = -1; // -1 serves as flag meaning the index isn't valid
```

A constant also makes it clear, and makes the comment unnecessary:

```
static final int INVALID= -1;
int index = INVALID;
```

This example brings us to a critical documentation guideline: *Some things should not be commented.* To keep comments with the described code in sync and up to date takes effort. Comments are always used to assist programmers, not programs. If a comment doesn't clarify or provides only redundant information, remove it. In all cases, clear, concise code that does not need comments is the best option.

History

In many cases, it helps to maintain a change history within a program. Some change-control systems automatically append a change history as files are checked in and out. In any case, a robust change history is an important tool that can provide enormous assistance with these refactoring activities:

- *Removal of dead code.* A change history can provide information about the existence of dead code, called lava flow in the *AntiPatterns* book.

- *Simplification.* Over time, simple methods can become needlessly complex. Rewriting such methods saves maintenance time and effort. Change histories can give clues to the complexities.

- *Consolidation, decomposition.* Sometimes, consolidation or decomposition can improve performance or improve readability. The history might reveal why two classes were separated in the first place, and help us decide whether to consolidate.

I prefer to keep as much of the change history as possible in the software change control system. This approach helps keep code uncluttered and as concise as possible. Many larger programming groups like to keep it in line. Either approach works, as long as it is diligently and uniformly applied.

Documentation

Many times, documentation in and out of the code shares a common purpose. With the development of frameworks and APIs, public methods can be explained once for both purposes. Then, JavaDoc can parse the comments in the code and produce amazingly robust documentation. The obvious benefit is a single point of maintenance. A more subtle benefit is that it's easier to keep an API document up to date if it's maintained with the code.

Still, some drawbacks should make us consider this approach carefully. For example, the audience reading the code and the programmers developing the application might have significantly different perspectives and needs. Realistically, the decision depends on many factors, including, but not limited to, the audience, the application's shelf life, and the stability of the code base.

9.2.5 Tabs vs. spaces

A detail like tabs versus spaces might seem trivial, but with the increase in team programming and publishing of code, this issue becomes much more important. Different editors will handle tabs differently. Some editors can set indentation levels and make it extremely efficient to indent and move code with the Tab key. Others are not so rich. In addition, tabs simply behave differently than spaces, and they can catch the unsuspecting programmer off guard. These tips can make it easier for teams to work together, where different editors are permitted:

- *Pick a standard, and stick with it.* Consistency is the most important rule.

- *In absence of other considerations, prefer spaces to tabs.* Spaces are interpreted the same universally. The same is not true of tabs.

- *If the editors in an environment are mixed, save code with a no-tabs option.* Most editors can save code with or without tabs. Some even convert tabs to spaces in real time, as they are typed.

These small sacrifices can make it much easier for teams to interact. They also make it easier to include code in technical documentation or published papers, should the need arise.

9.2.6   *Editors*

Few subjects can invoke passion in a programmer like the choice of editor. I mention them here not to state a preference, but to point out the role of the editor in good programming hygiene and readability. I've used everything from Emacs to Notepad. You can easily enforce many of the standards described in this chapter by using a good editor. If you don't already have a favorite, here are some factors to consider:

- Some development environments have built-in editors. In some cases, having a built-in editor is not as restrictive as it might otherwise seem, because the environment helps to manage such tasks as search and replace, class browsing, and hotlinking to related methods or classes.
- Better editors can enforce standards such as brace placement and indentation, usually with configuration files or parameters.
- An editor should give clues about the structure of a program. Colors, fonts, or other visual clues should make clear any comments, strings, variables, or keywords. An editor should also help identify matching braces or parentheses.
- The handling of tabs and spaces is important.
- The editor should be well integrated with the development environment. Useful features are the linking of a compiler error report with a line of code, the launching of compilation from within the environment, and syntax checking.

My choice of development environment, VisualAge for Java, doesn't have a pluggable editor, and many see that as a critical flaw. The editor in VisualAge is also not nearly as robust or configurable as the best programming editors. In future releases, it is my hope that this and other development environments will open up as interfaces between key components of the environment are exposed and formalized.

9.3   *Mini-antipatterns: Organization and visibility*

In the previous section, we examined commenting conventions that help us describe structure. In this section, we'll address standards that alternately ensure privacy and public utility as required. To understand our motivation, consider the following treatment of an instance variable:

```
public SomeClass {

  public int age;

  public SomeClass() {
    // code to correctly initialize age
  }
}

public AnotherClass {

  public void aMethod() {
    SomeClass anInstance = new SomeClass();
    Person person = new Person();

    person.age = anInstance.age;
  }
}
```

Two groups of programmers will cringe at this example. Purists will see that we are directly accessing our instance variable. Database programmers will see that we have implemented age as an integer attribute, meaning that for consistency, we will have to update the database yearly on the person's birthday. We'd probably want to change SomeClass to calculate the age based on the birthday, but that would make all users of SomeClass.age change. Instead, we should implement age with get and set access methods:

```
public SomeClass {

  private int age;
  public int getAge() {
    return age;
  }
  public SomeClass() {
    // code to correctly initialize age
  }
}
```

In this case, we do not need a set, because the value is initialized in the constructor and won't change. The implementation for age is then hidden. Our clients will access solely through the accessors, and we protect the instance variable with the `private` modifier. Then, we can safely refactor, as in listing 9.3.

Listing 9.3   This is a better implementation for getAge

We calculate getAge based on the birthdate, saving us from managing ever-changing ages.

```
private Date birthDate;
                                          ● Attributes are private
public Date getBirthDate() {                and wrapped.
  return birthDate;
}

public void setBirthDate(Date aBirthDate) {
  this.birthDate = aBirthDate;
}

public int getAge(){                      ● The implementation of
                                            getAge is hidden.
  Date today = new Date();
  int thisYear = today.getYear();
  int birthYear = this.birthDate.getYear();
  int age = thisYear - birthYear;

  if (! hadBirthdayThisYear()) {
    age = age - 1;
  }

  return age;
}

private boolean hadBirthdayThisYear() {   ● Intermediate elements
                                            are private.
  Date today = new Date();
  int thisMonth = today.getMonth();
  int birthMonth = this.birthdate.getMonth();
  int thisDay = today.getDate();
  int birthDayOfMonth = this.birthdate.getDate();
  if (birthMonth < thisMonth) {
   return true;
  } else if (birthMonth > thisMonth) {
    return false;
  }else if (birthDayOfMonth <= thisDay) {
    return true;
  }else {
return false;
  }

}
```

We are demonstrating the basic object-oriented principles of implementation hiding and visibility. Wrapping attributes with accessors is but one of many examples of information hiding. Let's now consider visibility of member functions and attributes. Java has three expressed levels of visibility and one implied level, as shown in table 9.5.

Table 9.5 Here are the visibilities supported by Java. Visibility is used to allow or deny access to the features of a class. In this way, we can expose useful interfaces for public use, or restrict intermediate results or useful but private features for security, safety, or design principle.

Keyword	Visibility	Usage
private	Private methods and attributes restrict visibility to the defining class.	Attributes and methods that compute intermediate results important only to another calculation. Methods that should be restricted to the defining class for safety or security.
protected	Protected methods and attributes restrict visibility to the defining class plus subclasses.	Attributes and methods that may be required for future subclasses. In general, protected should be preferred to private. Inheritance chains may need access to many aspects of the implementation, in ways that are not always easy to predict.
public	Public methods do not restrict visibility.	Only methods (not attributes) should be public. Methods that *must* be exposed to fulfill the contract for the interface are declared with public visibility.
Unspecified	Visibility is restricted to the package.	This visibility can be used like C++ friends. Coordinated frameworks within a single package can use this visibility. For example, a collection class utility set could use this visibility to ensure that iterators could see other collection types.

Figure 9.2 shows a conceptual view of visibility. Each widening bracket shows expanding visibility, going from private, to protected, to public. Package (unspecified) visibility is orthogonal, and helps to define visibility on another axis according to the packaging of the classes, rather than the inheritance relationships specified. Visibility modifiers do not make Java's runtime behavior more robust. Instead, through them, we can enforce policies that will help to ensure loosely coupled interfaces, effective implementation hiding, and good object-oriented principles.

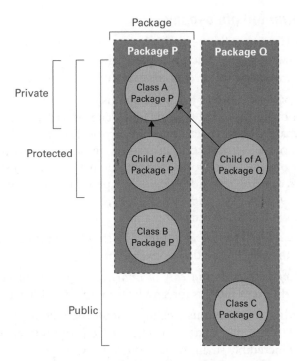

Figure 9.2 Java visibilities allow us to restrict access to attributes and methods. From strictest to loosest, we can restrict access to a class (private), a class and its descendents (protected), a package (unspecified), or all classes (public).

9.4 *Mini-antipatterns: Structure*

Bad object-oriented code can come in any number of shapes and sizes. Novice programmers make nearly universal mistakes as they try to mold the design process to what they know. Language is a surprisingly effective tool to help with the transition. Good object-oriented design is tough to dictate through coding conventions, but enforcing some guidelines can improve code simplicity, readability, and reuse. Some of the principles that can be enforced are elementary design, interface usage, and method complexity. In this section, we'll discuss individual conventions for Java interfaces, packages, elementary code structure, and basic design principles.

9.4.1 *Basic object-oriented philosophy*

Though standards cannot dictate good design, they can eliminate some bad designs. By following these basic principles, which may be targets for some coding standards, we hope to develop more straightforward, flexible designs:

- *In general, classes should be things.* It sounds elementary, but a surprising number of object-oriented designs try to encapsulate process. This type of design makes it easy to accumulate functionality into one, amorphous blob that does all of the work, instead of factoring the process across a number of objects. Two words that are commonly used to short-circuit this rule are *manager* and *process*. If a program has classes such as `RepaintingProcess`, `InventoryProcessor`, or `PurchaseProcessManager`, then usually it is time to refactor.

- *Methods should be single actions.* Methods should be actions that do one thing, and they should be descriptively named.

- *Methods should be short and easy to understand.* Different coding standards have different metrics for simplicity. Some that I like are:
  - The method body, minus cleanup, should be able to fit on a single screen. (I once met a lazy but innovative programmer who set his font size incredibly small to pass code reviews.)
  - A method should be understandable in 30 seconds.
  - A method should be less than a specified number of lines or words.

- *You should choose the simplest approach that will work.* This is an extreme programming technique that values readability and cycle time over a couple of bytes of memory and a few cycles of speed.

We are shooting for universal simplicity and clarity, and it is an elusive goal. The identifiers that we choose to *describe* our programs will have a surprising impact on the way that we *think* about our programs, all the way through the life cycle. Simple and descriptive names can help the cause for short, simple method implementations. Short and simple methods can make a dramatic difference in maintenance costs over time.

9.4.2 *Low-level design considerations*

We've discussed basic, high-level details, but we also need to examine conventions at a decidedly lower level. The application of these low-level concepts has some long-term implications that aren't always clear at implementation time. Let's look at some rules.

Interfaces vs. abstract classes

An interface is used to enforce a type contract between the caller and an object. An abstract class is used to provide a common parent, for behavior or interface, for a set of child classes. In general, interfaces provide a more flexible, general, and accurate mechanism for enforcing a type contract, whereas abstract classes provide a better mechanism for sharing partial implementation. Interfaces provide equivalent functionality to C++ multiple inheritance or Smalltalk mix-ins and must be used if you want to capture default implementations.

Here are some general guidelines to follow:

- Interfaces should be used whenever an implementation might change. Abstract classes can lock in an implementation.
- Interfaces should be used to describe add-on features (`Printable`, `Serializeable`, `Cloneable`).
- Interfaces should be used when no default implementation is specified.
- Abstract classes should be used when partial implementations are specified.
- Interfaces can sometimes be combined with an abstract class providing a fixed interface that can be used in a mix-in with a partial implementation. This combination can give you the convenience of a partial implementation with the full flexibility of an interface.

In the spirit of our continued refactoring of the bulletin board application, our command architecture can ideally be captured as a reusable interface. The last examples in chapter 6 can easily be modified to use a command interface. All of the command objects already use a common interface; we need only enforce them. To do so, we first define the command interface. Then, we can enforce this interface across the classes that use it with the `implements` keyword, as in listing 9.4.

Listing 9.4 Refactoring command objects

This program refactors our command objects to use interfaces. Then, our designs will be reusable, and the consistency will be enforced.

```
public interface Command {                    ● Interface definition
  public void initialize();
  public void execute();
}

public class AddPostCommand implements Command {  ● Enforcement of
  // code remains the same                            interface definition
}
```

The interface gives us additional punch in two ways. We maintain consistency across our implementations of common ideas, and we enforce the interfaces so that we can reuse our designs. Few novice programmers appreciate the power or simplicity of interfaces.

Consider the Cloneable interface

If our object might need to be cloned, then we should implement the Cloneable interface. This interface is used by several design patterns. We should often take the safer road by implementing from scratch rather than picking up the default behavior from Object.

Equality and hash codes

If we override Object.equals, then we should override Object.hashCodes, and vice versa. Equality is simply a stronger test than the hash code, so requirements for one but not the other are extremely rare.

The final modifier

The choice to use the final modifier is, well, final. Its use prohibits reuse of a class, attribute, or method, so take special care in using it. Conventions you might impose for final include:

- Use final only for the declaration of constants.
- Alternatively, allow guarded use of final, but only in cases where the superclass defines the interface of all of the methods (disregarding implementation-specific methods).

9.4.3 Exceptions

The Java language forces us to consider exceptions that might occur in our programs, but it cannot force us to handle exceptions well. In *Bitter Java*, the exception management is intentionally sparse. We do this to keep the examples short and readable, but at the cost of failing to communicate good exception-management practices. Here are a few rules of thumb:

- Exceptions should provide logical, predictable behavior. For example, a mistyped file name should not cause a dramatic stack trace and exit, because this behavior is neither logical nor predictable.
- Exceptions should be handled at a granular level. It is almost always poor practice to handle a raw exception, since logical behavior cannot be determined at this level.

- It is also usually poor practice to throw a raw exception (though we do so in this book to keep things as brief as possible).

The most complete and well-behaving Java code has predictable, logical exception management. Users and clients of an interface will appreciate the effort.

9.5 *Mini-antipatterns: Leaks and performance*

This section will depart briefly from design-oriented standards and will visit some of the rules discussed in chapters 6, 7, and 8. They are standards that help to prevent some of the antipatterns in this book. The nature of a project's coding conventions guidelines will determine whether this type of information is appropriate.

In general

- Optimize later. Optimization should be done at the tail end of the development cycle, with one caveat. If it is absolutely crystal clear that one area will be a bottleneck, then it should be attacked first and fully optimized, to allow recovery time. If you need to make code obscure for the sake of optimization, document the approach.

Leaks and cleanup

- Pair code that handles allocation and freeing of resources as closely together as possible, preferably in the same method.
- With collections, objects that are added should be removed as well. Add/remove pairs should remain in close proximity. The primary exception is a collection that uses weak or soft reference objects, or a collection that implements a fixed set that will remain fixed or that will grow throughout the life cycle of the collection. We need to document such cases clearly.

Looping and round-tripping

- EJBs should be accessed through a common command layer or facade so that collecting all of the attributes for a bean will not create a round-tripping situation.
- Keep redundant computations outside of loops and loop tests. For example, do not use this:

```
for (int i = 0; i < someCollection.size(); i++)
```

- When building strings within a tight loop, use string buffers instead of string concatenation to build the strings.

Synchronization

- For synchronization, pick a strategy and stick with it.
- Synchronization carries overhead. Use it where it is necessary, but never add synchronized to all of the methods just to be safe. Some standards prefer synchronization on a method level where possible. Others recommend locking specific objects for greater control.
- Know how Java handles synchronization. Two misconceptions are common. The first is that a synchronized section protects a block of code. It doesn't; it only protects code for the threads executing in *one instance* since all locks are on the object level. The second misconception is that atomic functions do not need protection. In truth, only very small byte movements are considered atomic.

Blocking

- Where possible, try to avoid blocking. For files, use the nonblocking IO package java.nio (beginning in Java 1.4).
- When a response is not required immediately, use a queue instead of a transaction or RPC.
- Wherever possible, spin off threads to handle tasks that are likely to block.
- Some applications require shared access for readers and exclusive access for writers. In these circumstances, use read/write locks (see the antipattern description in "Synchronized read/write bottleneck," in chapter 5) to limit the amount of blocking.

9.6   Conventions for testing

Still underwater on the Pine Creek rapid, I go through a mental checklist to make sure that my paddle, head, knuckles, and back are in the correct position. After 8 seconds that feel like an eternity, I sense my life jacket's buoyancy bringing my right side near the surface, giving me an opening to roll. I sweep out my paddle, snap my hips, brace with the paddle, and shoot upright. Feeling relieved, I position my kayak and resume the run.

I mention this story because we now go from a valued and respected topic to one that is … not. I hate practicing rolls and getting water up my nose, but when I was upside-down in the middle of a Class V- rapid in Colorado, I needed to know that my roll would work. Two things helped me hit that roll. The first was repeated use, or testing; the second was organization. Though it would be silly to test my roll in all different contexts, I did spend time perfecting my roll in turbulent water. I also spent time organizing my strategy. I knew to hold my paddle with the right wrist, rolled forward, next to my left knee. I knew to keep my head to my chest and my nose to the deck for protection. When the time came, it worked. These standards and tips can help us do the same thing for software. Some of the tips come from XP practices. Others come from coding conventions that I've used throughout my career.

- *Code unit tests first.* XP recognizes the value of embracing testing. Coding the tests helps us to consider exceptions when we design our classes. It helps us design all the way, code all the way, and test all the way. With a more accurate assessment of what we're building, we can even produce better schedules.

- *Include a* `main` *for unit tests.* Using a `main` can help when testing some stand-alone classes with the command line, to make sure that they fit specifications.

- *Organize test cases.* Some organizations will want to build test cases into the classes themselves, and some will want externally driven classes. Scaffold as necessary.

- *Append built-in test methods with a keyword like* `test`. It is important to be able to identify test cases versus production code for many reasons, and this practice helps us identify the tests quickly.

A combination of good design, effective test organization, and discipline will ensure that our classes perform when we need them. A first-rate unit testing application, such as JUnit or HTTPUnit, will make some of these steps unnecessary and will enforce others. Testing methodologies go well beyond the scope of coding conventions, or even this book. Many books are available that can supplement your knowledge on the subject, including:

- *Testing Object-Oriented Systems: Models, Patterns, and Tools* (The Addison-Wesley Object Technology Series), by Robert V. Binder

- *Object-Oriented Software Testing: A Hierarchical Approach,* by Shel Siegel and Robert J. Muller

9.7 *Building a good style guide*

Now that we've seen a good set of conventions, it's time to discuss ways to put them together into a style guide. A style guide exists to serve the programming community and the customer. It is intended to assist with the production of quality code. To accomplish that objective, it must be read and embraced by the entire organization. I believe in very short style guides for that reason. Here are some tips to consider:

- Keep style guides short.
- Everyone who touches code should read the style guide.
- Maintain the style guide like an application: fix it when it is broken.
- Use it and embrace it, but do not be overly rigid. Understand when exceptions apply.
- Make it appropriate to the toolsets and skill levels on the team.

Did I mention *short*? Nothing is more frustrating than a code cop screaming about section 145.265.23 of a style guide at 5:30 on a Friday afternoon. Long guides have the potential to turn into either unused boat anchors or crusading holy books. Instead, a style guide should take into account the tools, personalities, and skills of an organization. A style guide for a team of longhaired, 10-year Jolt-drinking veterans wouldn't need to preach about basic object-oriented design. A style guide for a team using an integrated development environment probably wouldn't need to mention make-file structure, because the development environment manages that.

9.7.1 *Buy, borrow, or steal?*

Many consultants sell programming style guides for a living. Some additional style guides are available in books or for free on the Internet. Which approach is best? Should you have a consultant build one? Should you combine from different sources? Should you build one from scratch? I've coded on teams that approached programming style in different ways. One team chose not to use a style guide; we failed. The successful teams used these methods:

- *Build it from scratch.* This is the approach that was taken at Contextual, Inc. (see the next section). Because the team was small and communication was good, this approach worked well.
- *Adapt a style guide from another assignment.* This is by far the most common approach. Most good programmers know what they like. A

leadership team is likely to have at least one member with an old style guide that can be adapted for use.

- *Buy one and modify it.* Out of the box, no style guide is going to work for a team of strong programmers with distinct personalities. I recommend the approach of taking a guide and trimming it, rather than adding to it or combining multiple guides. The idea is to build a short, concise guide that works. Did I mention *short?*

9.7.2 *A sample style guide from Contextual, Inc.*

This section contains the style guide used by Contextual, Inc., a startup based in Austin, Texas (http://www.contextual.com). I worked with the same people at allmystuff; they interview aggressively and tend to do a good job of screening for good understanding and hygiene. Therefore, their style guide reflects an advanced community. They use XP principles, including a shared code base, so their style guide reflects source code structure and spacing for consistency. They use Emacs extensively within their base development environment; therefore, advanced regular expression searches, which look for certain patterns as well as fixed text, are important to them. As such, punctuation rules dictating the use of white space and braces are prevalent in their style guide.

They decided to publish a short style guide that captured the basic essence in two short web pages. The guide resides on their intranet, so the whole team can get to it quickly.

My thanks to Brian Dainton at Contextual for providing this style guide.

▶ **Reviewing Contextual's style guide**

With slight modifications, this is the style guide used by Contextual, Inc., a startup based in Austin, Texas. The guide is short by design. All programmers can access the guide. Violations of the style guide are usually handled one-on-one, but frequent offenses or common community violations are broadcast. (Used with permission of Contextual, Inc., 2001.)

- Enclose statements such as `if`, `while`, and `for` within open and closed curly braces even if the body is a single line.
- Typically, import statements should import `java.util.*` rather than `java.util.Vector` to make maintainability simpler.
- Name all objects as if they were in the same package as all the JDK and other application objects.
- Make variables names descriptive and never abbreviate them.

- Spacing:

  1 Use two lines between the `package` statement and the first import.

  2 Use two lines between the last import and the `public class` section.

  3 Use two lines between each method.

  4 Do not insert blank lines after the class open curly brace or directly before the class closed curly brace.

- Method blocks should follow this format:

```
public String
doIt(String x,
     String y,
     Object somethingElse)
     throws Exception,
          OtherException
{
    ...
}
```

- Code should maximize the usage of short-circuiting. Error conditions should be at indentation level 8, the main path of execution should be at 4 (unless it is imbedded within a `try/catch`, `for`, etc.).

- Indentation level is 4.

- You should use // to indicate comments unless they are for JavaDoc purposes. Comments should begin no less than one full space after the second slash.

- Do not use underscores in class names, variable names, method names, and so forth. Use camel case syntax instead.

- Do not recompute the size of a vector each time you do the loop check; for example, don't do the following:

```
for (int i = 0; i < someVector.size(); i++)
```

- Use the syntax !!! in a comment to signify that the code needs to be revisited at that spot.

- Code should be less than 80 characters per line where possible.

- Declare variables where they are first used, not at beginning of a function.

- A cast looks like:

```
(Foo) foo
```

not like

```
(Foo) foo
```

- Any arithmetic operator should be surrounded by proper white space; for example:

```
for (int i = 0; i < x.size(); i++)
return x / y;
```

versus this:

```
for (int i=0; i<x.size(); i++)
return x/y;
```

- try/catch/finally blocks should look like this:

```
try {
    . . .
} catch (Exception exceptionType1) {
    . . .
} catch (Exception exceptionType2) {
    . . .
} finally {
    . . .
}
```

- Separate declarations, variable names, and default values by a single space.
- All fields in an object must be declared prior to the methods for the objects. Class fields should be declared prior to instance fields.
- When setting a local field, use the same parameter name; for example:

```
public void
setName(String name)
{
    this.name = name;
}
```

Contextual's code is extremely well designed, religiously refactored, and highly readable. It behaves well with the tools, and is easily learned by new hires. As you can see, a coding standards document doesn't have to be long to be effective. It should address issues that are important to the programming teams and their clients, both internal and external.

9.8 Summary of coding standards

Instead of listing a template of antipatterns, we'll provide a summary of the coding standards described in this chapter. The best way to use this information is to cross out those guidelines that are not important or compatible with the goals of your team, and then add any you like from one of the references in the bibliography or from the style guide in the previous section.

Guidelines for names

- For fields and attributes, use descriptive nouns with restrictive adjectives where appropriate.
- Use a descriptive test prefix for Booleans, like is, contains, or has.
- Make collection names plural for clarification.
- For methods, use descriptive verbs with restrictive nouns indicating targets where appropriate.
- Name accessors with get and set, followed by the field names.
- Name Boolean accessors with a descriptive test, like is, has, or contains.
- Exception: Single letters are acceptable for loop counters, for the economy of space, where readability remains clear.
- Use camel case to distinguish between words. Capitalize the first letter of acronyms.
- Capitalize the first letters of classes and interfaces, but not methods, variables, or attributes.

Guidelines for attribute name/automatic variable name collisions

- Use a leading or trailing _ for all attributes, or
- Precede all attribute references with this, or
- Access attributes solely through accessors, or
- Disallow the same attribute names in the method body.

Guidelines for braces

- Enclose such statements as if, while, or for within open and closed curly braces even if the body is a single line.
- Choose a style and be consistent.

Guidelines for comments

- Use */** */ documentation style comments* for comments that are useful in code, and in automatically generated documentation (JavaDoc).

- Use */* */ c-style comments* to block a piece of code from executing, or to document a long description or algorithm.

- Use *// end-of-line comments* to drop in annotations at the end of a line, or to drop in short comments between lines.

- Keep a change history in the header of each method, or choose a change control system that maintains an inline change history for you.

Guidelines for visibility

- Use *private visibility* for attributes and methods that compute intermediate results important only to another calculation, and methods that should be restricted to the defining class for safety or security.

- Use *protected visibility* for attributes and methods that might be required for future subclasses. In general, protected should be preferred to private.

- Use *public visibility* for methods that *must* be exposed to fulfill the contract for the interface.

- Use unspecified, or package, visibility for coordinated frameworks within a single package. For example, a collection class utility set could use this visibility to ensure that iterators could see other collection types.

- Do not use *public visibility* for attributes.

Guidelines for design

- Classes should be nouns. Watch words like *process* and *manager* that try to short-circuit this rule.

- Methods should be single actions.

- Methods should be short and easy to understand.

- Choose the simplest approach that will work.

- Interfaces should generally be preferred over abstract classes: when an implementation *might change*; to describe add-on features; when no default implementation is specified.

- Abstract classes should be used over interfaces when partial implementations are specified.

- Implement the `Cloneable` interface if an object might need to be cloned, and implement from scratch rather than picking up the default behavior from `Object`.
- If you override `Object.equals`, also override `Object.hashCodes`, and vice versa.
- Use `final` only for the declaration of constants. *-OR-*
- Use `final` only where the superclass defines the interface of all of the methods (disregarding implementation-specific methods).

Guidelines for packaging and file structure

- A `.java` file should contain a single class, and be named the same as the class, including the correct use of case.
- Place even private classes in separate files.
- Place interfaces in separate files.
- A package should contain a logical grouping of classes.
- Place files in a structure that mirrors package structure.

Guidelines for leaks and performance

- Pair code that handles allocation and freeing of resources as closely together as possible, preferably in the same method.
- With collections, `adds` should not be added to the code without associated `removes`. The primary exception is collections that use weak or soft reference objects.
- EJBs should be accessed through a common command layer or facade.
- Keep redundant computations outside of loops and loop tests.
- Optimize later.

Guidelines for testing

- Code unit tests first.
- Include a `main` for unit tests.
- Organize test cases. Pick a default organization and stay with it.
- Append built-in tests with the word `test`.

10

Bitter scalability

This chapter covers

- Topologies for high-performance deployments
- Antipatterns related to poor performance
- Antipatterns related to performance methodology and tuning

I am in Georgia, on the dreaded Chatooga, made famous by the movie Deliverance. I've aspired to one day go on a pilgrimage to the Chatooga from before I even started kayaking. But as we start our run I am on the verge of changing my mind. The river is stunningly beautiful, radiating power and a sense of awe at every turn. In spots like Seven-Foot Falls, the river slams against undercut ledges where the stream can pin and kill a boater. At Bull Sluice, jets of water are sucked through a hole in the riverbed large enough to swallow a boater and his boat. The water is then forced through an opening just a few inches across. Riverwide terminal hydraulics, like Woodall Shoals, look benign but are traps for paddlers and swimmers. By the time we reach the ominous Five Falls, I feel myself becoming paralyzed with fear. The river drops rapidly over five waterfalls, with little recovery time between them. Deep down I know I will always fear that mighty river.

This chapter will present a series of small antipatterns related to scalability. We'll focus on refactored high-level designs for scalability. Scalability issues require some coding finesse, but the larger examples to support them go beyond the scope of this book. Some good sources are *Core J2EE Patterns: Best Practices and Design Strategies; Concurrent Programming in Java: Design Principles and Patterns;* and *Java Performance and Scalability* (see the bibliography).

We can use several different techniques to make a solution more scalable. Many times, a faster, bigger box is a perfectly viable solution. Since many mainframes now support open standards and can even run Linux, they can run very large Internet applications with only mild rework. Because scaling in this manner doesn't usually require as many advanced design considerations, this chapter will instead focus on scaling through parallel design. We'll look at antipatterns in the area of performance and scalability, with some related to process and others related to programming.

10.1 Good topologies for performance

Internet topologies have varied dramatically, but they are starting to settle on slight variations of a common design. Many performance experts prefer a topology like the one in figure 10.1. In this configuration, all software on the web and application servers is redundant to achieve availability and better performance. The user's request comes through the Internet and goes through a firewall and a sprayer. Called *edge services*, these technologies have seen significant advances over the last decade.

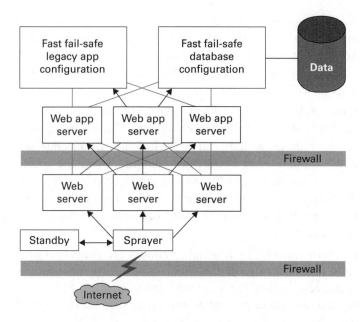

Figure 10.1 **A good topology for performance has layers that do one thing and do it well. This one has a sprayer, with a hot standby, that takes incoming requests and routes them to one of three identical web servers. The web server can then request services to build dynamic content from any of the available web application servers behind the corporate firewall, which in turn can use database or transactional servers.**

Edge servers can provide these functions:

- *Firewall.* A firewall is a hardware or software layer that sits between two zones. In our architecture, we have firewalls between our DMZ and the public Internet, and between our DMZ and the private intranet. Two major kinds of firewalls are *filtering* and *proxy.* A filtering firewall, usually implemented in a router, filters packets, or atomic TCP/IP messages, for security and performance. A proxy firewall allows or denies outbound traffic based on an existing security policy. For example, a systems administrator could block MP3 access with this type of firewall. In our architecture, we have two firewalls, which are configured with two different security policies. With such a configuration, only the most sophisticated attack penetrates both firewalls.

- *Spraying/load balancing.* A *sprayer* is a network node responsible for taking requests to a single destination and fanning them out to multiple physical machines. Usually, a sprayer is identified with a DNS name so that the user community doesn't need to be partitioned. A *load balancer* is a sprayer that makes intelligent decisions about where to route a request based on the load on a given system at any point in time. Among the popular sprayers available are Cisco's Local Director and IBM's Network Dispatcher. Many other vendors have solutions in this space as well.

- *Static caching.* Many vendors have boxes that can cache static content upstream of even the static web servers. These static caches can be independent boxes, or they can be included in other edge-server features. The combination of a proxy firewall and a cache for outbound requests (called a caching proxy) is fairly common. Since caching proxies bypass all of the existing communication within a firewall and free web servers and web application servers, they can have a significant impact on performance.

- *Dynamic caching.* Increasingly, vendors are providing innovative caching solutions for dynamic content and pushing those functions up closer to the edge server. JSP fragments and specialized EJB caches are becoming increasingly important as more pages are created dynamically.

An organization's security policy might specify that edge services satisfy requests via a cache. Other requests could be passed on to a web server, which would be responsible for strictly static content. Other requests could be passed to the application server to resolve any dynamic content. In a subtle configuration variation, application server software could be deployed jointly with the web server to handle the view, the controller, and a thin model wrapper (such as the command layer in chapter 3 or the facade in chapter 8). Alternatively, the web server might be deployed alone, with the model, view, and controller deployed on the application server.

The web application server houses the server-side model. EJB containers would be deployed here, as would wrapping technologies for legacy systems. The application server is usually deployed inside the innermost firewall for additional security, and for performance reasons that we will explore next.

10.1.1 *Layering hardware in homogeneous groups*

In our configuration, we achieve scalability through independent servers that do one thing well. When we have a performance problem, we can simply increase power by adding to the existing network a new system that performs the function we need. The key is that the configuration of the individual boxes must be identical.

Scaling Internet applications requires an architecture that uses independent software components as building blocks. Table 10.1 reviews the likely components. These pieces should stand alone, with only minimal standardized interfaces, or *touch points*, exposed to the rest of the system.

Table 10.1 Here are the controlled touch points between the elements of our architecture. The controller, JSP pages, and command layer form the interface between the static client and the model. The communication to the static client goes through the controller, while model communication is encapsulated in the command.

Touch Point	Shares Interfaces With	Uses This Interface
Static client	Controller	HTTP POST, GET
Controller (A.K.A. interaction controller, IC)	Static clients Commands JSP	HTTP Method calls Request object, URL parameters
JSP pages	Command beans Controllers	Data JavaBeans from controller Request object, URL parameters
Command layer (A.K.A. facade)	Controller JSP Model	Method call Data JavaBeans through controller Many
Model	Command layer	Many

Now let's explore each component's role in our system:

- *Static clients.* The clients communicate to the middle tier exclusively through HTTP POST and GET. The client scripting language can be generated dynamically. In the event that validation or complex user interface logic forces deployment of client-side Java, this too should communicate to the server exclusively through HTTP. In this way, the client can request a service via a single name and the request can be mapped by the edge services onto an appropriate server. This service can be completely independent of the client.
- *Servlets.* The initial touch points are the interaction controllers, which are implemented as servlets. They get input in the form of HTTP request form parameters. These servlets communicate with business logic through intermediate objects called commands, or facades. They also return dynamic content to the client by dispatching JSP pages. In addition, servlets can use services provided by the web server, such as

session state management. (In configurations with multiple web application servers, the session state can be problematic. We'll talk more about session state in the section "Chaotic session management.") The interaction controller may also access other web application services, such as naming and security services.

- *JSP pages.* Compiled to form servlets, JSPs build the return-trip view for the client. Additional JSP fragments can be embedded in the original to form a compound document. JSPs get input from the interaction controller in two ways. First, the interaction controller can embed beans, called *data beans*. Second, parameters can be passed through the HTTP response object; the compiled JSP then returns an output page that is returned to the client or embedded in another JSP.

- *Command layer (or facade).* The command layer is a thin wrapper around the model. It presents an interface to the interaction controller and JSP. It consists of `set` methods for input parameters, `prepare-to-execute` and `execute` methods to fire the appropriate business logic, and `get` methods that provide access to output parameters. Alternatively, a stateless session bean can be used to provide a remote interface to the EJB tier. This layer helps decouple the model and view, and also helps eliminate round-tripping.

- *Model layer.* This layer can consist of legacy code, proprietary Java, or EJB-centric code. Clarity of design, high performance, and reliability are the keys here. This layer has been the most prone to poor performance, and several antipatterns in this book have targeted it. Problems independent of EJBs include a lack of connection pooling, poor or missing caching strategies, poor algorithms and Java designs, and restrictive locking schemes. EJBs introduce more problems, including implementing the wrong EJB types, using full EJB entities for relationships, or choosing to use EJBs for trivial problems. The model layer tends to be fairly complex, so it's important to keep external interfaces clean and simple. The only interface to the rest of the system should be through the command layer.

Homogeneous units in layers often scale well because it's easy to determine where performance problems originate. Once we identify a problem, we can apply additional hardware or tuning to proportionally increase the system workload capacity.

10.1.2 *Other topology variations*

Several slight variations on our configuration are possible. Some systems combine all of the view logic onto a single presentation server, including a web server for static content and a web application server for dynamic content within the DMZ. This configuration is especially common for applications that directly access a legacy layer. The advantage is that all web services are encapsulated in a single layer. Of course, the downside is that enterprise connections are exposed in the DMZ, which can make certain hostile attacks easier.

Another variation combines the web application and web servers, with an array of servers housing the model inside the innermost firewall. With this configuration, all enterprise connections are made safely inside the corporate intranet. The command layer controls the round-tripping between the model and view layers.

You can optimize this configuration so that all web servers, or even web application servers, share a high-performance, highly available, distributed directory. This makes it easier to manage and serve static content. A distributed file system can mirror directories for HTML pages and images, for example, to simplify publication of new interface versions. The architecture also makes it much easier to configure for high availability. Performance through efficient caching is a significant benefit as well.

Books have been written about the topics covered in this chapter. Our bibliography contains excellent sources on deployment strategies.

In the next section, we'll look at performance-related antipatterns. Most involve high-level process issues, and others are specifically related to Java.

10.2 *Antipattern: Performance Afterthoughts*

I first learned the value of performance analysis as a member of a national support team for the predecessor to the Intel version of DB2. Our customers typically did not use capacity planning, and they rarely designed for performance.

One day, during an application design review for a Fortune 500 company, I asked about the firm's test plan. My contact replied that testing consisted of an intern's attempts to break the system. Slightly disturbed by that answer, I then asked about stress testing. He explained that stress testing involved five people trying to break the system at the same time. For performance testing, he'd ask 20 people to test the system the morning of production deployment, before the rest of the users arrived. The system would then be deployed to 300 concurrent users. Needless to say, over the next year I felt like Bill Murray in *Groundhog Day*, a movie about the same bad day repeating itself over and over.

This was not an isolated case. Out of an estimated 50 customers I visited during that period, only four had reliable performance-testing plans.

Ten years later, I am consulting. The problem domain is dramatically different. Performance analysis is one of very few areas that have become more complex with Internet deployment. For public deployments, the size of the user community for a given application generally cannot be determined in advance. The networks leading to the application servers are rarely under the sole control of the information technology staff. It's much more difficult to educate users about practices that are likely to stress a system. At the same time, for most companies performance- and stress-testing techniques have changed very little.

At allmystuff, we had very strong technical leadership but did very little performance testing. If we'd encountered significant success—and the ensuing traffic—I'm not sure that our architectures could have handled the load. Though our network topology was solid, our design model captured every object as a persistent EJB, and we did no dynamic caching. Our quality assurance department had tests for fail-over, but performed very limited tests for heavy concurrent use. Because our product never attracted enough customers to stress the system, we failed long before we were forced to pay for our errors. As a consultant, I find that my clients usually haven't performance-tested their applications, or they've been blindsided by the high number of users in their systems. This situation is normal, but it represents a very dangerous way of doing business. Sometimes, systems are designed well enough to scale as user needs grow. Other times, they are adequate to handle the needs of the initial community, but when the user base increases unexpectedly, scalability problems are uncovered. As with many relatively new technologies, performance problems mar Internet deployments all too often.

10.2.1 *Developing without performance planning*

The Performance Afterthought antipattern is process oriented. In general, architects focus on business and end-user requirements at the front of the cycle and give only marginal attention to performance considerations. Performance decisions are saved for the end of the cycle. In the Internet environment, this strategy can be fatal for a variety of reasons, as the following shows.

▶ **Considerations for early performance planning on Internet projects**

For Internet applications, performance cannot be treated as an afterthought without dire consequences. Here are some factors that complicate delayed planning, coding, and testing of performance components of a system:

- *Internet workloads can be inherently unpredictable.* If the target audience of an Internet application is not well defined, it's easy to underestimate the size of the community. At the height of the dotcom boom, technology companies dealt with workload prediction in different ways. Some hardware companies installed additional servers, free of charge, and allowed their clients to pay only when the servers were turned on. Designing for unpredictable performance can be a dicey proposition. It's tough to decide whether a constrained budget should focus on additional hardware or high-priority software features. This unpredictability, combined with the lack of a realistic performance plan, can throw off initial estimates considerably.

- *Some platform-dependent architectures can be difficult to scale and adapt to common Internet architectures.* Taking an early shortcut to build in a convenient platform-dependent feature can result in impaired scalability down the road. If the performance requirements aren't clearly communicated, this trap is much more likely to appear.

- *By failing to take performance into account, a company can underestimate hardware needs or development time.* Robust, scalable architectures take money and time. Without a clear understanding of what is necessary, under-budgeting is a real danger.

- *The most common highly scalable architectures require a number of assumptions about architecture and design.* Following a set of conventions for building highly parallel systems is much easier at the front of the development cycle. Decisions about session state management, persistence, locking, multithreading, loose or tight coupling, programming language, and dynamic content management will have a bearing on how a massively parallel architecture is built. Poor decisions on any of those fronts will limit the options available for creating parallel architectures.

10.2.2 Some real-world examples

Let's look at some real-world examples of companies that failed to adequately plan for performance. As a member of a database critical-situation management team and later as a consultant, I've dealt with many failures involving scalability. (Of course, I'll maintain the confidentiality of my customers for obvious reasons.)

Late performance design

Early in 2001, a large travel company implemented an EJB solution from the beginning. The architecture had many different complex layers and aggressive performance criteria. Though significant elements of the design were completed very early in the project, the first performance benchmark was not run until weeks before the project was scheduled to be completed. When the project was near completion, a performance snapshot revealed significant problems with production data volumes and workload. By that time, projected changes to the base object model and framework forced the team to scrap the EJB architecture, because not enough money was available to handle the extensive revisions. The project changed direction to use simple screen scraping front ends from 20-year-old technology. In a postmortem, the team agreed that an early-performance sanity check would have caught the problem in plenty of time.

No planning

In 2000, a small company built a complex user interface. The business analysts established few hard performance requirements, and they neglected to create a comprehensive performance plan. To complicate matters, no time was left at the end of the cycle to handle performance testing. In order to compensate, the programming team asked the entire company—board members and venture capitalists included—to assist in a companywide "test fest." This high-visibility event was the first time that the system was tested under load. It failed in several different ways; for example, a single JavaScript custom control took several minutes to populate. The company has since laid off more than two-thirds of its staff and is struggling to stay afloat.

Insufficient funds

In 1998, a large Fortune 100 energy company decided to release a companywide intranet infrastructure. The performance requirements were rigorous and stringent. The development team finished three major risky components early in the cycle, but they did not test the components under load. One of the components was a custom persistence framework. It failed, because many functions that would otherwise be handled by relational joins and low-level database functions were instead handled by the application. The alternatives radically changed the underlying persistence framework as well as the object model on top of it. The company completed the project only after significant schedule delays, penalties, and cost overruns that ran well into seven figures.

10.2.3 Solution: Plan for performance!

My early trip down the Chatooga reminds me of high-volume Internet applications. Scalability is one of the most technically demanding characteristics to build into web applications. The dangers are significant and real. Features such as concurrency control, session sharing, and sharable models have humbled many a competent programmer. In some cases, applications are built without consideration of the potential size of the user base. In other cases, performance is handled late in the development cycle without time to recover. Though the Chatooga is powerful and demanding, many boaters now run it with relative safety. Similarly, Internet experts are rapidly learning how to deploy highly scalable and reliable solutions with parallel clusters.

For both object-oriented applications and Internet applications, it is critical to plan performance from the beginning. It isn't enough to throw out loose requirements and bury them in some document. We must examine the hardware and software architectures in detail and compare them against the performance criteria. Here are performance-planning tips.

▶ **Performance planning tips**

I've accumulated these performance-planning tips over 10 years of consulting.

1 *Know your users* ... Good requirements are the key to meeting any user's needs. We should include formal response-time requirements, and we should interview and observe our end users.

2 *... but don't completely trust them.* This sounds contradictory to the first goal, but it isn't. It simply means that your information-gathering efforts should not end with your user community. In fact, your performance requirements may be *more stringent* than your users might recommend. Many sources suggest that customer performance expectations for generic consumer Internet sites are changing. For example, in 1999 *E-Commerce News* published *Performance Primer: Gone in 4 Seconds*, which stated that the typical Internet consumer spends no longer than 4 seconds at a site. Today, with high-bandwidth connections, the typical user will probably not wait even that long. Interview your user community, but also do your own research so that you won't be lured into false security.

3 *Plan for performance.* A performance plan is a critical element of any high-volume Internet application. All major stakeholders should sign off on the plan early in the design cycle. Performance plans should be written in advance of the application architecture, because performance requirements will dictate the application architecture. Hard metrics for response time should be included.

4   *Assume eventual parallel deployment.* In designing for scalability, it's
    much easier to plan for eventual parallel deployment in advance, even
    if the added scalability is never needed. Even if you don't initially
    deploy on a parallel architecture, it pays to keep that option open for
    the long term. That means addressing the following:

    - Database designs should assume shared access with reliable concur-
      rency control.
    - Session state should be deployable across multiple machines, with a
      strategy for ensuring session affinity or keeping track of a multipart
      conversation in a parallel architecture.
    - Operating system services and other services should be deployable
      in a parallel configuration.
    - The model should have a clear path to a sharable, scalable solution.

5   *Tackle high-risk elements first.* With all projects, risk mitigation
    involves planning for the worst possible contingency. That means
    addressing high-risk elements as early as possible in the development
    cycle, with sufficient time to recover.

6   *Perform a sanity check on key assumptions as needed.* While a full-blown
    performance test belongs at the end of the cycle, frequent sanity
    checks of critical risk elements are a good idea. Identify these key risk
    elements in the performance plan. System architects need to under-
    stand what elements are likely to break.

7   *Plan for contingencies.* Internet workloads are inherently unpredict-
    able, and aggressive contingency plans should mitigate that risk. Make
    contingency plans for any highly performance-sensitive components
    with completion dates scheduled later in the development cycle. Risk
    mitigation can often provide for a delayed delivery of a subset of sensi-
    tive components in order to protect the whole application. All stake-
    holders should sign off on aggressive schedules.

8   *Plan to test the system and key touch points.* Several tools can help you
    test parallel architectures under load with enough time to recover.
    Many Internet applications enable access to legacy systems. These sys-
    tems were frequently not designed for the type of access or the scale
    that the enabling technologies provide. Testing the *back end* in the
    new context is critical; ensure that you have enough time to adjust for
    any problems.

9 *Save time for performance*. Regrettably, but inevitably, something will go wrong. It's important to have enough time and money to make modifications. The time a company dedicates to performance issues depends on several factors, including the competence of its staff and the consequences for failure.

These suggestions don't take the place of a strong development culture and plain old common sense. We can help a project succeed by encouraging developers to watch for performance concerns and allowing them to step forward without repercussion. I've worked with many teams in a variety of development cultures. Some managers tended to staple messengers to the wall; under those circumstances, problems did not get reported. Other companies encouraged developers to find problems and even had formal reward systems for bringing suggestions to managers' attention. The balance probably lies somewhere in between, with reasonable accountability and an atmosphere that focuses on fixing problems rather than assigning blame.

10.3 *Antipattern: Round-tripping*

The Round-tripping antipattern is a combination of earlier antipatterns in this book, but it merits special attention here because of its significant impact on performance. Round-tripping occurs when a design requires significant iteration across an interface boundary. In figure 10.2, the model is deployed on a different system than the view.

For our purposes, it doesn't matter whether the view logic is implemented as a proprietary client, an applet, or a distributed application across multiple servers. The key is that the design will require multiple round-trip communications across the interface boundary between the model and the view. As the view grows in complexity, the communication costs will rise. Because we're iterating through the fields of our view across a major interface boundary, this is a classic example of the Round-tripping antipattern.

10.3.1 *Solution: Cache and Facade*

The antipattern we just described is technically the same problem that occurred twice in earlier chapters. In chapter 5, we discussed the Cacheless Cow antipattern and used our bulletin board example to illustrate a round-tripping scenario without a cache to compensate. The Everything Is an EJB antipattern in chapter 8 iterates through the fields on an EJB. Three solutions to the round-tripping antipattern exist:

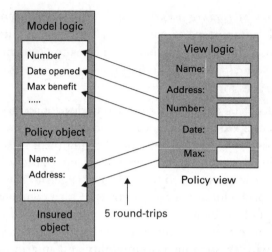

Figure 10.2 **Round-tripping is considered the top EJB performance problem by many consultants. It occurs when significant iterations occur over major interfaces. In this case, we iterate through a list of fields, and set or get them independently across a client-server boundary.**

- Caching, described in detail in chapter 5, eliminates the need for the round-trip communication for the expected case by keeping a local copy of frequently accessed data the first time it's fetched. Parallel implementations can somewhat reduce the effectiveness of a local cache. Multiple servers require multiple copies of the same data, and multiple round-trips to build them. Updates to cacheable data are more expensive because the cached copy on each server must be invalidated. Still, for applications with high read/write ratios and extremely high volume, caching is effective. Further, edge servers offer caching solutions that eliminate the need for multiple cached copies.

- The Facade design pattern, discussed in chapter 8, refactors a round-tripping architecture to make a call to a facade object, which then encapsulates many request and response distributed calls into a single distributed call. Stateless session beans are good choices for facade objects. We can also use distributed command objects to solve this problem; this approach requires only a single round-trip. (The stateless session bean requires an initialization round-trip in addition to the round-trip for the actual communication—not a perfect solution, but still a significant improvement.)

- The third solution to round-tripping is to simply refactor. In some cases, it's possible to redefine the major interface boundaries so that they fall in places with fewer round-trip communications. In rare cases, we should sacrifice packaging for performance if we can eliminate a large number of round-trips, but as a rule, refactoring should produce a cleaner, more readable architecture. For this type of refactoring, the UML sequence diagram, like the one in figure 10.3, is extremely useful.

UML sequence diagrams clearly show round-trip communication layers between major interface points. The rectangles across the top of the graph represent objects. The vertical lines under each are timelines. The horizontal arrows represent flow of control. For optimization, iterations and chatty interfaces between objects can be shifted off an interface boundary. In other cases, we can add a facade or cache. The detail and layout of good sequence diagrams makes it all possible.

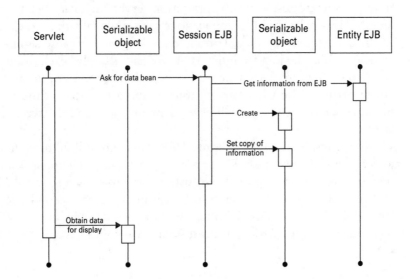

Figure 10.3 Sequence diagrams are ideal for dealing with round-tripping. The interfaces between objects can be clearly seen, and we can determine if we have iteration or major activity across them.

10.4   *Antipattern: Bad Workload Management*

At McDonald's, there may be five lines, but I always seem to wind up behind the kid who orders 27 Big Macs. Sure, other lines may be longer, but mine always seems to move the slowest. In this instance, the cash registers are resources, and one person is taking a disproportionate share of the resources.

Web servers generally don't have this problem because the content is static and all of it is served relatively quickly. Web application servers, on the other hand, experience this problem in spades. Some jobs simply take more time to complete than others—for example, database write operations are often considerably longer than reads. Enterprise applications behind the server may dictate transaction length; enterprise transactions may be synchronized, forcing application servers to wait for completion. Some database architectures force a connection to be held for the entire duration of a recoverable transaction (called a *unit of work*), which can encompass many different atomic operations. In some cases, the web application server itself can dictate transaction length. Heavily layered EJB applications can simply take time to execute.

In any case, highly variable transaction lengths can cause significant problems. Consider the jobs in figure 10.4. We have 20 jobs, each of one unit, distributed evenly across 4 queues. Two metrics are significant: total throughput and waittime. The total throughput is operating at maximum efficiency because each of the servers will be working on a job, and the average wait time is 2 units.

Now, consider the jobs in figure 10.5. There are still 20 total units, but the jobs are of variable length. There are 11 jobs, one of 10 units, and the rest of one unit each. In the figure, we distributed the work in a round-robin fashion and generated the order randomly. In this instance, the second queue got the larger job. Since we were distributing work round-robin, two additional jobs were added to the queue. In this instance, we could have finished the job in

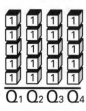

Figure 10.4
Good load balancing ensures that all servers will have a proportionate workload.

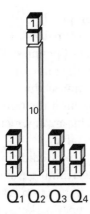

Figure 10.5
Odd jobs like the one at Q2 can disrupt balance by giving
disproportionate loads to random servers sporadically.

Q_1 Q_2 Q_3 Q_4

10 units, but because the second queue received additional work, the total length of time required to process all of the work was 12 units. Our throughput has suffered. In addition, our average waiting time has been extended to 7 units, because smaller jobs have to wait for larger ones to complete.

In practice, workload distribution that is not uniform can cause additional problems. A single system that receives a disproportionate load can bog down and become slower, and throw the balance further out of kilter. Symptoms include inferior throughput for the combined matrix of systems and sporadic performance for any given user. Real-world scenarios with the sporadic long job like this are common; examples include an account report on a stock trading system, or a new post on a bulletin board (where reads frequently outnumber writes by a margin of 100 to 1). We must develop an effective strategy for dealing with workload disparity when performance requirements are stringent and high throughput is necessary.

10.4.1 Solution: Workload Management

We can use various techniques to help us distribute workloads uniformly. We might attempt to isolate transactions that are unusually long; these techniques fall under the umbrella of workload management. Some techniques will use hardware, called load balancers, and others will require us to break down longer transactions or isolate unusually long transactions to specialized queues. In all cases, our goal is an even distribution of work, leading to better efficiency.

Queue specialization

To understand solutions for queues and workloads, let's turn to the real-world queue experts. They employ a practice called *queue specialization* to keep workloads going smoothly. In our McDonald's example, I've often wondered if each restaurant could start a single line for the terminally slow, for the customers who pay for 27 Big Macs with a shoebox full of pennies. That's probably not enforceable, but supermarkets do essentially the same thing, in reverse. Because the majority of the work consists of longer transactions, supermarkets offer express lanes for short transactions. These lines limit the number of items per customer and may limit the form of payment. This arrangement makes the workloads for the various queues much more predictable.

We can simulate the express lane in our systems by dedicating servers to workloads of similar sizes. The key is to isolate long-running transactions to a subset of the servers. If a specialized long-duration-transaction server is idle, it can then take on short transactions, just like in the supermarket. The reverse is not true, because the long-duration transactions can adversely affect our overall balance. Figure 10.6 shows our workloads with Q1 functioning as a specialized server for long transactions.

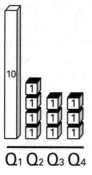

Q_1 Q_2 Q_3 Q_4

Figure 10.6
A dedicated server (Q1 here) for longer tasks can smooth out the workload and ensure that a single odd task cannot throw the entire system out of kilter.

Partitioning jobs

Another possible solution to the distribution problem is to break larger jobs into smaller ones. In many cases, it makes sense to break huge user interfaces down for other reasons. A well-known trick that Disney uses is *hiding the line*. The customers for a popular ride enter a short line to a building with lots of displays of interesting things, which again goes outside into a garden, which then enters another building with actors talking about the ride experience itself. The larger line is broken into many smaller ones. The authors of the most effective surveys also hide the length of the survey by breaking it into smaller chunks and branching conditionally. A "yes" answer to "Did you buy model 4045A?" could lead to more questions about that model. We can do the same with long business forms. Other times, poor distribution of work can be a case of a facade or command doing too much work. If a command's granularity is too coarse, then meaningful reuse is significantly reduced. Figure 10.7 shows the impact of partitioning combined with specialization. In this case, we've dedicated half of our service queues to managing large loads, and we've partitioned the larger, 10-unit job into two smaller jobs.

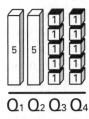

Figure 10.7
With dedicated odd job service queues (here, Q1 and Q2), workload partitioning can add balance to a system. This may be as simple as adding commits to a longer transaction, if the application can tolerate the unit-of-work implications.

Of course, we should reserve partitioning the workload for cases where the partitioning makes sense structurally. Readability and ease of maintenance are prices too high to pay for a slight improvement in performance. Also, transaction partitioning should not break transactional integrity. For instance, let's consider a business transaction—a bank account transfer, for example. A transfer consists of a debit and a credit transaction. We should not partition the transfer transaction into two because both things should succeed or fail in a transactional unit. If either succeeds while the other fails, the bank or the customer (or both) will not be happy with the results.

10.4.2 *True load balancing*

True load balancing involves distributing workload intelligently, based on an individual system's capacity, workload, and performance, as well as the bandwidth to the server. Earlier we mentioned round-robin scheduling. These dispatchers have been popular for three reasons:

- The nature of web applications has been primarily static content, so the jobs have been relatively uniform. With a uniform collection of identically configured servers, this type of algorithm does a decent job of uniform work distribution.
- Round-robin load balancers are very fast. The same has not always been true of more sophisticated true load-balancing dispatchers.
- In general, job durations have been very short. In these instances, dispatchers have needed to make very fast decisions to avoid creating a

bottleneck. In general, the dispatcher needs to be as fast as the average service time, divided by the number of servers.

Application traffic is getting more dynamic and workloads are getting more diverse. At the same time, true load-balancing technologies are getting much faster, making them an attractive option. The load-balancing dispatcher can take distribution and expected performance into account, as well as the existing performance of a system. Load balancing is a difficult problem to solve. To achieve the most complete job, we must be able to estimate transaction duration and accurately measure the workload on a system. Even this measurement can be problematic: what resources are constrained? An I/O bound system may show a relatively low CPU utilization, though it is swamped. Most load balancers opt not to solve all of these problems, and instead settle for effective compromises and rich tools for specialization, configuration, and tuning.

Other interesting problems arise. If a system remains up but loses the ability to do work (for example, if the database network connection goes down), it will "complete" its tasks rapidly, though not with the desired results. If the load-balancing algorithm is too primitive, this system will get most of the work, with the load balancer systematically directing most of the traffic to the wrong box. For this reason, load balancers usually are built to deal with some aspects of reliability as well. The dispatcher can detect whether a given system is down and dynamically take that system out of the rotation. It can also repeatedly route the same user to the same server, increasing the impact of caching and simplifying implementations. Even so, queue specialization and workload partitioning are still effective tools for solid, predictable performance.

10.5   *Antipattern: Chaotic Session Management*

When multiple web application servers are maintained, a user can be routed to a different system with each subsequent request. In this case, load balancing can make session state management much more difficult, or vice versa. Several options are available for distributed session management.

10.5.1   *Solution 1: Dispatching with session affinity*

Some dispatchers will route a given user to the same server for every subsequent request. An association between the user and a server is called session affinity. Dispatching with session affinity solves the problem by essentially localizing the solution. If a given user will always hit the same server, the application is masked from the distributed architecture.

This approach greatly simplifies the programming for session state management. This is because the architecture completely insulates the programmer from distribution issues.

Despite the fact that this technique has been widely and successfully deployed, it does have its limitations. Proxy architectures can sometimes lead to sporadic behavior. If a user's Internet service or company can route through several different proxies, the dispatcher may route contiguous requests to different servers, leading to unpredictable results for the user. (Some dispatcher technologies do not have this problem.) Also, because there is no replication of the session data, session data can be lost if the user's first application server crashes.

10.5.2 *Solution 2: Using a distributed state management service*

Most web application server vendors have distributed state management services. The services provide a dictionary (a session ID associated with data) for state management. A framework either replicates this data or makes this data available through distributed requests.

This solution also frees the programmer from having to deal with the distributed architecture. The performance of distributed state management services will probably improve over time as vendors iterate on them. These vendors also use approaches that are easily adapted to open standards. Some of these solutions add failure safety by replicating the state to another site.

Keep in mind that distributed replication and communication comes with overhead. This performance penalty can be severe compared with localized session state management. Also, performance suffers for very large blocks of session data.

10.5.3 *Using custom session bean solutions*

Another approach is to use a session bean to communicate with a persistent store, state table, or database elsewhere. Session beans can be relatively lightweight alternatives to entity EJBs. With this solution, we can support much larger session blocks than by using the native alternatives. Since the session bean is custom, it is very flexible.

Using a custom session bean does have disadvantages:

- Stateful session beans can be difficult to clean up.
- Memory leaks are common with this type of architecture.
- Data in stateful session beans is not transactional or fail-safe.

- This solution forces a level of programming that other solutions don't require.

10.5.4 *Using custom entity bean solutions*

Another solution is to use an entity EJB to store session data. This is the most robust solution. Frequently, entity beans are used to handle transactional data related to a session, and one of the lightweight alternatives is used to cache housekeeping session data, such as user preferences.

However, using custom entity beans is also the most heavy-handed solution, and it comes with a definite performance penalty.

10.6 *Antipattern: Thrash-tuning*

Performance analysis often seems like a black art. With so many different variables, it's difficult to determine which parameters have significant impact and which make things worse. Add the inherent unpredictability of the Internet, and things get dicey at best. Slight improvements in performance can result in increased traffic, which in turn harms performance. Unstructured performance-tuning is sometimes called thrash-tuning. Here are some characteristics of thrash-tuning:

- *Results of major design or parameter changes are unclear.* Though fairly significant changes are made, many times all at once, it isn't clear whether a real performance improvement has been made.

- *Attempts to improve performance go in circles.* In many instances, an administrator or developer may tune a parameter and put it back again several times, without settling on an improvement.

- *Performance tuning consumes much more of the schedule than it should.* Performance improvements can be elusive, and performance improvements are not always readily apparent.

In general, the performance-tuning methodologies are the cause of the problem, though the symptoms can sneak up on us quickly. These practices can get us into trouble:

- *Changing more than one parameter at a time.* This approach has tripped veterans and novices alike. Though it seems counterintuitive, this practice takes more time than it saves because it's extremely difficult to determine the impact of parameters.

- *Working without a baseline.* This practice is a close second in the performance antipattern area. Without a baseline, it's impossible to tell what progress is being made toward the goal.

- *Undisciplined choices for performance improvement.* It's easy to work into a cycle of making expensive, low-impact fixes. Ironically, some of the best programmers fall into this trap.

- *Working on performance for too long.* It's equally important to know when to stop. Firm exit criteria will save time and money.

10.6.1 Solution: Use sound performance methodologies

With parallel architectures, solid performance-testing methodology is much more important because so many variables are involved. Two investments for high-volume applications are imperative: a strong performance-testing methodology and an isolated performance environment. The methodology, and the will to use it, allows efficient testing and rapid improvement, and controls the performance-tuning expenses. It will also protect part of the testing budget and schedule to ensure that stakeholders will be satisfied with the application speed. With an isolated, stable environment, system performance can be closely controlled and measured. In general, the steps shown next have worked well for me.

▶ **Performance Enhancing Methodologies**

I have used many performance methodologies in the past, and these rules represent some of the most effective parts of each. Two keys to success are attention to frequent measurements and repeatable steps after a good baseline, and a focus on items with high reward/cost ratios.

1 *Decide on the metrics for success.* An often-overlooked key to success is defining success.

2 *Set up the base environment, and stick to a code base.* This is the base environment. The process will measure the base; make single, controlled modifications; and then measure the base again. This process is repeated until success is achieved. Sometimes, it's cheaper to rent the equipment and lab space than to build a specialized lab. That option is perfectly acceptable as long as the testing conditions are at least as stringent as the production conditions.

3 *Take a snapshot of the controlled environment.* For the environment to be a valid baseline, it must be completely repeatable, from configuration files to database data.

4   *Take baseline measurements.* Before you attempt anything else, you must measure the system. The baseline will show either progression or regression in subsequent tests. The baseline measurements should include enough detail so that you can isolate problems to individual components. Code profilers can assist with this process. Other tools, such as Page Detailer, can break down the individual load times for objects on a web page. The point is to have enough information to spot the bottlenecks.

5   *Test with repeatable scenarios.* Testing with repeatable scenarios makes it much easier to understand when a change has improved the performance of the system.

6   *Work on the most important scenarios first.* This should go without saying, but many programmers waste valuable time on meaningless administrator functions or unimportant error conditions, and ignore the critical test cases.

7   *Work on the bottlenecks with the highest reward/cost ratio.* Again, it should go without saying that many smaller low-cost, medium-reward fixes can often improve the system as much as a high-reward fix with a high cost.

8   *Quit when you are done.* Performance testing can go on indefinitely if you let it. Establish criteria that will make your customers happy and quit once you've satisfied those criteria.

9   *Once a system is in production, do not stop measuring and tuning.* Production systems will probably have different behavior from sterile tests. It's difficult to predict how caching models will hold up, how workloads will be distributed, or how end users will use a system. You should periodically measure your production systems and, where possible, tune the systems with information learned from the sterile test environment. If a system must be tuned in production, it's important to keep the methodology strong; change one variable at a time, and measure between changes. For production systems, response time in a vacuum is not enough, since the workload can also change. Other metrics, such as page views per second, may be more valuable.

10 *If necessary, get help.* Because Internet performance tuning can be such a demanding discipline and is becoming more specialized, it pays to spend a little money up front to prevent a long-term disaster.

10.7 *Taming the performance beast*

In this chapter, we discussed performance antipatterns. Some were related to code, but most were related to process. The unpredictable growth and workloads inherent in high-volume Internet applications make achieving good performance tuning more difficult. Planning and testing are mandatory, leaving enough time at the end of the cycle to tune the system to predefined specifications. Many Internet architects are turning to parallel architectures to provide scalability, with a dispatcher serving multiple web servers, which in turn serve multiple web application servers. The complexity of these solutions makes the architectures ripe for antipatterns. We should pay special attention to even workload distribution, round-tripping across interface boundaries, and session state management. A world-class performance-testing environment, built or rented, and a solid performance-testing methodology are critical.

10.8 *Antipatterns in this chapter*

These are the templates for the antipatterns that appear in this chapter. They provide an excellent summary format and form the basis of the cross-references in appendix A.

Performance Afterthoughts

DESCRIPTION: Poorly defined performance plans, poor requirement specification, and inattention to performance throughout the cycle can lead to nasty surprises at the end of the cycle.

MOST FREQUENT SCALE: Application.

REFACTORED SOLUTION NAME: Performance Planning.

REFACTORED SOLUTION TYPE: Process.

REFACTORED SOLUTION DESCRIPTION: Gather performance requirements, plan, and prepare for the future. Sanity-check key components, and address the riskiest elements of the architecture early.

TYPICAL CAUSES: Poor planning.

ANECDOTAL EVIDENCE: "We'll have plenty of time to performance-tune at the end of the cycle." "It is a good design. We don't need to tune for performance." "We'll let our unit testers probe for performance." "We've done all of our test cases except our performance test case."

SYMPTOMS, CONSEQUENCES: Repeated delivery of software with poor performance; performance-tuning activities that are unfocused and ineffective; inability of low-level developers to articulate the performance requirements for a component they're building.

Round-tripping

RELATED ANTIPATTERNS: The Cacheless Cow. Some specializations of this antipattern exist. The lack of a cache can also cause round-tripping.

DESCRIPTION: Round-tripping occurs when a chatty interface falls on a major interface boundary, such as a distributed interface. For EJBs, a client (usually a controller or JSP) accesses the remote interface of a distributed entity bean. Since an entity bean usually exposes many fields and sometimes collections, this results in many round-trip communications, absolutely murdering performance.

MOST FREQUENT SCALE: Application.

REFACTORED SOLUTION NAME: The Facade.

REFACTORED SOLUTION TYPE: Software.

REFACTORED SOLUTION DESCRIPTION: The most common solution to this problem is the facade. This interface is implemented with a distributed call, such as a session bean. The interface combines many chatty communications into a single, consolidated call.

TYPICAL CAUSES: A common cause is the use of major frameworks, such as EJBs, near interface boundaries without modification.

SYMPTOMS, CONSEQUENCES: Applications are slow.

ALTERNATIVE SOLUTIONS: The distributed command can also be used to control round-tripping. In addition, refactoring can frequently shift an interface so that logical tasks are grouped into a single physical round-trip. Other alternatives can help performance. A cache can help after the first load. (Often, both a cache and facade are desired.) The EJB can also be deployed on the same box, though many times, strong reasons motivate separation.

Bad Workload Management

DESCRIPTION: Poor distribution of work occurs when one server of a cluster receives a disproportionate share of the work.

MOST FREQUENT SCALE: System.

REFACTORED SOLUTION NAME: Workload Management.

SOLUTION ALSO KNOWN AS: Even Load Balancing.

REFACTORED SOLUTION TYPE: Technology.

REFACTORED SOLUTION DESCRIPTION: True load-balancing dispatchers help. Partitioning larger jobs into smaller ones can even out a workload, and the specialization of certain servers to handle longer jobs can produce significant benefits.

TYPICAL CAUSES: Dynamic content is much more uneven. When the same primitive techniques are used to balance static and dynamic jobs, uneven distribution of work can be the result. In addition, if odd long jobs are treated the same as other jobs, they'll throw off round-robin load-balancing schemes.

SYMPTOMS, CONSEQUENCES: Sporadic performance and inconsistent performance across identically configured servers are the most common symptoms.

SOLUTION ALTERNATIVES: Server consolidation to a single high-powered server eliminates this problem completely, at the price of convenient scalability.

Chaotic Session State Management

DESCRIPTION: Certain state management techniques with distributed architectures have different strengths and weaknesses. Some alternatives include dispatching with session affinity, distributed state management, stateful session bean state management, and entity bean state management. These techniques can easily be misapplied.

MOST FREQUENT SCALE: Enterprise. In many cases, an enterprise implementation will dictate an approach.

REFACTORED SOLUTION NAME: Correct Choice of Technique.

REFACTORED SOLUTION TYPE: Software.

REFACTORED SOLUTION DESCRIPTION: Choose the right tool for the job. Understand the problem domain and the technologies that will be applied to the problem.

ROOT CAUSES: Ignorance.

SYMPTOMS, CONSEQUENCES: Improper choice of technique can result in poor performance, difficult application maintenance, and difficult extensibility.

Thrash-tuning

DESCRIPTION: Performance tuning is difficult without a solid baseline or when multiple configuration parameters are changed at once between measurements. Attempting performance tuning in these conditions can result in similar or identical tests run several times, giving the appearance of thrashing.

MOST FREQUENT SCALE: Application.

REFACTORED SOLUTION NAME: Good Performance Methodology.

REFACTORED SOLUTION TYPE: Process.

REFACTORED SOLUTION DESCRIPTION: Good testing methodology and a good testing environment are the primary keys. Baseline measurements are mandatory. All tests should start from a common configuration and change a single parameter at a time.

ROOT CAUSES: Haste, ignorance.

ANECDOTAL EVIDENCE: "What did we change for that last test?" "Didn't we just do that?" "We're right back where we started."

SYMPTOMS, CONSEQUENCES: Inefficient performance testing and tuning, longer-than-expected performance tuning cycles, and unclear results of performance improvements.

Sweet parting thoughts

We are on the nearly flooded Barton Creek in Texas. Considering that its bound-aries are almost entirely within the Austin City limits, it is an amazingly isolated run. The creek normally has plenty of fun, intermediate-level rapids when the water is at sane levels. Today it is freight-train loud. We'd run it many times before, but never with this much water.

Years before, in much easier conditions, I'd been trapped in a hydraulic, where I struggled in vain, panicked, and was beaten badly on the river bottom before I swam clear. Today, I have a healthy dose of nervous anticipation, but not so much as to be incapacitated. After all, I am on a familiar creek with some very strong boaters. There are few dangerous places on the river where I cannot be reached from the bank with a short throw rope or from another boat, and I am prepared. I know where the challenges are hiding.

As we descend I see the mist rising just behind a horizon line. It is the first dan-ger spot, an 8-foot waterfall with a nasty hole at the bottom. At the top of the fall my approach and speed are good—I get a nice jump off the edge of the drop. I flip as I clear the hydraulic but I roll routinely, without much effort. Now we are approaching the second danger spot called Twin Falls.

A mass of water surges violently to the left over a 4-foot waterfall with a com-plicated hydraulic. I do not want any part of it, but some of the stronger paddlers head that way. I go right instead. The move is intricate, but plenty of water sweeps through the main channel to guide my boat. In spite of that help, I misread the current and get swept into the hydraulic behind a pour-over. It is a particularly nasty and sticky formation today. My momentum is gone. I shudder at the power and suction of the hydraulic, and focus on staying upright. Barton Creek now has my undivided attention.

11.1 Antipatterns help us on many levels

Throughout this book, we've looked at Java programming processes and prac-tices that break under pressure. We've refactored the problems to solutions that work. At this point, let's step back briefly and take one final look at the big picture.

By now, the value of the antipatterns presented here should be clear, but this list is in no way comprehensive. Now that we understand the negative impact of individual antipatterns on projects, management, and programmers, we can begin to appreciate the value of integrating antipatterns on many dif-ferent levels. They can jump-start careers, save projects—make us into better programmers. Study and application of antipatterns in advance of a program-ming venture can steer us around the swamp-like traps that have mired so many projects of all dimensions and sharpen our skills by hammering home the reasons behind the rules for good hygiene and program structure.

11.1.1 Antipatterns ignite careers

For most of my career, I've sought difficult problems and honed my skills in finding practical solutions to those problems. As a database systems programmer at IBM, I learned about database performance and the common problems that plague database applications. My management team liked my initiative and deployed me on a highly visible national team chartered to solve these problems. After publishing an article on performance-related antipatterns, I was approached by a publisher to write my first book.

These days, I am a consultant. My professional focus is on antipatterns and the application of refactored solutions. The first rule of consulting and sales is "Hurt, then rescue." We must be able to see a customer's problems, communicate the impact of the problems, and show that the impact is sufficient enough to warrant a decent commissions check for the solution. Then, we must solve the problem. The best consultants recognize a pattern of behavior that they can leverage across many enterprises. Does this process sound familiar? It should.

Software engineers and architects who are well versed in antipatterns can be of considerable value. They have the foresight to steer the troops away from many software development ambushes, often while upper management is watching. The most respected programmers seem to know why an idea is good or bad. I like learning from my mistakes as much as the next person, but I would much rather learn from *your* mistakes.

11.1.2 Understanding antipatterns improves programs

Many of the bad practices outlined in this book can be exceedingly expensive mistakes. We know that a tight coupling between the model and view can be crippling or even fatal under many circumstances. We have seen the impact of round-tripping. The code may be easy to refactor, but the problem may not be easy to find—I've worked on projects that involved *months* of trying to locate the source of performance problems of this kind. Often, a caching strategy should be considered from the beginning, so that strategies for stale data and invalidation will be compatible with the architecture. Many of the EJB antipatterns are also easy to fix, but very difficult to isolate without advanced knowledge because so many layers and variables complicate the search. It is not rare for a single decision leading to an antipattern to cost hundreds of thousands of dollars over the life cycle of a project. Crisis meetings with high-ranking management and highly paid technical staff can burn money at a frightening rate. So can schedule overruns and consultants.

By far the best way to solve antipatterns is to avoid the conditions that allow them to occur in the first place. This requires that we allocate time in our careers and projects to perform adequate research. We should also ask questions about key antipatterns that share our project's domain when we interview and phone-screen job candidates, and we need to reserve time after a project to identify and capture key antipatterns that plagued its design. Publishing the worst problems where the whole team is able to read them is a good idea.

11.1.3   *Understanding antipatterns makes you a better programmer*

Good programmers learn from their mistakes, but that costs time. Great programmers learn from the mistakes of *others*. The study of antipatterns gives us insight into the patterns of behavior that lead to failure. Few programmers are motivated enough to follow style guides and programming practices *if they don't understand why they should*. If we understand the Split Cleaner design pattern in chapter 7, then we also understand why we must aggressively pair adds with removes and know when it's okay to break those rules. Understanding Model-View-Controller can lead to cleaner architectures, and learning some of the variations in chapter 4 can help us understand the ways that design patterns can break.

Antipatterns can also help us look at coding in a whole new light. We can empower ourselves to make a difference by learning to spot patterns of trouble in our domain and find solutions to those problems. Becoming more productive will be valuable—making a whole team more productive will multiply the value. Learning to apply antipatterns to a new domain need not be difficult. We can see direct relationships between Round-tripping and the Cacheless Cow. We can identify the common root cause in Lapsed Listeners, Leak Collections, and Split Cleaners: a failure to pair the preparation and cleanup. Testers will note similarities between some of the performance analysis antipatterns and the general testing process. With enough exposure over time, we can spot and solve antipatterns quickly. This ability makes us more efficient, productive—and valuable.

11.2   *Integrating antipatterns with process*

We can indeed make a significant impact by studying and applying the theory of antipatterns. While individual pockets of value can make a difference, we can do much more by integrating them into our processes and organizations. Figure 11.1 illustrates the six stages in which we can improve our process with antipattern-related activity.

Figure 11.1 shows a common iterative development process that we reviewed in chapter 2. The eight-ball symbols identify the likely places that a development process can be modified to include protection from antipatterns. Some deal with prevention or early detection of antipatterns, and some deal with capturing and refactoring them.

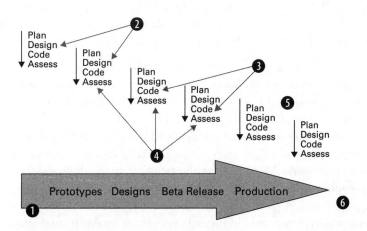

Figure 11.1   An antipattern can be addressed in at least six stages in the development process. At initialization, we can research antipatterns in our chosen domain. At design and code time, we can use annotations and inspections to prevent them. At testing time, we can establish patterns. Between cycles, we can refactor. At the end of the cycle, postmortems help to identify antipatterns.

❶ *In the project initialization.* We can identify antipatterns related to a technology or approach. By aggressively seeking out likely problems, we can short-circuit many of them before they start. This is a highly recommended practice that helps prevent antipatterns.

❷ *In the design stage.* In our design documentation, we can provide a place in our design artifacts to capture likely antipatterns. We should also capture annotations to warn against antipatterns in likely places (for example, the use of a publish/sub-scribe design pattern could have an annotation to watch for Lapsed Listeners, as in chapter 6). This practice also helps prevent antipatterns.

❸ *In the implementation stage.* Code inspections are a good way to find occurrences of existing antipatterns. Senior developers and leads should know about the antipatterns related to a technology and react accordingly.

❹ *In the testing stage.* An occurrences field in a bug database can allow us to capture information on how many times a certain type of problem has cropped up. This flag motivates us to look beyond the scope of a single fix and look to the causes of the bug. This way, we can identify new antipatterns.

❺ *Between iterations.* At allmystuff, we did some refactoring between iterations of our framework. Between iterations is an ideal time to refactor antipatterns, and this practice helps us refactor identified antipatterns early. Remember, extreme programming teaches us that refactoring *saves time*; it does not *waste* time.

❻ *After delivery.* After a project, we should take the time to do a *postmortem*. This meeting gives developers a chance to look back at a development process and modify it for the next cycle. This process should be dedicated to *fixing the problem rather than placing the blame*. At allmystuff, our postmortems were often combative and confrontational. Upper management was also watching, making it difficult for engineering or client services management to release control long enough for the process to work. Managers' involvement pretty much guaranteed that certain issues would not be addressed, or discussion would be killed shortly after those issues were raised. A good postmortem should be free from management influence and politics. Managers should instead concentrate on ensuring that each identified problem and associated task has appropriate ownership and attention.

To thrive, an antipattern must *infect* a process in three ways:

- *It must be injected into a system.* An antipattern will not hurt us if it is never introduced. Knowledge, common sense, and diligence are the best inoculations against infection.
- *It must go undetected long enough to cause harm.* If an antipattern is refactored before it causes damage or is copied, then it will cost us only the refactoring time. If it goes undetected or if we allow it to persist, then the meter is running: the costs will accumulate over time.
- *It may be repeated, multiplying the damage.* If we solve an antipattern after it has only bitten us once, we are ahead of the game; otherwise, the impact will be multiplied across many implementations.

We can attempt to break an antipattern's cycle in one of these three places. At stages 1, 2, and 3, we prevent the antipattern from ever making it into the design. Stage 5 refactors the antipattern, preventing the damage from spreading. At stages 4 and 6, we try to find patterns and break the cycles before the antipatterns can be repeated.

11.3   Next steps, last steps

This collection of intermediate antipatterns is an attempt to encourage the Java community to use antipatterns. To establish momentum in this area, we must work together. If you want to help build this community, make an effort to participate in the discussion boards, such as the one at http://www.bitterjava.com (for Java antipatterns) or http://www.antipatterns.com (for general process antipatterns). The *Bitter Java* message boards have been recently created for you. If you'd like to publish, there are a number of opportunities to do so. You can start small with online services, like http://www.bitterjava.com, and vendor pages such as IBM's developerWorks at http://www.ibm.com/developer and Middleware Co.'s TheServerside.com at http://www.theserverside.com.

We need to collect Java antipatterns as vigorously as we do design patterns. We should also collect success stories about the application and use of antipattern research. As the momentum builds, tool vendors, authors, and programmers will help strengthen the movement.

As I am violently tossed about on Barton Creek, I clear my mind. My boat now points to the east bank, perpendicular to the current, with my forward momentum completely arrested. I let my training take over.

Though I am rarely on a body of water large enough to practice, my earlier obsession with hydraulic-escape techniques tells me that instinctively leaning too hard on my downstream paddle will separate my shoulder. Instead, I brace and test my lateral freedom. I find that though downstream momentum is limited, I can work back and forth, toward either bank, with a combination of bracing and sweeping strokes that I've studied but seldom applied on bigger water. After a couple of strokes, I reach one side of the hydraulic. I lose momentum and slide back toward the center. However, I use that backward momentum to move toward the other bank.

The hole still holds firm, but it turns my boat 90 degrees to face it. My instincts scream at me to paddle away from it, but on this day, I trust my training. I paddle hard, right into the teeth of the turbulent hole in the river. My boat stands up on end, and my weight and the downward turbulence conspire to drive me deep into the creek. Then suddenly the buoyancy of the kayak drives me high into the air, and I dramatically pop free.

My friends look at me as if I am Lazarus, raised from the dead. I recognize the look and feel the same, but I shrug my shoulders as if to say, "No big deal." I turn my back to them, allow myself a wide grin, and paddle on down the river, ever closer to the safety of our cars below.

A
Cross-references of antipatterns

319

Table A.1   Cross-reference of antipatterns by name

Name	Description	Solution	Symptoms	Location
1. Bad Workload Management	Poor distribution of work occurs when one server of a cluster gets a disproportionate share of the work.	Even load balancing, job partitioning	Sporadic performance and inconsistent performance across identically configured servers	Chapter 10, Section 10.4
2. Cacheless Cow	Caches can be used to provide a significant performance boost with very little effort, but many developers neglect this basic enhancement. Most Internet applications take advantage of hardware and web servers for caching of static content, but caching of dynamic content takes more time.	Dynamic command cache	Poor performance	Chapter 5, all sections
3. Chaotic Session Management	Certain state management techniques with distributed architectures have different strengths and weaknesses. Some alternatives include dispatching with session affinity, distributed state management, stateful session bean state management, and entity bean state management. They can easily be misapplied.	Choose the right tool for the job. Understand the problem domain and the technologies that will be applied to the problem.	Improper choice of technique can result in poor performance, difficult application maintenance, and difficult extensibility.	Chapter 10, Section 10.5
4. Coarse or Fine Commands	Commands can be divided too coarsely or finely for optimal performance, readability, or reuse.	Optimal command granularity	Poor reuse/poor performance	Chapter 4, Section 4.4
5. Compound JSPs	When a command's execution can lead to one of many pages being returned to the user, sometimes a programmer will express this decision logic in a JSP.	Push decision-making into controllers	Poor separation of concerns	Chapter 4, Section 4.3
6. Connection Thrashing	When database connections are created from scratch with each new user connection, the performance can be poor, because database connection costs are prohibitive. This antipattern can happen for other connection types as well.	Connection pooling	Poor performance	Chapter 7, Section 7.2

Table A.1 Cross-reference of antipatterns by name *(continued)*

Name	Description	Solution	Symptoms	Location
7. Everything Is an EJB	This is the generic form of the Round Bean in a Square Hole antipattern. If a problem is not well suited, an EJB solution is likely to be too difficult or will perform poorly.	Use alternatives to EJBs	Poor performance, high expense for simple solutions	Chapter 8, Section 8.5
8. Excessive Layering	Object-oriented systems are easy to layer with excessive complexity that is not required to adequately describe the relationships and behavior in the model. The complexity of the software can easily outpace the capabilities of the hardware platform.	Refactor; integrate early and often	Poor performance, poor readability	Chapter 2 Section 2.3.4
9. Fat Commands	Functionality that belongs in the model or controller can creep into the command layer.	Refactor into model-based commands.	Command layers change with every change in model. The command layer looks like a utility collection.	Chapter 4, Section 4.5
10. Hardwired Connections	For business-to-business connections, a common implementation is to enumerate all of the fields in an entire interface, complete with parameter and return types. The connection is then made through some form of a remote procedure call. This approach makes the connection difficult to maintain and support as the interfaces change.	XML messages or web services	Multiple versions of the same interface; interface support lagging the capabilities of both the client and server systems.	Chapter 7, Section 7.4
11. Incomplete Process Transitions	Many fail to get the full benefits from object-oriented technologies and iterative processes because they fail to make a full transition to the new development process.	Education, leadership	Long cycles, analysis paralysis, overruns	Chapter 2, Section 2.5.2

Table A.1   Cross-reference of antipatterns by name *(continued)*

Name	Description	Solution	Symptoms	Location
12. Lapsed Listeners Leak	The publish/subscribe design pattern requires applications or classes with an interest in an event to register. The Lapsed Listener is one form of memory leak where an event listener is registered without being removed. If the life cycle of the listener registry is long, then a memory leak will occur.	Weak references, or pairing `register` with `remove`.	Some objects are not garbage-collected, causing the system to slow over time, until the app is terminated or eventually dies.	Chapter 6, Section 6.3
13. Leak Collection	If a collection has a long life cycle, it can have long-lived references that are never removed. These will prevent large blocks of memory from being freed.	Weak references, or pairing `add` with `remove`.	Some objects are not garbage-collected, causing the system to slow over time, until the app is terminated or eventually dies.	Chapter 6, Section 6.4
14. Magic Servlet	The Magic Servlet is a Java servlet that does all of the work itself. The servlet has elements of model, view, and controller. Servlets created in this form should be approached with extreme prejudice: they are simply evil.	Model 2, the Triangle, Model-View-Controller	Poor readability, rippling impact of minor changes	Chapter 3, all sections
15. Monolithic JSPs	Like the Magic Servlet, the monolithic JSPs show a complete absence of any trace of model-view-controller separation. In this case, all of the code is in a tag language.	Model 2, the Triangle, Model-View-Controller	Poor readability, rippling impact of minor changes	Chapter 4 Section 4.2

Table A.1 Cross-reference of antipatterns by name *(continued)*

Name	Description	Solution	Symptoms	Location
16. Performance Afterthoughts	Poorly defined performance plans, poor requirement specification, and inattention to performance throughout the cycle can lead to nasty surprises at the end of the cycle.	Gather performance requirements, plan, and prepare	Repeated delivery of software that performs poorly, performance-tuning activities that are unfocused and ineffective, and inability of low-level developers to articulate the performance requirements for a component that they are building.	Chapter 10, Section 10.2
17. Rigid XML	Some design choices can restrict the extensibility of XML. Namespaces can collide, and some constructs are more restrictive than others.	Extensible, flexible XML	Difficult maintenance and changes that ripple into other parts of the system	Chapter 7, Section 7.6
18. Round Bean in a Square Hole	Many times, the wrong classification of EJB is used inappropriately. There are several different variations of this problem. A complex object relationship may fit bean-managed persistence better than container-managed persistence. In other cases, a problem may not require the full support of an entity bean. Similarly, entity beans may be overkill for applications that exclusively read or write.	Use the correct EJB for the job	Poor performance or readability	Chapter 8, Section 8.4
19. Round-tripping	Round-tripping occurs when a chatty interface falls on a distributed boundary. For EJBs, a client (usually a controller or JSP) accesses the remote interface of a distributed entity bean. Since an entity bean usually exposes many fields and sometimes collections, this results in many round-trip communications, absolutely murdering performance.	Command layer, facade, refactoring, caching	Poor performance	Chapter 8, Section 8.3 Chapter 10, Section 10.3

Table A.1 Cross-reference of antipatterns by name *(continued)*

Name	Description	Solution	Symptoms	Location
20. Split Cleaners	When a resource is allocated separately from where it is freed, cleanup can be potentially lost.	Pairing allocation with free	Resource leaks	Chapter 7, Section 7.3
21. Synchronized Read/Write Bottleneck	The Java programming language locks on the object level for synchronization, but does not distinguish between readers and writers. This locking mechanism is too restrictive for applications like databases and caches.	Read/write locks	Poor performance	Chapter 5, Section 5.5
22. Thrash-tuning	Performance tuning is difficult without a solid baseline or when multiple configuration parameters are changed at once between measurements. Attempting performance tuning in these conditions can result in similar or identical tests run several times, giving the appearance of thrashing.	Good testing methodology and a good testing environment are the primary keys. Baseline measurements are mandatory. All tests should start from a common configuration and change a single parameter at a time.	Inefficient performance testing and tuning, longer than expected performance tuning cycles, and unclear results of performance improvements	Chapter 10, Section 10.6
23. Too Many Webpage Items	Many web designers have no concept of the costs associated with loading web page items like graphics or animations. Since items have incremental load costs, too many objects can doom performance.	Eliminate extraneous objects	Poor performance	Chapter 2, Section 2.2.7
24. XML Golden Hammer	XML, like many powerful technologies, can be misused. In this case, we are using XML to do large-scale search or summary missions.	Databases, indexed XML	Poor performance	Chapter 7, Section 7.5.1

Table A.2   Cross-reference of antipatterns by scale, name

Name	Scale	Location
2. Cacheless Cow	Application	Chapter 5
4. Coarse or Fine Commands	Application	Section 4.4
5. Compound JSPs	Application	Section 4.3
6. Connection Thrashing	Application	Section 7.2
7. Everything Is an EJB	Application	Section 8.5
8. Excessive Layering	Application	Section 2.3.4
9. Fat Commands	Application	Section 4.5
11. Incomplete Process Transitions	Application	Section 2.5.2
12. Lapsed Listeners Leak	Application	Section 6.3
13. Leak Collection	Application	Section 6.4
14. Magic Servlet	Application	Chapter 3
15. Monolithic JSPs	Application	Section 4.2
16. Performance Afterthoughts	Application	Section 10.2
17. Rigid XML	Application	Section 7.6
18. Round Bean in a Square Hole	Application	Section 8.4
19. Round-tripping	Application	Section 8.3 Section 10.3
20. Split Cleaners	Application	Section 7.3
22. Thrash-tuning	Application	Section 10.6
24. XML Golden Hammer	Application	Section 7.5.1
3. Chaotic Session Management	Enterprise	Section 10.5
10. Hardwired Connections	Enterprise	Section 7.4
23. Too Many Webpage Items	Enterprise	Section 2.2.7
21. Synchronized Read/Write Bottleneck	Micro-architecture	Section 5.5
1. Bad Workload Management	System	Section 10.4

Table A.3   Cross-reference of antipatterns by symptom, name

Name	Symptoms	Location
11. Incomplete Process Transitions	Analysis paralysis	Section 2.5.2
9. Fat Commands	Command layers change with every change in model. Command layer looks like utility collection.	Section 4.5
11. Incomplete Process Transitions	Cost overruns	Section 2.5.2
3. Chaotic Session Management	Difficult maintenance	Section 10.5
17. Rigid XML	Difficult maintenance	Section 7.6
7. Everything Is an EJB	Expensive simple solutions	Section 8.5
16. Performance Afterthoughts	Ineffective tuning activities	Section 10.2
22. Thrash-tuning	Inefficient performance testing and tuning	Section 10.6
10. Hardwired Connections	Interface support lagging the capabilities of both the client and server systems	Section 7.4
11. Incomplete Process Transitions	Long development cycles	Section 2.5.2
22. Thrash-tuning	Long development cycles	Section 10.6
12. Lapsed Listeners Leak	Memory leak	Section 6.3
13. Leak Collection	Memory leak	Section 6.4
10. Hardwired Connections	Multiple versions of the same interface	Section 7.4
1. Bad Workload Management	Performance is sporadic and inconsistent across identically configured servers	Section 10.4
16. Performance Afterthoughts	Performance requirements are not known by responsible programmers	Section 10.2
2. Cacheless Cow	Poor performance	Chapter 5
3. Chaotic Session Management	Poor performance	Section 10.5
4. Coarse or Fine Commands	Poor performance	Section 4.4
6. Connection Thrashing	Poor performance	Section 7.2
7. Everything Is an EJB	Poor performance	Section 8.5

Table A.3   Cross-reference of antipatterns by symptom, name *(continued)*

Name	Symptoms	Location
8. Excessive Layering	Poor performance	Section 2.3.4
12. Lapsed Listeners Leak	Poor performance	Section 6.3
13. Leak Collection	Poor performance	Section 6.4
16. Performance Afterthoughts	Poor performance	Section 10.2
18. Round Bean in a Square Hole	Poor performance	Section 8.4
19. Round-tripping	Poor performance	Section 8.3 Section 10.3
21. Synchronized Read/Write Bottleneck	Poor performance	Section 5.5
23. Too Many Webpage Items	Poor performance	Section 2.2.7
24. XML Golden Hammer	Poor performance	Section 7.5.1
8. Excessive Layering	Poor readability	Section 2.3.4
14. Magic Servlet	Poor readability	Chapter 3
15. Monolithic JSPs	Poor readability	Section 4.2
18. Round Bean in a Square Hole	Poor readability	Section 8.4
3. Chaotic Session Management	Poor reuse	Section 10.5
4. Coarse or Fine Commands	Poor reuse	Section 4.4
5. Compound JSPs	Poor separation of concerns	Section 4.3
20. Split Cleaners	Resource leaks	Section 7.3
14. Magic Servlet	Rippling impact of minor changes	Chapter 3
15. Monolithic JSPs	Rippling impact of minor changes	Section 4.2
17. Rigid XML	Rippling impact of minor changes	Section 7.6

bibliography

My goal for *Bitter Java* is to provide a book that informs and communicates in clear, understandable language. For this reason, many of the books and articles that I consulted provide interesting angles to old ideas. Some of the books and articles helped me shape ideas, while others provided new language that worked in this forum. Many antipatterns, after all, are not yet named. Still other sources provided organizational insight.

Among the sources I've listed are some of the standards in the industry, as well as some relatively unknown sources. Some that you might not have seen before are Eric Allen's bug pattern on the Split Cleaner (part of a perceptive series on bug patterns on developerWorks); Michael Conner, et al.'s article on caching of dynamic content; and a well-executed book on the command pattern for a specific architecture, by Joaquin Picon. Some of my favorites are on this list, including Skip McCormick, et al.'s *AntiPatterns*, which keeps some tedious topics fun to read; Kent Beck's book on extreme programming, which takes a necessary step back toward simplicity; and Walker Royce's *Software Project Management*, which has shaped many of my ideas about managing iterative projects.

NOTE   Links are provided for convenience. All were tested before the book was published, but may not remain current.

Allen, Eric E., *Diagnosing Java Code: The Split Cleaner Bug Pattern*, on IBM developerWorks: July 2001.
Link: http://www.ibm.com/developerworks/java/library/j-diag0717.html?dwzone=java.

Ambler, Scott W., *Writing Robust Java Code*, self-published. January 2000.
Link: http://www.ambysoft.com/javaCodingStandards.pdf.

Beck, Kent, *eXtreme Programming eXplained*, Reading, Mass.: Addison-Wesley, 2000.

Binder, Robert V., *Testing Object-Oriented Systems: Models, Patterns, and Tools*, The Addison-Wesley Object Technology Series, Reading, Mass.: Addison-Wesley, 2000.
Link: http://cseng.aw.com/book/coverpic/0,3831,0201809389,00.html.

Bos, Bert, *XML in 10 Points*, World Wide Web Consortium (W3C), at http://www.w3.org/XML/1999/XML-in-10-points.

Brooks, Fredrick P., *The Mythical Man-Month*, Reading, Mass.: Addison-Wesley, 1995.

Brown, William J., Raphael C. Malveau, Hays W. "Skip" McCormick III, and Thomas J. Mowbray, *Anti-patterns: Refactoring Software, Architectures, and Projects in Crisis*, New York: John Wiley and Sons, Inc., 1998.
Link: http://www.antipatterns.com.

Clark, Roger, *A Primer on Internet Technologies*, at http://www.anu.edu.au/people/Roger.Clarke/II/IPrimer.html. February 1998, Xamax Consultancy Pty. Ltd., 1997, 1998.

Conner, Mike, George Copeland, and Greg Flurry, "Scaling Up E-business Applications with Caching," in *Developer Toolbox Technical Magazine*: August 2000.
Link: http://www6.software.ibm.com/devtools/news0800/art7.htm.

Costello, Roger L., *XML Schema: Best Practices Homepage*, November 2001.
Link: http://www.xfront.com/BestPracticesHomepage.html.

Henry, Ethan and Ed Lycklama, *How Do You Plug Java Memory Leaks?* in *Dr. Dobb's Journal:* February 2000.
Link: http://www.ddj.com/articles/2000/0002/0002l/0002l.htm.

Lea, Doug, *Draft Java Coding Standard*, released to the public domain, February 2000.
Link: http://g.oswego.edu/dl/html/javaCodingStd.html.

Leung, Tony K. T., *Plugging Memory Leaks in JavaPro*, at http://www.devx.com/upload/free/features/javapro/1999/06jun99/tl0699/tl0699.asp.

Metz, Cade, "Performance Primer: Gone in 4 Seconds," in *PC Magazine*: February 20, 2001.
Link: http://www.zdnet.com/ecommerce/stories/main/ 0,10475,2682126,00.html.

Monson-Haefel, Richard, *Enterprise Java Beans*, Cambridge, Mass.: O'Reilly & Associates, Inc., 2000.

Picon, Joaquin, Regis Coqueret, Andreas Hutfless, Gopal Indurkhya, and Martin Weiss, Design and Implement Servlets, JSPs, and EJBs for WebSphere, Armock, N.Y.: IBM Redbooks, 2000.
Link: http://www.redbooks.ibm.com/abstracts/sg245754.html.

Royce, Walker, *Software Project Management: A Unified Framework*, Reading, Mass.: Addison-Wesley, 1998.

Sharma, Rahul, *J2EE Connector Architecture*, Sun Microsystems, Inc., at http:// java.sun.com/j2ee/connector/.

Siegel, Shel and Robert J. Muller, *Object-Oriented Software Testing: A Hierarchical Approach*, New York: John Wiley and Sons, 1996.

Singh, Amandeep, "Implementing Read/Write Locks in Java," self-published.
Link: http://www.asingh.net/technical/rwlocks.html.

Sun Microsystems, Inc., *The Java Programming Reference* at http://devel- oper.java.sun.com/developer/infodocs/?frontpage-main#docs.

Williams, Kevin. *XML for Data: Four Tips for a Smart Architecture*, on IBM developerWorks, August 2001.
Link: http://www-106.ibm.com/developerworks/xml/library/x-xdtips.html.

Additional references by subject

This group of books represents many of the industry standard books for Java design, refactoring, performance, and standards. Some, like *Design Patterns* or *Refactoring*, provide blinding flashes of insight and clarity. Others, like *Core J2EE Patterns*, are clean and practical. In every case, the source communicates something important to the technologies and disciplines that provide a foundation for this book.

Design patterns and refactoring

Crupi, John, Dan Malks, and Deepak Alur, *Core J2EE Patterns: Best Practices and Design Stratgeies*, Englewood Cliffs, N.J.: Prentice Hall, 2001.

Cooper, James William, *Java Design Patterns: A Tutorial*, Reading, Mass.: Addison-Wesley, 2000.

Fowler, Martin, Kent Beck (Contributor), John Brant (Contributor), William Opdyke, and Don Roberts, *Refactoring: Improving the Design of Existing Code*, Reading, Mass.: Addison-Wesley, 1999.

Gamma, Erich, Richard Helm, Ralph Johnson, and John Vlissides (The Gang of Four), *Design Patterns: Elements of Reusable Object-Oriented Software*, Reading, Mass.: Addison-Wesley, 1994.

Grand, Mark, *Patterns in Java, Volume 3, A Catalog of Enterprise Design Patterns Illustrated with UML*, New York: John Wiley and Sons, Inc., 2001.

Lea, Doug, *Concurrent Programming in Java: Design Principles and Patterns*, Reading, Mass.: Addison-Wesley, 1999.

Preiss, Bruno R., *Data Structures and Algorithms with Object-Oriented Design Patterns in Java*, New York: John Wiley and Sons, Inc., 1999.

Performance

Bulka, Dov, *Java Performance and Scalability Series*, vol. 1, Reading, Mass.: Addison-Wesley, 2000.

Crupi, John, et al., *Core J2EE Patterns*.

Lea, Doug, *Concurrent Programming in Java*.

TCP/IP

Stevens, Richard, *TCP/IP Illustrated Series*, vol. 1, Reading, Mass.: Addison-Wesley, 1994, ISBN 0-201-63346-9.

UML

Arrington, C. T., *Enterprise Java with UML*, New York: OMG Press/Wiley, 2001.

Booch, Grady, et al., *The Unified Modeling Language User Guide*, Reading, Mass.: Addison-Wesley, 1998.

Fowler, Martin, and Kendall Scott, *UML Distilled: A Brief Guide to the Standard Object Modeling Language*, Reading, Mass.: Addison-Wesley, 1997.

XML

http://xml.org: This website contains information about all of the XML specifications, as well as some great instructional documents.

index

Supporting technologies and frameworks

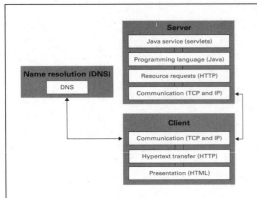

Java servlets rely on many standards, adding tremendous flexibility and some overhead. Read about Internet technologies in section 2.2, page 28.

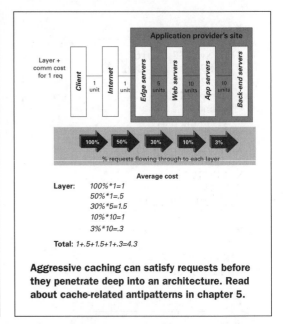

Aggressive caching can satisfy requests before they penetrate deep into an architecture. Read about cache-related antipatterns in chapter 5.

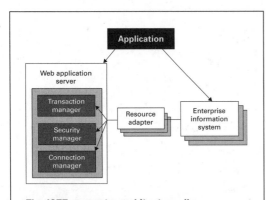

The J2EE connector architecture allows application servers to provide general pooling, security, and transaction support for connectors. Read about it in section 7.2.5, page 180.

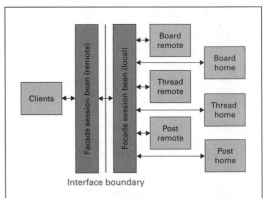

Round-tripping is the most bitter of the EJB antipatterns. Facades can dramatically reduce this problem by providing a local interface and making many communications at once. Read about them in section 8.3, page 225.